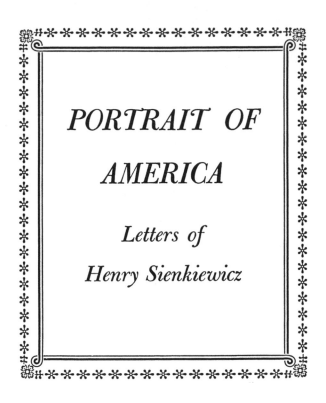

PORTRAIT OF AMERICA

Letters of Henry Sienkiewicz

HENRY SIENKIEWICZ   JOHN DEPOL

PORTRAIT OF AMERICA

Letters of Henry Sienkiewicz

EDITED & TRANSLATED BY

CHARLES MORLEY

1959

Columbia University Press · New York

PREFACE

IN 1955, Julian Krzyzanowski, Professor of Polish Literature at the University of Warsaw, completed a task upon which he had been engaged for eight years: the editing of a new, definitive edition, in sixty volumes, of the works of Henry Sienkiewicz. It was the publication of this edition that made the present book possible. Now for the first time all of Sienkiewicz's reports from America were assembled in a single unit. They were published with the title *Listy z podrozy do Ameryki* (*Letters from my travels in America*) as volumes 41 and 42 of his *Dziela* (*Works*). Most of these reports or *feuilletons*, as Sienkiewicz preferred to call them, originally appeared in the Warsaw *Gazeta Polska*. Under the misnomer "letters," they were printed in serial form between 1876 and 1878. Others appeared in those same years in the *Kurier Codzienny*, *Przeglad Tygodniowy*, and *Gazeta Handlowa* (all of Warsaw); one was printed in the Lwow *Przewodnik Naukowy i Literacki* in 1879.

Although translations of the *Letters* have appeared in many languages, there has been only one previous English translation, that of Casimir Gonski. This version was published in the New York monthly *Poland* in 1925–1926 (volumes 6 and 7) and went only as far as Sienkiewicz's discussion of American women.

The present translation includes approximately three-fourths of Sienkiewicz's reports from America and is based exclusively on volumes 41 and 42 of his works, mentioned above. In my selection and occasional abridgment, I have omitted some of the lengthy geographic descriptions and such matters as might be of little interest to American readers. Because Sienkiewicz wrote for several newspapers and even to private parties who on their own initiative had his letters printed, the material in the reports is sometimes repetitious. I have endeavored to exclude most of this duplication though this was not possible in every instance.

Two recent books greatly facilitated my work of editing Sienkiewicz's account. Professor Krzyzanowski's *Henryk Sienkiewicz, kalendarz zycia i tworczosci* (Warsaw, 1956) provided a kind of timetable of the author's whereabouts and activities in the United States. Zdzislaw Najder's edition of the *Letters* (*Henryk Sienkiewicz. Listy z podrozy do Ameryki*, Warsaw, 1956) clarified many allusions and obsolete Polish expressions.

Like every book, this one, too, is the product of many hands. To Professor Krzyzanowski who read most of my manuscript and made many important corrections and valuable comments I acknowledge my deep appreciation. To three students at The Ohio State University, Krystyna Conklin, Edward Winnicki, and Elizabeth Piotrowski, who gave me the benefit of their knowledge in the translation of obscure passages, and to my wife, Ruth Clarkson Morley, who provided indispensable assistance at every turn, I express my sincere gratitude. No one other than myself, of course, is responsible for any deficiencies which the book may possess.

I wish to thank the California Historical Society *Quarterly* for granting permission to reprint, with modifications, the article on the Chinese in California which originally appeared in the December, 1955, issue of the *Quarterly*. Finally, I wish to acknowledge a grant for the Autumn Quarter of 1951 of a Faculty-Study Fellowship from the American Council of Learned Societies to read extensively in Polish literature. It was then that I discovered the *Letters from America*.

CHARLES MORLEY

The Ohio State University
Columbus, Ohio
January 1959

CONTENTS

viii   Contents

INTRODUCTION

AMERICANS have always had an almost insatiable curiosity to know what other peoples think about them. As a result, books by foreigners describing their impressions of this country have usually attracted considerable attention among the American reading public. This has been true of all the notable travel accounts, whether they were harshly critical as were Mrs. Trollope's and Dickens', or laudatory like those of De Tocqueville and Lord Bryce. All of these accounts were written by West Europeans; those written by East European authors, on the other hand, are practically unknown in the United States.

The reasons for this neglect are easy to understand. Travelers from distant eastern Europe have neither been as numerous nor generally as famous as those from England, France, and Germany. Written in difficult Slavic languages with which few Americans were familiar, their works were rarely translated into English. Nevertheless, it is astonishing that a book about America by so prominent a literary figure as Henry Sienkiewicz should have remained in relative obscurity on this side of the Atlantic.

As the author of the Nobel Prize-winning novel, *Quo Vadis?*, Henry Sienkiewicz needs no introduction to Americans. But very few of those who have been thrilled by his tragic drama of early Christians, whether from reading the novel or viewing its most recent screen version, realize that he visited the United States in 1876–78 and, more important, that he recorded his impressions in his *Letters from America*.

Born in 1846, Sienkiewicz was thirty years of age when he came to the United States. His literary reputation still remained to be made, but his writings as a journalist had already attracted

wide attention in the pages of the Warsaw *Gazeta Polska* for
which he wrote a column, "The Present Moment," under the
pseudonym, "Litwos." [1] Under the editorship of Dr. Edward
Leo, the *Gazeta Polska* proved to be an excellent medium of
expression for the talented young writer. Allowed complete freedom by his editor, Sienkiewicz did not hesitate to write on
controversial subjects nor to voice unorthodox views. In the
cafés and salons literate Varsovians engaged in animated discussions of the opinions expressed in Litwos' latest *feuilleton.*
Only the strict Russian censorship and the resourcefulness of
his mind and imagination placed limits on the scope of his
literary activity.

One may well wonder what motives prompted this well-
educated Pole, descendant of an impoverished gentry family,
to journey such vast distances to settle in California at a time
when, to most East Europeans, America was still a land of
mystery. As the writer himself acknowledged, "A person who
is leaving for America is still a rarity among us." Yet for a
venturesome and imaginative young man, eager for new sights
and experiences and unencumbered by domestic ties, the name
America had a bewitching attraction. The young man's curiosity was further heightened by the ecstatic accounts of California appearing in a local newspaper from the pen of Julian
Horain, a fellow journalist, and by the appearance in 1875 of
a highly colored account entitled *In America* by a woman
writer, Christine Narbutt, who told alarming tales of gunfire
below the windows of her New York hotel room.

Two of Sienkiewicz's close friends, Helena Modjeska, the
actress, and her husband, Count Charles Chlapowski, shared
his intense interest in this country. Madame Modjeska describes how one winter night in 1875 the writer and a group
of young men were at her Warsaw home when the subject of
the approaching Centennial Exposition in Philadelphia was

[1] "Litwos" may be translated as "The Lithuanian." The original home
of the Sienkiewicz family was in Lithuania.

brought up. Immediately an enthusiastic discussion of the United States was begun in which Sienkiewicz took a leading part, describing the country, and especially California, in the most glowing terms. The consensus was that California was indeed the Promised Land where game of all kinds might be had for the shooting, fruits of every variety grew at least three times larger than anywhere else, coffee, pepper, and castor-oil beans grew wild, and gold was to be found almost everywhere. The eventual outcome of the evening's conversation was that Sienkiewicz, the Chlapowskis, and several other enthusiasts decided to seek adventure by going to California. When Count Chlapowski proposed the formation of a tiny utopian colony on the model of Brook Farm, the idea was acclaimed by the others. Endless discussions ensued; statutes were written to regulate the life of the colony; the journey was planned in detail; happy fantasies of a new idyllic life close to nature were dreamed. Madame Modjeska's expectations were typical:

Oh, but to cook under the sapphire-blue sky in the land of freedom! What joy! To bleach linen at the brook like the maidens of Homer's 'Iliad'! After the day of toil, to play the guitar and sing by moonlight, to recite poems, or to listen to the mockingbird! And listening to our songs would be charming Indian maidens, our neighbors, making wreaths of luxuriant wild flowers for us! And in exchange we should give them trinkets for their handsome brown necks and wrists! And oh, we should be so far away from every-day gossip and malice, nearer to God, and better.[2]

The participants imagined everything except what really lay in store for them.

Sienkiewicz and a companion, Julius Sypniewski, were designated to proceed to America ahead of the rest and to select a suitable location for the proposed colony in California. What helped to make the trip financially possible for Sienkiewicz was the suggestion by his editor that he send back a series of articles

[2] Helena Modjeska, *Memories and Impressions* (New York, 1910), pp. 250–51.

on what he saw in the United States for publication in the *Gazeta Polska.*

Early in 1876 Sienkiewicz sailed for the New World. After a brief stay in New York City, he and his friend set out for California via Chicago over the recently completed transcontinental railroad. Upon reaching the West Coast, the two selected the small but thriving community of Anaheim in southern California as the most promising place to launch the utopian experiment. Not only did this location offer a sunny and salubrious climate, but it also had the advantage of being predominantly German. Since all of the colonists knew the German language, communication with their neighbors would be no problem during the interim they were learning English. Enthusiastic letters were dispatched to those who remained behind, urging them to come at the earliest opportunity. Sypniewski returned to Europe to give a firsthand oral report and to assist his family in making the long move to California. The colonists, eight in number, arrived early in the fall of that year, equipped for the dangerous exigencies of American life with two huge boxes of medicine, an assortment of surgical instruments, telescopes, and a formidable armament of several rifles, brass knuckles, and six revolvers!

It was almost a foregone conclusion that a project so lightheartedly embarked upon was doomed to failure, for the softhanded intellectuals who composed the group possessed no previous knowledge of practical agriculture, nor were they accustomed to the strenuous physical labor involved. These amateur farmers did not know how to milk their cows or kill the poultry they raised. Neighbors' cattle trampled and munched upon the winter barley crop, while the animals' owners helped themselves freely to the fruit in the vineyard. As a result, many of the food supplies for the group had to be purchased. Aching backs and blistered hands soon took a toll of the colonists' early enthusiasm, and within a few short months the disillusioned idealists were ready to admit their defeat. Madame Modjeska, alarmed by the steady diminution of her husband's capital invested in the farm and the complete absence of any financial return, announced her intention of going to San Francisco to study English and to recoup their fortunes by resuming her acting career. Sienkiewicz, for his part, went off to investigate new aspects of life in the American West and to write up his findings for his readers back in Warsaw.

Most of the European travelers who wrote accounts about America had several characteristics in common. They were generally well-educated and therefore their interpretations of what they witnessed and experienced tended to reflect the viewpoint of the educated class. All of them arrived with certain preconceptions about the United States firmly entrenched in their minds, derived from the accounts of earlier travelers with which they had familiarized themselves or based upon the prevailing image of America in their native land. As Europeans, they were all bred under political and social systems quite different from what they encountered in the United States. Thus, the entire background and experience of the visitors, the information or misinformation with which they came equipped, the nature of the government under which they had lived, their own niche in the social milieu—all of these were factors which inevitably affected the observations even of those travelers who endeavored to give a true and objective account of what they saw. In spite of these handicaps, or perhaps because of them, the more perceptive and penetrating analyses of the institutions and meanings of American life have usually come from foreign observers. All too frequently the vision of native commentators was obscured by their very familiarity with the American scene, their matter-of-fact acceptance of phenomena they deemed commonplace, and their ready assumption that certain facets of life in this country were not in the least unique.

The *Gazeta Polska's* reporter labored under the same handicaps as had his predecessors in writing of the New World.

Sienkiewicz wrote as a professional author and intellectual educated in philosophy at the University of Warsaw. He, too, arrived laden with a preconceived picture of America gleaned from the accounts of others. Those specifically mentioned by him were the works of De Tocqueville and Charles Dickens, both of which described the America of a generation earlier. Also there were the superficial reports of Julian Horain and Christine Narbutt, cited earlier. His image of the United States was likewise colored by the fiction works of two American authors, the highly romanticized accounts of James Fenimore Cooper and Bret Harte. Sienkiewicz was to experience considerable disillusionment when he at last encountered Cooper's "noble savages" in the flesh.

Perhaps the most important factor that determined Sienkiewicz's reaction to America was the environment of his native land. Russian Poland, like the rest of the Russian Empire of which it was an integral part, lagged far behind most of Europe in its political, social, and economic evolution. A highly centralized and autocratic form of government dominated all aspects of life, affording no concessions to local diversities or needs. The oppressive dictums of the St. Petersburg government were carried out by a vast bureaucracy of civil servants that had assumed the status of a separate caste, superior and unresponsive to those it ruled. Society in Russian Poland was rigidly divided into separate social strata, and the glaring contrasts of wealth and poverty, education and illiteracy, refinement and uncouthness, served to perpetuate this outdated class structure. Since the economy of the country still remained predominantly agricultural, the scarcity of land attendant upon rural overpopulation had reduced much of the peasantry to the most dire poverty. Meat, for example, was a rarity in their diet, and most peasants were vegetarians not by choice but by necessity.

Toward the subjugated Poles the Russian government followed a policy of Russification. Compulsory service in the Rus-

sian army, strict censorship of the press, use of the Russian
language in the schools and of Russian officials in the public
administration, surveillance by an omnipresent police—all were
designed to inhibit Polish cultural development and to mold
the Poles into a Russian pattern. Even more oppressive was the
policy of the Russian government toward the vast numbers of
Jews in Poland. Highly discriminatory legislation made their
position almost intolerable and soon forced many thousands
to emigrate. Nor was their lot made easier by the attitude of
the Poles who regarded them as an element outside of the
Polish nation. This, then, was the background from which
Sienkiewicz looked upon society and institutions of the United
States.

It is easy to understand, therefore, why certain aspects of
American life made such a strong impression upon him. He
saw at once that here were many lessons to be learned by his
own countrymen. The democratic system of government attracted his particular attention, and he returned to this subject
in several of his letters. For Sienkiewicz, it was no longer a
question of whether or not the American experiment would
succeed—as had been the case with some of the earlier European travelers—but why the experiment had proved so successful. He immediately realized that American democracy was not
merely political but social as well, that it was more than just
an "institution and a theory"; in his words, American democracy was apparent "in men's relations with one another." In
seeking to determine what was the essence of this democracy,
Sienkiewicz came to the conclusion that three ingredients were
basic to it: esteem for work in any form, absence of any great
differences in education, and lack of marked disparity in manners. His comments on these elements, together with numerous
examples to support his argument, make some of the most
interesting reading in the *Letters.*

The young Pole's imagination was likewise stirred by the
great natural resources of this country, especially the vast tracts

of western lands which still awaited the touch of human hands. Here land was to be had practically for the asking, yet Sienkiewicz was quick to perceive that the settlement of these lands was no simple matter. Recent European immigrants who crowded the Eastern cities and stood to benefit most from going West sometimes did not even know of the existence of the Far West. Or, having expended their meager funds, they could not pay the cost of transportation from the seaboard to the frontier, a cost which exceeded the ocean passage itself. Or, most important, they did not possess the capital and equipment to set up husbandry. Homesteaders found initial hardships and sacrifices almost unbearable but, once these were overcome, a decent livelihood could be earned and even a certain degree of wealth achieved. In general Sienkiewicz found the economic level of life in the United States to be infinitely higher than elsewhere, so that even the poor were unfamiliar with the kind of poverty that existed in Europe, a poverty that "makes teeth chatter from cold, bloats bodies from hunger . . . begs, steals, murders."

Sienkiewicz singled out the policy of the American government toward minority groups for particular praise. Here he found no attempt at forced assimilation. Each national group was allowed complete freedom to live where it pleased, to establish its own communities, to publish its own newspapers, to found its own schools, churches, and social organizations. Despite this freedom and despite all efforts of minority leaders to preserve national identity, the process of Americanization moved rapidly forward. Even before the large influx of Slavs began, Sienkiewicz foresaw that they, too, like the immigrants who preceded them, would lose their national identity within a generation or two.

Finally, what manner of people did Sienkiewicz find in this vast new land? The character and behavior of these extraordinary Americans alternately intrigued, repulsed, and attracted him. In his early letters he delivered denunciatory blasts upon the uncouthness and boorishness of their social conduct, their informality on occasions of ceremonious significance, the men's exclusive preoccupation with matters of business, the women's laziness and love of ostentatious finery. On the other hand, the boundless energy of the Americans, their readiness to experiment with new approaches to old problems, their courage and enterprise in tackling seemingly insurmountable tasks, inspired the young man's keenest admiration. Eventually, even most of his harsher views (with the exception of those on American women) underwent a slow but steady mellowing as he became more intimately acquainted with various types of individual Americans, especially the frontiersmen of the West. The lack of formality he had once deplored, he now came to regard as admirable forthrightness and a sensible rejection of dishonest subterfuge. The social equality that had originally startled him was now comprehensible and praiseworthy. Even the crudity of manners and the element of violence he found so prevalent he ascribed to the boisterousness of a youthful society rather than to any inherent viciousness in the American character or to any deficiency in democratic institutions. Everything Sienkiewicz observed during his visit here convinced him that a great future lay in store for this country. Though institutions and resources might contribute to this greatness, it was rather the nature of the Americans themselves that made him confident in the accuracy of his prophecy.

The extended sojourn in the United States had beneficial effects upon Sienkiewicz himself and upon the development of his literary career. Nothing is so productive of new ideas as travel, and his visit to a vigorous, expanding America served to broaden his horizons and provide new subjects for his pen. Nature on a grand scale such as he encountered in the vast prairies and forests possessed a special fascination for him. This kinship with nature was later to be reflected in descriptions in his great historical novels. Even though he hailed from a landlocked country, he established a familiarity with every mood of the sea from his life at Anaheim Landing and his ocean crossings, and his pictures of the sea are considered by some to be unrivaled in the literature of his own nation. His creative imagination was ever alert to the literary potentialities in the events and people he encountered along his travels in the New World. Certain of the best loved characters in his famous Trilogy, for example, are believed to be modeled upon prototypes he met in this country.

The majority of Sienkiewicz's short stories were written early in his career during or shortly after his residence here, and as a result, eight of these tales deal with American themes. For instance, the mannerisms of his German neighbors at Anaheim, California, provide the subject of his amusing farce, "The Comedy of Errors." Sacramento of the 1870s is the setting for "In the Gold Country," a sentimental tale of love and heroism. The great trek of American settlers westward as he glimpsed it from the windows of a transcontinental train and gleaned details from old-time pioneers and Indian fighters is depicted in "Across the Prairies." The visit of a circus to Anaheim gave rise to the story entitled "Orso," while "Sachem" concerns the ruthless extermination of an Indian tribe in early Texas. Polish political exiles with their profound homesickness and longing for the sound of their native tongue supplied the material taken from life in "Memories of Mariposa" and "The Lighthousekeeper of Aspinwall." Frightened and bewildered peasants packed in the steerage of an ocean vessel as they crossed the terrifying Atlantic in quest of bread and freedom provide the heroic theme of "In Search of Bread." [3] The original source

---

[3] No single volume contains all of these short stories in English translation. With the exception of "In Search of Bread" they are found in volume 3 of the latest Polish edition of Sienkiewicz's *Works* (*Dziela*, Warsaw, 1947–1955. 60 vols.). This volume also contains "The Cranes," a self-revealing fragment describing Sienkiewicz's nostalgia for his homeland while living in faraway California.

materials from which most of these sketches were adapted are clearly discernible in the *Letters from America.*

Equally important was the psychological impact that his prolonged exposure to American life had upon the young writer. Like so many Poles in the period following the failure of the 1863 Insurrection, Sienkiewicz was depressed about the future of his homeland; indeed, much of his early writing inclined to a morbid, pessimistic tone. His visit to America served as a fresh breeze bestirring him from the doldrums of pessimism. Here he found none of the inertia of an old and settled civilization; instead, change was everywhere proceeding at a whirlwind pace. The surging vitality of the people, the energy they displayed in surmounting all misfortunes and disasters, and, above all, their prevailing spirit of optimism and confidence in the future inspired him with new hope. "Everybody looks to 'tomorrow,'" Sienkiewicz remarked with wonderment, "'yesterday' to them means only deserts, primeval forests and the vast silence of the prairies." That the author was infected by this optimism was apparent in his Trilogy, written immediately after his return to Warsaw. Through this epic narrative of Poland's struggle for survival during the seventeenth century, Sienkiewicz endeavored, as he himself affirmed, "to strengthen the hearts" of his compatriots. As Poles read the Trilogy, the courage and achievements of their forebears revived their faith in Poland's future. Thus Sienkiewicz succeeded in transplanting in the minds and hearts of his fellow countrymen some of the optimism that he himself had gained during his travels in America.

✻✻✻✻✻✻✻✻✻✻✻✻✻✻✻✻✻✻✻✻✻✻✻✻✻

AS the train for points west pulled out of Warsaw's station on Saturday afternoon, February 19, 1876, a fluttering cloud of handkerchiefs was waving adieu to a young man leaning out of a coach window. Friends and colleagues who had given a gay farewell party in his honor were seeing him off on the first lap on a long journey. Henry Sienkiewicz, columnist and reporter of the *Gazeta Polska,* was on his way to the United States.

It was with an air of astonishment and delight that Sienkiewicz informed the readers of his column of his projected trip. "I should sooner believe almost anything than that I should journey to America," he exclaimed, and jocularly wrote that he expected to be viewed as a kind of Count Ferdinand Cortez upon his return. And yet what had once seemed fantasy was now being transformed into reality. On February 23, Sienkiewicz with his companion, Julius Sypniewski, set sail from Liverpool on the Cunard steamer *Germanic* bound for the New World.

In the course of several humorous installments, the *Gazeta Polska's* reporter relayed to his readers the tribulations and pleasures generally experienced by trans-Atlantic tourists. He described luxury life on the high seas, alarming storms, seasickness, eccentric fellow passengers, and shipboard concerts by amateur performers whose falsified renditions of Chopin "literally caused our Polish ears to wilt." But he did not overlook the unfortunate emigrants packed in the steerage; their misery touched his heart and later he would poignantly tell about them in his writings.

During the crossing Sienkiewicz had his first encounters with Americans and got his first taste of American manners. He was astonished to note that some of the men sat down to dinner with their hats on, and after dinner had been cleared away, they customarily read their newspapers with feet propped up on the table! But when at last the ship docked, he copied the example of these same Americans and rid himself of the customs inspector with a two-dollar bribe. Then, "Upon our second step in New York," Sienkiewicz wrote caustically, "we were robbed by the hack driver, and the hotels were to take care of the rest." He had indeed reached New York.

Letter I

SOJOURN IN NEW YORK

MARBLES, bronzes, rugs, and mirrors—these are what make American hotels. Along with the banks and the post offices, the hotels are the most beautiful buildings in New York. In addition to the sleeping rooms, each hotel has many large salons where the guests may receive their callers, and sumptuously furnished boudoirs set aside for the ladies. The Central Hotel where I stopped for a few days is so large that it resembles a small city. Besides the permanent and transient guests, every evening a great many inhabitants of the city congregate in its magnificent lobby to read newspapers, to meet their acquaintances, to smoke or chew tobacco, and to rock back and forth in the numerous rocking chairs.

The hotel is located on Broadway, the widest and busiest street in New York, and one of the longest. Since it was already too late to tour the city on the evening of my arrival, I had to be satisfied with exploring only the hotel; my companion and I, therefore, proceeded to the dining room. It is indeed an enormous hall, with a seating capacity of several hundred, furnished with magnificence but without taste. The pillars supporting the arches are of stone, but are too thick and short, making the ceiling seem low and oppressive; the tremendous double doors, rounded at the top, remind one of the entrance to a barn.

Three times a day all the guests of the hotel descend to the dining room. In American hotels there is no separate charge for meals, for their cost is included in the price of the room. Each guest who has engaged a room has the privilege of dining here five times daily at no extra charge, but the majority come down only for breakfast, lunch, and dinner. At the table the guests converse with one another as though already acquainted, but this does not lead to any closer relationship. Upon finishing the meal, the guests rise and go their way, without waiting for the others or thanking them for the pleasure of their company.[1] Women frequently visit the dining room without escorts; in fact many women, even though unmarried, travel unchaperoned. All dress more elaborately than anywhere in Europe. Since none of them wears hats, dinners take on the appearance of private, formal affairs. Here one does not tip the servants, who in practically all hotels are Negroes. Colored help is employed because it is cheaper than white. At each table stand two or three Negroes whose heads resemble those of black rams. They are very polite, they serve quickly and efficiently, and in their dress coats and white ties they look, if not handsome, at least very original. But the work is not difficult. According to American custom, numerous porcelain dishes filled with a variety of foods are placed simultaneously before the guest. You have before you all at one time soup, meats, fish, eggs, puddings, tomatoes, potatoes, ice cream, strawberries, apples, almonds, coffee—in a word, a countless variety of dishes in small servings. Begin with whatever dish you please, eat what you like; nobody pays any attention to you. A Negro stands over you like an executioner over a condemned man. He keeps filling your glass with ice water whenever you take a sip and replies invariably, "Yes, sir!" to all your requests. As a result of this mode of serving, everything you eat is cold, stale, and unappetizing, even in the best restaurants. American cuisine is the worst on earth. It ignores all consideration for your health and well-being in order to speed you through your meal so that you can return as quickly as possible to business. Everything is determined by the need for speed, and only the evening dinners are served somewhat more carefully, for all business ceases at the stroke of five.

---

[1] In Poland, it is customary to express thanks to your fellow diners as you leave the table.

On the day after my arrival, instead of sitting in the reading
room and writing a monograph on American customs (as did
a certain lady correspondent of a Warsaw newspaper, who with
truly miraculous intuition was at once able to fathom these
customs),[2] I left the hotel to take at least a fleeting glance at
everything in town. It is true that during the night I had not
experienced such strong impressions as the aforesaid correspondent, who was unable to sleep a wink during the first
several nights of her sojourn in the United States because of
the gunfire of Americans who were blasting each others' brains
out. I had slept so peacefully that I am led to doubt whether
the nocturnal sounds which the lady correspondent heard actually had such tragic implications. Without passing final judgment on this question, however, I left the hotel and ventured
forth to see the city.

But New York not only did not enthrall me, it disappointed
me greatly. Every European city possesses certain sights peculiar
to itself which are really worth seeing. Paris and London have
thousands of them. Vienna has its St. Stephen;[3] Berlin, its
Kaulbach;[4] Brussels, Wiertz and St. Gudule;[5] Venice has its
canals; Rome, the Pope and her ruins; Cologne, the foremost
cathedral in the world; Cracow has its Wawel and Matejko;[6]
and Warsaw its good intentions with which it is paved, its
important people for petty affairs, the longest tongues in the

[2] The allusion is to Christine Narbutt; see Introduction.
[3] St. Stephen's cathedral is especially famous for its 450-foot Gothic spire.
The original building dates from the twelfth century.
[4] Wilhelm von Kaulbach (1805–1874) was a German historical painter
and illustrator. He decorated the grand staircase of Berlin's New Museum
with a series of paintings depicting the evolution of civilization.
[5] Antoine Wiertz (1806–1865) was the most famous Belgian historical
painter of his day. St. Gudule's cathedral, named for the patron saint of
the city, is one of the finest examples of pointed Gothic architecture; it
was built in the thirteenth century.
[6] Wawel is the hill on which stand St. Stanislaus' cathedral and the royal
palace. The Polish kings were crowned in this cathedral which is today the
pantheon of Poland. Jan Matejko (1838–1893), the "Sienkiewicz of Polish
painting," was born, lived, and died in Cracow.

world, the Saxon Gardens,[7] and social welfare resembling a
nut full of holes on which anyone may whistle whatever tune
he pleases. Everything is infused with tradition; centuries look
down upon you from the ramparts; history is imbedded in every
wall and stone; everywhere can be seen some distinctly national
trait or some exalted concept whose origin lies in the dawn of
history. Nothing of this sort can be found in New York. The
city's main attractions are its hotels and banks; in other words,
there are no historical monuments or sites here. You must look
for the history of the United States in Washington; in New
York you will find only merchants. Business, business, business,
from morning till night, that is all you see, read, and hear. At
first glance, this is not a city inhabited by a particular nationality; rather it is a collection of merchants, industrialists, bankers, officials—a cosmopolitan market place which impresses you
with its vastness, activity, and industrial civilization, but bores
you with the onesidedness of its life, productive only of money.
In describing this city, you do not know where to begin or
what the mind and eye should take for a starting point. One
street resembles the next; all are filled with carriages and omnibuses, and teem with the activity of noisy throngs. With
agitated faces and movements the citizens rush about feverishly
as though they had taken leave of their senses. This haste is
apparent in everything, even in the construction of houses,
streets and sidewalks; one thing is scarcely completed when
another is already begun. On Broadway, for instance, next to
the hotel built completely of white marble stands a row of
red brick homes and, a little farther on, a heap of charred ruins.
Yesterday there was a fire here; today they are already erecting
a new building. If this one should burn tomorrow, the following day they would build again.

Yonder is a church in which people praise the Lord by

---

[7] The Saxon Gardens, one of the most beautiful parks in all Europe,
cover an area of seventeen acres in the center of Warsaw. They date from
the eighteenth century when the Saxon dynasty ruled in Poland.

bellowing like calves; in another, they shake and tremble; in still a third they worship in the Catholic manner. But these churches are closed, for today is a weekday, and business leaves no time for prayer. Nor are they distinguished for their size or antiquity; one suspects that they too were built in a hurry. Near the churches are small cemeteries which here, more than elsewhere, serve truly as places of rest. Farther down the street are funeral parlors, businesses dealing in coffins and tombstones.

Along another street can be seen store windows with rich and dazzling displays which are arranged, however, without taste. On the sidewalk in front of the plate glass windows lie heaps of rubbish. The streets are muddy, dirty, and badly paved; here and there stand small puddles of black mud that cannot flow away through the clogged sewers. Quantities of torn newspapers, orange skins, and apple peelings litter the sidewalks and pavements. The roadway is filled with heavily laden wagons, splendid carriages, and omnibuses. Ownerless pigs with battle-scarred ears amble about—and there are plenty of them here. "Here is a solitary swine lounging homeward by himself," says Dickens in his description of New York. "He has only one ear; having parted with the other to vagrant-dogs in the course of his city rambles. But he gets on very well without it; and leads a roving, gentlemanly, vagabond kind of life, somewhat answering to that of our club-men at home. He leaves his lodgings every morning at a certain hour, throws himself upon the town, gets through his day in some manner quite satisfactory to himself, and regularly appears at the door of his own house again at night, like the mysterious master of Gil Blas. He is a free-and-easy, careless, indifferent kind of pig, having a very large acquaintance among other pigs of the same character, whom he rather knows by sight than conversation, as he seldom troubles himself to stop and exchange civilities. . . ." [8]

[8] This passage is taken from Charles Dickens' *American Notes*, first published in 1842. Dickens had visited the United States the previous year.

There are certainly fewer of these animals now than during Dickens' time, but even today one encounters more of them, especially on the streets of the Lower East Side, than in ten European cities. In short, I have never in my entire life seen a more untidy city, and I predict at the outset that all the efforts of the Warsaw municipal authorities to compete with New York in untidiness will be of no avail—New York will always hold first place, having the advantage of being a port city. And yet no city spends as much as New York for the maintenance of order and municipal services. But unfortunately, like other government administrations, the municipal authorities here consist of thieves so skilled in their profession that European corruption pales into insignificance in comparison. If, for example, in some European city a small, private town hall is born from the official town hall, here the official mouse needs must give birth to a private mountain, even though the mouse itself should fail to survive the delivery. Public money and public welfare here are nothing more than fat for greasing the boots of those who wish to pass dry-shod through the mire. Later I shall have occasion to speak again of similar abuses and of the causes which evoke them. But now I must resume my description of the town.

Let us continue along Broadway. Not far from the City Hall looms the magnificent post office building, containing facilities unsurpassed anywhere else in the world. All the larger stores and firms, and even wealthy private citizens, have their own numbered boxes where every day they receive letters, packages, and even money. Similar facilities exist in banks. For a certain annual fee one is given access to a granite vault with an iron door fitted with an intricate lock. Here in individual small boxes one may keep his most valuable papers, gold, jewelry, and the like. The owner may come at will, take out or add as much as he wishes, clip his coupons whenever he pleases; in a word, although keeping his money in a bank, he has complete control over it. It is protected from robbers first by locks, then

by iron bars, and finally by guard. Fire is no threat because
the banks here are built of massive stone.

In the vicinity of the City Hall, brick buildings surrounding
a beautiful square contain the editorial offices of such powerful
daily newspapers as the *Herald*, the *Tribune*, the *Times*, and
the *Staats Zeitung*. All of these papers print hundreds of thousands of copies daily, using machines the like of which are unknown in the whole of Europe. The *Herald*, owned by the
Bennett family, is considered the outstanding American daily,
employing thousands of people and producing millions of dollars of annual income for its owners. Its editors are considered
the greatest power in the nation, with whom both the Congress
and the President must reckon. Innumerable telegraph lines
bring the news daily from all over the United States and from
the entire world. It frequently happens that not only the
Herald but also the *Tribune* and the *Times* (which has long
since surpassed its English namesake) describe European events
ahead of and more accurately than European newspapers.

A whole army of reporters, paid their weight in gold and
stationed throughout the world, are constantly on the watch
so that nothing worthy of attention may escape them. The
number of copies printed weekly by any one of these dailies
exceeds the annual output of all the Warsaw papers put together. Among the reporters of the *Herald* are such celebrities
as Stanley, who, at the expense of the publisher, is at this
moment penetrating the interior of Africa. Americans recount
with pride that even many European ministers serve as corre-
spondents and send political news to American newspapers.
Of course, this is sheer myth, but it goes to show the tremendous scale on which political publications operate.

And yet, from a literary standpoint, these newspapers are
inferior to European ones. Literary talent does not as yet play
so prominent a role here as in Europe. In the American press
news content takes precedence over literary form; speed and
accuracy in obtaining news are regarded as more important.

Thus, these papers serve rather as agencies than as congenial hearths around which literary figures gather. Individuality is submerged in the complex organization of a paper; reporters are merely hirelings whose activities, taken collectively, are enormous, but whose names can seldom become known for their literary talent.

One of the main differences between the American and the European press is the former's preponderantly political and informative rather than literary character. American journalism accurately reflects the requirements of the American people, who read their newspapers for specific information relating to their political, industrial, and commercial affairs, and not for stylistic gems, wit, or literary flourishes.

Still another distinction results from the limited interests of the people and their newspapers: in Poland a newspaper subscription tends to satisfy purely intellectual needs and is regarded as somewhat of a luxury which the majority of the people can heroically forego; in the United States a newspaper is regarded as a basic need of every person, indispensible as bread itself. This attitude explains the millions of readers and the thousands of papers which are published not merely in the larger cities, but also in settlements that sprang up only yesterday.

From the newspaper offices let us now walk over to Wall Street, a short, narrow street, but perhaps even more important than Broadway. It is the street of the bankers. From early morning it is thronged with people. Here are treasures with which entire countries could be bought. The transactions of the various commerical houses reach an annual total of 170 billion francs. We shall gain some conception of this sum if we recall that Bismarck hoped to ruin France forever by the imposition of a war indemnity of only five billion francs.[9] Outwardly nothing would reveal the importance of this thor-

---

[9] This was the indemnity imposed on France by the Treaty of Frankfort (1871) following the Franco-Prussian War.

oughfare, unless it be the thousands of feverish people who greet each other hurriedly, exchange a few words, and rush on. Obviously something significant is going on here which is of the utmost importance to them.

Here, too, is the stock exchange, or what might better be called an insane asylum for those afflicted with *febris aurea*.[10] The peaceful onlooker is gripped with fear at the sight of what is occurring here. All is noise and tumult, as though a battle were impending. Faces are flushed, voices harsh; men rush at each other, yelling like madmen and shaking their fists. Each tries to outshout all the others. One would judge that these crowds had been overcome by some incomprehensible madness under whose influence they will murder each other. And who would ever think that this is nothing more than a method of making a commercial transaction, and that all the shouting and shaking of fists serve merely to make oneself better understood! When finally the president rings his bell to close transactions, these same people, after a brief interval, go their ways peacefully, arm in arm.

Other than the banks, the stock exchange, the gold room, and the grain, wool, and cotton exchanges, there is nothing else worth seeing on Wall Street.

We now walk down to the streets leading to the harbor. There is less activity here, but the disorder is much greater. The mud is often so deep that it is impossible to cross the street. Negroes are more common in this section of the city. They are employed as coachmen, laborers, stevedores, and the like. For the most part they are clad only in trousers and flannel shirts. Their kinky heads, unfamiliar with comb or scissors, resemble balls of black wool. Some of them are working, while others stand idly in front of houses with hands in their pockets, smoking short pipes, moving their jaws stuffed with tobacco, and staring at the passers-by. All of them look ugly and slovenly. The women, even uglier, differ from the men more by their

---

[10] Gold fever.

dress than by their faces, for they have the same flat noses, the same short, kinky hair, and black skin. These black "ladies" are just as dirty as their menfolk. They wear no hats; they use their heads instead for carrying all kinds of packages, merchandise, containers, and even food. Where a white man uses his back and hands, a black man generally uses his head, which apparently is the hardest part of his anatomy. I saw a Negress who, having bought an orange, instead of carrying it in her hand, immediately placed it in her mop of hair. The orange rolled from left to right, but, being embraced by strong, twisted wool, it could not fall out. Seeing that I was looking at her head, the black "miss," still balancing the orange, began to do a jig. At last she called out: "All right, sir!" and showed me a row of large, white teeth; she then departed, obviously much pleased with her accomplishment.

Side by side with the Negroes in these districts of the city live also the poor immigrants, overcrowded in houses which are wretched and dirty beyond description. Lured by the news that money could be earned easily here, they set out for America with scarcely enough funds to pay their ocean passage. Earning a living is, in fact, much easier in America, but this is true only of the interior of the country and of the Far West. New York itself, on the other hand, is overpopulated. For this reason, the poorest of the immigrants, who have no funds for costly railroad transportation into the interior, die of starvation, cold, and want. These districts reminded me of the London slums, with this difference: Here it is a hundred times dirtier and, as the inhabitants consist of the scum of the proletariat of all nations, they look even worse than those of London. All kinds of diseases, epidemic and nonepidemic, constantly decimate these unfortunates. If they could reach the Western states, which are sparsely populated and in some areas even entirely uninhabited, they would constitute a working force equally beneficial to the nation and to civilization.

The one salvation for these people is enlistment in the army, but this remedy is inadequate—first, because the entire army of the United States totals only 25,000 soldiers, and secondly, because only young men without dependents are eligible to enlist. Thus the majority live without steady wages, working irregularly, looking with envy and certainly with hatred at the millionaires who have more money than they can count. Such a state of affairs is responsible for the many crimes and transgressions of the proletariat, committed in some instances for monetary gain and in others, as I have been informed, for the sole purpose of getting into prison where at least food and shelter are assured.

A goodly majority of these unfortunate people are Irish, of whom there are said to be almost ten million in the United States. They are easily recognized by their dress, or, rather, by the remnants of their national garb, and by their blue eyes, beautiful blond or dark hair, strong physique, and typical Gaelic liveliness of speech and gesture. These traits so sharply differentiate the members of this nationality from the Anglo-Saxons that it is practically impossible to mistake them. Addicted to drinking, gambling, and all sorts of excesses, and possessing a fiery temperament, these people would certainly commit many more crimes were it not for their religious devotion which never deserts them. All of them are very devout Catholics, and for future heavenly bliss they patiently endure all kinds of earthly woe and affliction.

In the Western states there are likewise many Irish, but they do not suffer the same misery as those in New York. Some of them have achieved a good livelihood, others considerable fortunes, and still others even millions. They set an example of clannish solidarity; they help one another, they always flock together, and they vote alike, i.e., as the priests tell them. They never forget their nationality or their motherland; they love Ireland and hate England, even in the tenth generation. They constitute an element America must already reckon with and will have to reckon with even more in the future.

The reason for this lies in the exceedingly rapid increase in numbers of this people. The Irish are as prolific as rabbits, while the native Americans are exactly the opposite. While American families have two, or at most three children, pious Irish parents, who regard children as God's special blessing, bring them into the world like poppy seed; "each year brings forth a prophet," as the saying goes, and the years follow in rapid succession.

This extraordinary fecundity has thus far been beneficial to America, whose territories need to be populated in the national interest. The Irish are already playing an important role in the United States and in addition are necessary and advantageous to the States in ways Americans perhaps are not even aware of, or, being aware, do not appreciate. The Irish contribute a certain element of idealism to this thoroughly materialistic society, thereby maintaining a desirable measure of equilibrium. I can imagine how my positivist colleagues are smiling at this moment; nevertheless, I stand by my opinion. A preponderance of idealistic tendencies is harmful to any society; it gives rise to dreams, political Don Quixoterie, expectation of divine intervention, longing for spring in the midst of winter, but in springtime, only laziness, poverty, and weakness. All of this is unquestionably true, but it is also true that all onesidedness is harmful. The Chinese, for example, are a people lacking all elements of idealism. Among them realism has been developed to the highest degree and has so permeated the national character that it has obstructed all progress and the formulation of powerful ideas for which European peoples are willing to sacrifice their lives. The Chinese, by destroying their national imagination, have at the same time destroyed all initiative, not only in the realm of social relationships, but also in technology, science, and art; in short, they have lost creativeness, the child of imagination.

Perhaps their character predisposed them to the course they have followed. Inherent traits, however, are not the sole deter-

mining factor, for, just as they may influence the nature of a
civilization, so the latter in turn may affect national characteristics either favorably or adversely. In my opinion, the American people, despite their many truly great virtues, are likewise
creating a very onesided civilization in which the Irish character serves as an antidote both necessary and beneficial to the
welfare of American society.

But the Irish, too, have their weaknesses. They are lazy,
especially in the first generation. Incomparably more boisterous
than the Americans, they are given to indulging in political
disturbances. Thus they constitute a very dangerous element,
especially in a republic. Moreover, since they are entirely in
the hands of their priests, they may in time form a strong
clerical party. Such a party is harmful in any state because it
considers its own particular objectives as surpassing all others
in importance. In the United States such a party might with
the passage of years disrupt that harmony which now prevails
among the various religious denominations.

But let us return once more to New York. However unfavorable an impression this city makes because of its lack of historic
monuments, splendid edifices, churches, galleries or museums,
and because of its disorder and its lack of taste in everything,
it does have certain admirable aspects. Foremost among these
are its tremendous industrial development and the spirit of
enterprise and energy of its inhabitants, all of which give
evidence of this young society's unprecedented vitality.

The extraordinary growth of the city, as well as its world-
wide commercial significance, is not explained by its geographi-
cal location alone. Rio de Janeiro and Buenos Aires are equally
well if not more favorably situated for purposes of commerce,
and yet they are not one-tenth so important, for the simple
reason that their inhabitants cannot be compared with the
Yankees either in enterprise or energy. Today New York, together with Brooklyn and Jersey City, numbers more than a
million inhabitants. If some unusual circumstances do not im-

pede its growth, in fifty years New York will be larger than London and Paris combined.

My five-day sojourn was, of course, inadequate for a careful inspection of this gigantic city which calls itself the "Empire City." I did become acquainted with the most important districts, however, and to me this seemed sufficient, especially as I had been assured that the other districts differed only in their greater neglect and untidiness. Indeed, so extreme is this neglect that on the streets often lie dead animals on whose bloated carcasses enterprising businessmen, taking advantage of every opportunity to advertise, post handbills. This is a very typical incident which, in truth, I have not seen myself, but about which I have read and which I have heard described by eyewitnesses.

Of public municipal institutions Central Park deserves mention. It is located on Broadway and is for New York what the Bois de Boulogne is for Paris. It differs little from most municipal parks, but in my opinion it cannot be compared with London's Hyde Park nor even with Berlin's Tiergarten. It is frequented less than either of these, for New Yorkers are occupied with business on weekdays, while on Sundays, according to American custom, they stay at home.

Among the churches, excluding those of Brooklyn (which here is called the "City of Churches"), not one of them merits special attention. The most famous is Trinity Church, founded by the English in colonial times. It is a rather spacious edifice with high, sharply pointed steeples, built in a style approximating the Gothic. It is surrounded by a small cemetery no longer used for burial purposes, but in which are found the graves of several prominent Americans.

There is no national American theater in the strict sense of the word either in New York or elsewhere in America, so far as I know. Theaters do exist, of course, and indeed are elaborately designed and furnished, but the actors and singers who perform in them are, for the most part, celebrated European artists who are paid their weight in gold. Even the plays which are presented come from the pens of European dramatists. Although original American plays are occasionally staged, they do not merit serious attention; they are but awkward beginnings which promise nothing great for the future.

Not only the city of New York, but also its inhabitants impress the visitor unfavorably. To be sure, they possess many fine qualities, but these can be appreciated only after closer acquaintance. Every European traveler is immediately struck by their lack of refinement, their boorishness, and certain crude, offensive habits. Of course, members of the wealthy upper classes who have traveled or spent the greater part of their lives in Europe do not differ at all from Europeans of the same social status; but the conspicuous lack of good manners and graciousness among the people in general makes even the most enthusiastic admirers of the Americans admit that in this respect European nations surpass the United States. The customs and habits which I shall now describe are those which I observed after longer residence among Americans and not merely during my five days' stay in New York.

First of all, the foreigner who comes to the States will seek in vain for that affable readiness to direct and explain which he finds in France, for example. The New Yorker is eternally in a hurry, and when asked for directions he usually replies offhand, "Oh, I don't know," not because he really does not know but because he does not want to be bothered to explain. French politeness is practically unknown here. If a foreigner chances to meet with a certain consideration, it is so coarse, so distasteful, so full of boorish familiarity, that involuntarily one is tempted to say, "plus de confidence que de connaissance!" [11]

In general no one here troubles himself about foreign visitors. The reasons for this are obvious. Paris and other European cities are accustomed to wealthy tourists, who travel for their own pleasure and belong chiefly to the upper social classes. In

[11] More confidence than knowledge.

America, on the other hand, the most numerous class of travelers is composed of poor, ill-mannered immigrants, ofttimes with a very dubious past, who inquire about everything with the object of inquiring themselves into the Americans' pockets. For this reason the newcomer is viewed by native Americans with a measure of suspicion. If, on the contrary, the newcomer happens to be a person of wealth and high birth, he looks down disdainfully from the lofty pedestal of his European conceptions and of his own importance on the uncouth, democratic children of America. None of this promotes harmony in mutual relations and understanding. Add to this the innate crudeness of Americans and you will easily understand why relations with them, especially on first acquaintance, are practically intolerable.

The Americans themselves are well aware of this boorishness. Some of them, especially the better educated, even try to cure themselves and their countrymen of it. The majority, however, consider it a kind of republican and democratic national trait and therefore display a preference to be proud of it rather than a readiness to correct it.

This is a foolish symptom of self-esteem which is very common. Through inordinate egotism whole nations as well as individuals reach such a degree of stupidity that they look through rose-colored glasses even upon their defects as though the latter were unique attributes making them superior to others. It is easy to observe the signs of this weakness in every individual. If Jack drinks a whole jug of wine at one time, he merely proves to sensible people that he is a hog. Yet Jack always takes pride in reminding people of this ability of his and is even prepared to challenge to a fight anyone who disparages it. This admiration of one's own imperfections is carried to such an extreme that people frequently speak of "my palsy," "my influenza," "my bad temper," not apologetically but almost boastfully. Among nations the same thing is true.

Americans are no exception. They consider themselves the

foremost nation on earth. Yet the majority of the better-educated visitors are inclined to maintain that the United States is a political entity but not a nation in the strict, European sense of this word. In their opinion America is a large conglomeration of people of all nationalities, trading, selling, working in agriculture or in industry, united in a great partnership, organized under their own form of government and law, but lacking those traits which generally characterize a unified nation. There is some justification for such an opinion, but I shall go no further into this matter at present. Instead, I wish to speak of certain individual customs which will, I hope, be of greater interest to my readers.

How does that lack of refined manners which I referred to earlier manifest itself? I can answer—in every way. But let the reader judge for himself. Until four or five o'clock in the afternoon practically all the inhabitants of New York, indeed of the entire country, work with feverish zeal to accumulate a fortune. Wealth is the chief criterion by which men are measured, and even the idiom of the language reflects this sentiment. Here people do not say a man *has* a certain amount of money, but that he is *worth* so many thousands. In the evening all business ceases; then comes dinner, followed by a period of relaxation for everyone. Every American (here I am referring only to the middle class) then takes out of his pocket a plug of tobacco, cuts it with his penknife, stuffs it into his mouth, and begins to chew with gusto. Seated in a rocking chair with his feet on the table or the window sill, he begins to whittle with his penknife whatever may be at hand, even the arm of the chair, the window frame, or the table. If he happens to be outdoors, it is the lattice of the veranda which suffers. This practice of whittling with a penknife is so deeply engrained in the character of these people that many of them carry pieces of wood specifically for this purpose. Frequently such an occupation serves also as a screen for stupidity or lack of intellectual resources. If an American happens to find himself in the com-

pany of Europeans whose intellectual attainments he cannot
match, then he will invariably resort to whittling and remain
contemptuously silent as though to demonstrate that, as a true
republican and democrat, he is completely indifferent to their
culture and refinement. Yet in the depths of his soul he envies
these qualities in others and is ashamed that he himself does
not possess them.

The disgusting custom of chewing tobacco is steadily declin-
ing, especially in the larger cities, but today it is still rather
common. If you glance at any group of people, you will notice
that a majority of the men are moving their jaws rhythmically,
as though they were some species of ruminating animals. Every
few moments they expectorate the abominable juice; stuffed
with tobacco, their cheeks seem swollen. Wherever hotels and
restaurants have a marble decor, there are printed signs request-
ing the public to have the kindness to spit into the cuspidors,
not on the marble, which becomes stained and marred. Cuspidors are found in large numbers everywhere, in private dwellings as well as in public places.

But these are not the only customs in which American vul-
garity is displayed. Americans leave the dinner table without
expressing thanks for the pleasure of each other's company;
they greet each other simply by a nod of the head or a wave
of the hand; while conversing, they grasp each other's coat
buttons or lapels, a habit so universal that it is practiced even
between master and servant. They do not take off their hats
even in private homes, and yet they remove their coats everywhere, even in the presence of ladies or in places where dignity
would require otherwise.

In New York, because of lack of time I was unable to see
any governmental institutions in action. But several months
later I had occasion to attend a jury trial in Sacramento, the
capital of California. You will be amazed, dear readers, at what
I saw. The presiding judge, ensconced in a chair on a dais, was
tormented by a loud hiccough; rhythmically moving his jaws

like a cow chewing its cud, he stared vacantly upon the audience. The coatless jurors, likewise chewing tobacco, were lying rather than sitting on their chairs with their feet propped up on the railing. The attorneys, too, were only in their shirtsleeves, while the spectators, without troubling to remove their hats, sat with their feet higher than their heads. Everyone was coughing and spitting as though being paid to do so. To me, accustomed to the dignity and solemnity of European courtrooms, the whole scene gave the impression of some dirty German ratskeller from which the sooner one emerges, the more freely one breathes.

I have been assured that in smaller cities conditions are incomparably worse. This democratic simplicity and uncouthness of the courts might be forgiven if their consciences were equally democratic and their verdicts just. But Americans themselves admit that nowhere in the world is there a court system so corrupt as their own. He who wishes to pass dry-shod through the mud must grease justice, as Old John says, and justice will grease his boots. This is a universal truth. In the United States this axiom applies not only to the judiciary but to the entire system of administration, for certainly nowhere else is the public conscience so dormant as here. My readers will readily understand the reasons for this. The salaries of government officials are generally very low and do not entail pensions. In addition, the continuous struggle between the Republican and Democratic parties, in which victory smiles first on one side and then on the other, never permits an official to remain long in office. On assuming power each party immediately drives out all the incumbent officials and fills the posts with its own henchmen as a reward for their services. Knowing that they will not warm these seats for more than a year or two, the new office-holders try to extract from their positions all possible profit.

This system is an extremely pernicious one, which gives rise to all of those fantastic scandals about which American and foreign newspapers write so much. But this system has become so integral a part of American republican institutions that it constitutes the very essence of them; to change it would be practically impossible.

But even if the spoils system were to be altered, other evils would arise. In any republic, whatever its nature, all officials must work in harmony with the government, that is, with the governing majority. Otherwise a situation is created similar to that which prevails in France where the government is republican and the officials monarchical.[12] And in this tug-of-war the bewildered nation wavers, knowing neither how to extricate itself from this vicious circle nor whither to proceed.

Not by changing the system nor by overthrowing government institutions will the salvation of the republic be achieved, but by radically reforming the education of future generations of citizens and by combating the universally accepted opinion in America that money alone constitutes the worth of a man and that material gains and enjoyment are the sole objectives worth striving for. It must be admitted that the Americans themselves have realized this and therefore have entrusted education mostly to women who, being by nature more idealistic, influence the youth in this same spirit.

For this identical reason I should regard it undesirable to entrust education in Poland to women, inasmuch as our people's national character is exactly opposite to that of the Americans. To adopt foreign institutions bodily and blindly simply because they have proved salutary elsewhere can be very harmful for us, and whoever should attempt to do so would be like that American doctor who treated all ailments with aloe, asserting that whether the patient recovered or died, he as a doctor was merely helping nature take its course. This should be remembered by those in Poland who are the leaders in the movement for public education.

---

[12] Although the constitution drafted in 1875 provided for a republican form of government, monarchical sentiment was still strong among aristocratic elements in France.

By entrusting education to women in America, still another enduring benefit is achieved, that is, the promotion of social amenities which here are so sadly neglected. A male teacher cannot have the same influence on his pupils as a gracious and well-educated woman whose very presence restrains the crude, impetuous tendencies of her semibarbaric charges. This is easy to understand when we recall the respect shown to women in America. Indeed, through their influence on conduct women teachers in the United States perform a real mission. I myself am familiar with a little school in California on the Cosumnes River. The surrounding countryside is still wild. Here and there Indians can still be seen. The settlers consist of poor farmers, sheepherders, gold miners, and large numbers of Chinese. Naturally, a newly created settlement with so motley a population has rough and uncouth ways. Now picture for yourself in this primitive settlement a little schoolhouse which the children are compelled to attend, and in this little schoolhouse is the teacher—a young "miss," delicate and slight, sensitive as a mimosa, accustomed to a different kind of life and other surroundings. But you should see how embarrassed any ruffian is in her presence, how he turns his hat in his hands, not knowing what to do with himself, nor what to think of this apparition so unfamiliar to his eyes. In her presence no one takes the liberty of telling a crude joke or of using profanity, for everyone instinctively feels the inappropriateness of such conduct. But should someone not conform to this code, the fists and revolvers of his neighbors would quickly teach him wisdom. One may safely conclude that both the present and future generations will mellow and acquire gentler ways under such influence.

Roaming with a gun on my shoulder along the banks of the Cosumnes and in the neighboring hills, lured by curiosity and—shall I confess?—by the charms of the teacher, I frequently stopped at the solitary little school. It is a small building, consisting only of one room. The benches are arranged according to the latest scientific methods. On the walls are maps of the United States, Europe, and other parts of the world. Between two maps hangs a motto made out of dried flowers by the children: "Knowledge is power." Facing the benches is the teacher's elevated desk, which, however, she seldom occupies; instead, walking among the pupils, she conducts the lessons in a peripatetic manner, so to speak. Moreover, since the children vary in the degree of their mental development, almost every one requires individual instruction. Reading, writing, and arithmetic are, of course, the main subjects, but the lessons also include zoology, botany, geography, and the like.

The accepted system of teaching is by demonstration, an exceedingly practical method which is now in common use. The teacher's starting point in a lesson in geography is the schoolhouse itself. The children learn how houses are built and for what purposes the rooms are used. After learning about the school, they become acquainted with the country-side in which the school is located, the towns, the rivers, then the entire state, next the United States. The teacher constantly extends the horizon of their knowledge until it includes the whole earth. In the study of zoology and botany the children learn first of all about the fauna and flora of their own vicinity. They study a large number of plants which they see daily on their way to and from school, and the teacher describes the harmful and useful properties of these plants. In the same manner she acquaints her charges with animals and minerals.

Thanks to this excellent system there is in the entire United States scarcely a person among the younger generation who cannot read, write, or calculate, who does not understand politics, and who, in short, is not more or less prepared for his duties as a citizen. The hope is well-founded that such schools and teachers will awaken civic honesty and public conscience, which at present are apparently being bandied about by playful young kittens.

There are many schools like the one described above. Where-ever several farms are established on the prairie, there among the Indians, buffaloes, grizzlies, jaguars, and rattlers a small school is immediately erected which the children attend daily, even from a distance of several miles. The United States spends more money than any other country on education, and remarkable results may be expected from this investment in the not-so-distant future.

The education of youth, especially on the elementary level, is almost exclusively in the hands of women. I have already discussed the good features of this system; I shall now speak of the bad, for every medal has two sides. Each teacher is generally an "interesting young lady" in whom loneliness nurtures a very romantic disposition. Youth and blood cry out for fullfillment even on the prairie. As a result it frequently happens that some young knight of the prairie, some trapper or farmer, adorned by the maiden's imagery with rainbow colors of heroism, sinks into this imagery as torrents of rain into the ground, and then occur trysts under the sycamore tree, then a hushed "I am yours—you are mine" and other possessive pronouns, declined through all the cases. Then a whispered, "Eternally, ah, eternally!" And finally, as Slowacki says:

> . . . things evil and sinful
> Concerning which the Bible speaks.[13]

The result is that the morals and the duties of the teacher suffer in so far as the devil gains. As a result of the laws of this country, however, such relations are a ladder from which one either breaks one's neck or, more generally, goes to the altar. It is well to write this, if only for the benefit of my compatriots who, when abroad, are astonishingly enterprising in this respect.

And now a few words about American women. That cogent

[12] Juliusz Slowacki (1809–1849) is one of Poland's greatest poets. The lines cited are taken from the stanza on "first love" in Song II of the poem *Beniowski*.

Roman description *domiseda, lanifica, pia* [14] in no way applies to American women. Here the usual pattern is for the husband to work, the wife to reign and to use God's gifts as she pleases. Following the example of the Austrian governor [15] who hung his hat on a pole and ordered the Swiss to bow before it, here one could in all seriousness hang a woman's slipper on the pole. An order to pay homage to it would be entirely unnecessary, for every husband, following his own sentiments, would voluntarily remove his hat.

American women dress most ostentatiously. Standing a half hour on Broadway in New York I have seen a greater variety of silk and cashmere dresses—black, yellow, green, and red—than could be seen on the boulevards of Paris. In all of this there is little taste but much display. In the hotels women come to dinner as though dressed for a ball, bedecked in golden bracelets, earrings, and other ornaments. They are such bold, provocative coquettes that truly the roles of the sexes have been reversed and here the woman is the aggressor. Nor is there any lack of bluestockings, but the rumors circulating in Europe about the education of American women are much exaggerated. In my opinion, secondary education of European women is of higher caliber.

Girls here lead a very free life and there are few whose past does not include some episode resulting from a too enthusiastic practice of a relationship called a "flirtation"—and even without a flirtation. "I do not look into my husband's past; let him not look into mine," is a very common sentiment among American women. Such an attitude would certainly lead to greater abuses if their energetic but cool temperament and a certain preponderance of reason over sentiment did not constitute a very strong deterrent.

Foreigners have great appeal for American women because of

[14] Keeping house, spinning wool, saying prayers.
[15] The Austrian governor was Gessler, the tyrant in Schiller's *William Tell*.

their polish and refinement, in which they excel Americans. Frequently, however, a foreigner mistakes counterfeit for good money; but even if he finds good money, so much the worse for him since here, as I have indicated, the altar is the consequence not only of guilt but even of slight indiscretions.

Finally, American women are unattractive. Without breeding and distinction in appearance, their despotism becomes all the more intolerable. And this despotism is felt everywhere: in homes, on trains, in coaches, and even on the streets, where women drive at a mad pace, indifferent to the safety of pedestrians. The law not only places no limit on this despotism but even fosters it. In California a law was recently passed to the effect that a man who beats his wife shall receive twenty-one lashes with a rawhide whip. Why twenty-one? Why not twenty or twenty-five? These are mysteries of American legislation. In a word, he who did not make haste early, now finds the road forever closed to him. If the cruelty of husbands here really were excessive, and if such a law had been passed as a result of actual abuses, one might understand such legislation. But in a country where the husband works like four horses, while the wife idles away the entire day in a rocking chair and greets her husband when he returns from work in whatever humor she pleases, such a law only adds oil to the fire. Sensible people ridicule this inappropriate flight of philanthropy; some of the newspapers have asserted that henceforth every husband who has the desire to thrash his better half must leave California for another state and return only after the operation has been completed. They predict as a consequence a notable increase in train travel. I doubt, however, that railroad officials, especially those who are married, place any credence at all in this prediction.

The respect with which a woman is treated here is easily explained by the fact that the demand for the fair sex is far greater than the supply, to speak in economic terms. There are comparatively few women in America, and in newly settled regions the ratio is only one woman to twenty or thirty men. This explains why rough, unmannerly fellows treat women just as though they were made of glass.

American politeness toward women, however, must not be confused with French or European etiquette. The American will remove his coat in the presence of ladies or do other things, according to his habit, which a European woman would regard as impoliteness or indifference. But whereas French politeness generally has deception as its goal, and is eager to take advantage of a good opportunity, here a woman is entirely safe: a hundred fists and revolvers will threaten the impertinent fellow who dares to offend her in any manner whatsoever. Of course, the women are aware of this and it is not surprising that they consider themselves select beings entitled to adulation.

Europeans have many false impressions about Americans and their country. I have referred to religion; allow me, therefore, in passing, to speak of this aspect of American life. American society is generally considered the most religious in the world. Agnostics are few, religious regulations are strictly observed, and on Sundays and holidays a dead silence descends upon the cities and villages—stores are closed, cabs and omnibuses run only occasionally, theaters are dark, public places are deserted; in short, nowhere else have I seen such gravity and solemnity. But upon closer examination we see in this solemnity the influence of unreasoning habit rather than a living, fervent, conscious faith. The American people are extraordinarily matter-of-fact. No one troubles himself about things which have no connection with reality or material benefits or which cannot be grasped and calculated. Such questions as the origins of the universe, the existence of the Creator, the immortality of the soul, all of which are agitating the minds of European youth, professors, philosophers, and the intelligentsia—these ideas, which so often lead first to philosophical bankruptcy and then to widespread doubt among the people, here carry no weight at all. No other people are less capable of philosophical reflection than Americans. Tangible activity prevails over abstract contemplation. Occupied with commerce, industry, and agriculture, they do not inquire about the validity of religious formalities. Thus, when Sunday comes, the American goes to church because such is the custom; he reads his Bible for the same reason; he stays at home because everybody stays at home. But who can tell in all of this outward observance of the Sabbath whether mechanical routine and empty formality do not predominate over genuine piety?

On the other hand, the great number of sects and the competition among them and the struggle with an ever growing Catholicism color religious feelings with a partisanship which, it must be admitted, produces a purely secular stimulus. The communicants of an old sect try to maintain and extend it; therefore, they must set an example to others. A faction always ties followers to itself, and, as a result of the entanglement of their general and individual interests, it creates partisans who eventually find themselves attached by so many ties that they are neither willing nor able to separate themselves, even though they may have become indifferent to the main principle.

On the other hand, every American regards religious liberty as the jewel in the Constitution of the United States, and, wishing to demonstrate this freedom, he feels obligated to observe assiduously all the rites of the sect to which he belongs. However, my original contention that Americans possess only the outward semblance of deep religious sentiment still stands. Business leaves no time for resolving transcendental questions. Hence they remain unresolved, and religious matters will continue to be dictated by habit and tradition.

I now conclude this cursory sketch of America and Americans in general and of New York in particular. I shall have occasion to return more than once to the many questions raised in it. Here I shall only remark that although I have criticized many shortcomings, I entertain not the slightest doubt about this nation's future. America possesses the capacity for unlimited expansion; it is young, courageous, and energetic beyond description. It understands its faults and is trying to correct them. And because it is courageous, it tries all possible ways and means. Many of these means will undoubtedly prove erroneous, but nobody will shrink from an experiment. Here progress does not wait on God's mercy or on other countries to set an example. No one calls out to France, England, or Germany: "Hey there, fellow; wait for me; I too shall try." Americans are the first to try the new. Blind and decayed conservatism which shakes its head at the sight of any innovation, as at the newly invented pancakes of Mme. Cwierciakiewicz,[16] and says: "Good heavens, in my generation one did not eat pancakes!"—such petty conservatism, I repeat, does not weigh down Americans like a millstone about the neck. For this reason they are able to consider new ideas and to adopt those which are best.

In my next letter I shall describe my impressions from my trip on the transcontinental railroad.

[16] A Polish "Fanny Farmer" who introduced many new recipes in her book entitled *360 Dinners*.

Letter II

ABOARD THE TRANSCONTINENTAL: NEW YORK TO OMAHA

WHEN I realized that I was to be the first Pole to give an eyewitness account of the famous transcontinental railroad, the thought imparted great energy and speed to my actions. Five days after my arrival in New York, I found myself, accompanied by my friend, at the Western Station from which trains leave for Chicago. Here we had an argument with the station master who, like a true Yankee, kept trying to sell us some excessively priced rope with which to tie one of our bags. Having settled the matter of baggage, we started our journey in the direction of the Great West.

We left New York at night, and I was able to see the banks of the Hudson River only by moonlight. Fortunately the night was bright, illuminated by the moon and the snow which covered the ground. I could therefore feast my eyes to my heart's content on the gorgeous views stretching on both sides of the tracks. The immense, broad river glistened like a silver ribbon. Along its banks stood mysterious, silent, dark forests. The region appeared to me quite wild and primitive, especially at night, and in my imagination it swarmed with Indians and buffaloes. Actually, their traces have already long since disappeared from these regions, and they are as unfamiliar to the local inhabitants as to the residents of Warsaw or Lublin.

Because of my meager knowledge of geography, which is on a par with that of the average third-grader, I had imagined the climate of North America, or at least that of the United States, to be much warmer. Spring with its murmuring streams and sprouting wheat fields had already come to Belgium, France, and even England when I left Europe. Yet in this area, which

is on the same latitude as southern Italy, snow covered the
fields, the air was raw and penetrating, and, in the darkness of
night, the trees stood silhouetted in sharp, leafless outlines.
The Hudson River, however, was not frozen over, for I saw
large steamers quietly cleaving through this deep, wide river
which presents a magnificent sight, especially at night. But
soon the river was lost to our view. The train ran along a road-
bed carved through rock whose walls, rising high above both
banks, completely hid the scenery. From time to time we sped
through tunnels, but not with that much-advertised American
speed about which I had heard and read so much. On the
contrary, having by now traveled extensively on all kinds of
American trains, I can say with certainty that all the accounts
of terrific speed are veritable myths. American trains not only
do not travel faster but incomparably slower than the regular
European trains. Only the special trains travel faster, such as
those which traverse the long stretch between New York and
San Francisco in three days and three nights. But such speed is
primarily for the sake of publicity, novelty, and the profits to
be gained.

We traveled seven days and seven nights, with hardly a stop
longer than an hour or two, but at approximately the same speed
as our own trains. In my calculations I do not include the
forced stopover of several days at one station where we were
snowbound. Throughout the seven-day period you live, sleep,
and eat in the coach. You become so accustomed to all this that
later you are unable to fall asleep for several nights without the
familiar roar and vibration of the train. He who travels in
sleeping cars finds the trip quite endurable; he sleeps in a bed
quite similar to, or perhaps even better than, his own at home.
But he who must spend the night in an ordinary coach is
subjected to real torture. There is about as much truth in the
accounts of the conveniences and comforts of American trains
as about their speed. The regular American, first-class coach is
a huge shed, along either side of which is a row of small seats,

each accommodating two people. Down the center of the coach runs a passageway. The seats are covered with faded plush or with shabby green oilcloth. They are so narrow that two persons of average weight can scarcely squeeze into them. They are so close together that a mortal blessed with legs of somewhat more than average length actually doesn't know what to do with them, particularly if he does not wish, as is customary among many Americans, to rest them on the top of the seat in front of him, thereby clasping as in a pair of pincers the head of his fellow-traveler.

At each end of the coach stands a small iron stove and day and night the attendant stuffs it with as much coal as it will hold. The heat is unbearable and the foul air even worse. Passengers stroll up and down the entire train. The conductor keeps opening and closing the doors and the cold air, bearing a whole store of ailments in its wake, sweeps through the coach. Your companions chew tobacco, spit, eat, sleep; everywhere is the greatest untidiness and disorder; the floor is littered with skins of various fruits, shells of nuts, and porcelain cuspidors over which you stumble with every step. Some whistle, others sing, still others snore; the children scream, the men remove their coats, the women are disheveled—in short, a veritable street in bedlam.

In the morning, especially, such a coach looks like a real battlefield. Amidst this chaos the conductor makes his rounds. He does not resemble in the slightest the amiable old fellow we have in Europe who classifies passengers as "good" or "bad" and seats them accordingly, or to whom we give a cigarette so that he will not allow any additional passengers into our compartment. Instead, he is an imposing conductor, a personage of consequence, a veritable captain of a ship, who walks back and forth throughout the train, ensconces himself in the sleeping car or the drawing room, props his feet at an incredible angle, takes off his coat, sits down beside the ladies; frequently he is magnanimous, sometimes arrogant, sometimes majestic, sometimes condescendingly familiar or mildly reproachful, and sometimes battered and bruised after a disastrous exchange of blows with a trapper who, for his part, is unimpressed even by persons of such exalted station.

This is a normal occurrence on these trains. If you insult the conductor, he will attack you with his fists, blacken your eyes, and throw you out of the coach. But if you are the stronger, you may smash his jaw and eject him instead. The same is true of the gentlemen who fire the stoves and make the beds in the sleeping cars. But in America, as elsewhere, if one minds his own business and doesn't look for trouble, he will not find any. To be sure, if you are a foreigner, you will be treated with politeness.

In the sleeping cars, or better still in the so-called "silver-palace Pullman," a certain comfort and orderliness prevail. A Negro appears in the evening, pulls out various drawers from the sides of the coach and transforms them into beds, set one above the other in the long, side walls of the coach. Each pair of beds constitutes a section and is separated from the others by damask curtains. The lower berth is the more desirable. When two persons are traveling together, they reserve such a section and have for the night what amounts to their own damask boudoir. Persons traveling alone, however, and unwilling to pay the cost of an entire section are entitled only to one berth. This may prove inconvenient and even embarrassing, for it frequently happens that the same section is assigned to two passengers of different sex.

I am not exaggerating in the least. An old German cigar salesman who traveled with us as far as Omaha was the co-occupant of a section of which the lower, more desirable, half was occupied by an equally old, scrawny spinster. Every morning each cast disapproving glances at the other. Every evening the poor old German had to climb laboriously into the upper berth. In doing so, he would muss up the bedding of the lower berth and groan as though the trip would be the death of him.

In Europe all kinds of scandalous consequences would surely ensue from such a custom. Yet Americans see nothing strange in it. The explanation lies in the exceptional honor and respect which here surrounds a woman. Every woman, even the youngest, if she is traveling alone, is under the protection of all the men. Even simple miners or farmers will take bloody vengeance with their fists or revolvers (or where lynch law prevails, with a noose) for any insult offered to her. This honor and respect should not be regarded as identical with the cultured manners of the French. The gentlemen who were traveling with us, although belonging to the upper classes of society, did not consider it at all improper to be without their coats or even their boots in the presence of ladies. When we called their attention to these practices, they replied that such things were of no real consequence and that the observance of empty forms was only a false mask concealing trickery and deceit. We, however, did not observe the American code of manners, but retained our Polish and European courtly etiquette which the women here regard most favorably.

The morning following our first night we awoke quite late. Most of the berths were already made up. Some of the ladies, already dressed, were drinking coffee or tea at small tables placed between the settees. The gentlemen, some wearing coats and others in shirtsleeves, were entering or leaving the small men's dressing room at one end of the coach. The conductor sat by the window with his hands in his pockets, sleepy-eyed and hiccoughing. I went to the window to see what America looked like by day.

The train now ran along a low, open road, through a plain enclosed by forests of bare trees. The region was well populated. On both sides you could see farms with attractive small homes of Swiss design. The landscape was, in fact, quite similar to that of Poland. The farms, if they can be judged in the winter, are not to be compared with the farms of Germany, Belgium or France. The buildings are poor; good fences and drainage ditches are lacking. One is reminded of the neglected areas of Podlasie or Pinsk.[1] The soil is evidently fertile, but perhaps for that reason inadequately cultivated. It presents a depressing picture to anyone familiar with the excellent agriculture of western Europe. Everywhere are to be seen evidences of haste in the setting up of the farms which have not yet acquired an appearance of permanence and charm. While still traveling through New York, the most populous and developed state in the Union, here and there in forest clearings we saw small, solitary homesteads which evidently had just emerged from under the settler's ax. Around them were neither shade trees nor orchards; nor was there even a trace of a garden—only the virgin forest. But if you look more closely, you will see rows of burned out stumps, piles of branches and kindling wood, here and there large pools of dark, muddy water, framed by heaps of grey, dirty snow.

Such scenes reminded me of the denuded forest regions which I have seen so often in Poland. Here, however, they have a different, less ominous meaning. Forests are still so abundant here that the pioneers who clear them are rendering a real service to the country. Occasionally, in the midst of the forest lonely cabins can be seen, surrounded by cultivated fields which only a year ago were covered with undergrowth. Day and night these regions resound with the ring of the ax; the frightened animals and birds keep retreating westward; and practically every day new lands emerge from the forest darkness into the sunlight and await only hands and plows to transform them into grainfields.

On the basis of my inquiries and from what I have seen with my own eyes, I can frankly say that Americans are not model farmers. They are too ambitious, they do not like to remain long in any one place, they are too eager for profits. Thus, when an American buys land, his purpose usually is speculation. He is not interested in settling on it and leaving

---

[1] Regions in Eastern Poland containing many forests, marshes, and lakes.

it to his children and grandchildren. The speculator acquires a large section of forest or virgin prairie which costs him very little or nothing at all. He puts a fence around it, builds a house, scratches the soil a little, and then proceeds to sell it at a huge profit to an immigrant or a local capitalist as if it were a genuine "farm" ready to operate. It must be pointed out, however, that although uncultivated virgin lands belonging to the government can be acquired in many states for an incredibly low price or even without charge, income-producing lands located in the vicinity of large cities attain values which are unheard of in Europe. Many fortunate persons who acquired as much free land as they wished afterwards could sell it at $500, $600 and even $1,000 per acre, if nearby there suddenly arose, as so frequently happens in America, a large, commercial city. Such was the case, for example, with the lands on the outskirts of Chicago, which only a short time ago the government considered worthless and distributed to war veterans as a reward for their services; today, the lands are practically worth their weight in gold.

But many speculators who took up immense tracts of land in the vicinity of a newborn town have lost enormous fortunes, for Americans make little ado over abandoning a town. It frequently happens that a town appears somewhere on the prairie and for a time grows like a mushroom. Then, perhaps the location proves unsuitable, or the climate is unhealthy, or the natural wealth of the region becomes exhausted, and without any compunction whatsoever the inhabitants load their wives, children, and old furniture on their wagons and move forward, wherever fancy leads them. The town, which only yesterday had several thousand inhabitants, declines into a miserable settlement or even disappears completely.

But he who takes up land not for speculation but for cultivation, and who has at least some means, seldom loses. Frequently an immigrant who lived in poverty all his life in Europe, or some wreck from life's storm, seeking tranquility and solitude, purchases a wagon, some livestock, agricultural machinery and equipment; then with his wife and children he sets out across the prairie for the Far West. Selecting a suitable spot, usually near a forest or a stream, he builds a house, fences a piece of land, and thus becomes a squatter. From this time on this land is incontestably his own property and whosoever should try to take it from him may expect, not a lawsuit, but a bullet through his head. Or if the region is governed by lynch law, an even more dreadful penalty awaits him at the hands of the vigilantes who enforce this draconic law.

Although such a settler rarely acquires great wealth, on the other hand he seldom suffers financial ruin. Even if there is nobody to pay cash for his grain and cattle, of what use would money be to him out on the prairie? He has food and clothing; his children grow as strong as oaks, and upon reaching maturity, they fly from the nest and settle nearby. The whole of life, though somewhat primitive, is peaceful and untroubled about the morrow. Imperceptibly his twilight days come upon him and life fades away as serenely as a prairie sunset.

It frequently happens that two, three, ten, or a hundred squatters will drift in and settle close to such an isolated prairie farm. The land, which each had acquired without charge, begins to take on value. Its value rises rapidly and in a few years the farm which cost the owner only his labor may be worth as much as a hundred thousand dollars.

Identical conditions do not prevail everywhere, however. In the state of New York through which I traveled by railroad in the direction of the Great Lakes and in the Eastern States generally, practically no unoccupied or government land is available to settlers. Every nook and cranny has been explored and surveyed; all is in private hands; and because of the fertility of the soil and the excellent communication facilities, the land is as expensive as in Europe, and even more so.

As I have indicated, the farms compare unfavorably with

those of Europe. Perhaps if I had seen the countryside during the summer, they would have seemed more attractive and cheerful to me. But in the wintertime the landscape as far as Syracuse appeared monotonously flat, grey, and depressing.

In Syracuse the train made a half-hour stop for breakfast. We then moved on toward Rochester, a city situated on the shores of Lake Ontario. As we approached Rochester, the elevation gradually decreased, although the landscape remained unchanged. The abundance of water in fields and forests indicated that we were approaching the lake region. In some places stretched vast forests, many of which were inundated with water, giving the illusion that the trees grew out of the lakes. From the window of the train I saw large and small flocks of water fowl—wild ducks and sea-gulls that had flown inland from the sea. Sometimes the train emerged abruptly from the forest and ran through low meadows overgrown with thick grass, sweet flag, and last year's withered reeds. The farms are rather close to one another, even more so than are the villages in Poland, but being surrounded by puddles of water, they looked even more desolate than those east of Syracuse. Here and there the black, upturned soil was beginning to emerge from beneath its cover of melting snow; the water-filled furrows glistened in the sun. The wind blew warmer now; you could feel the first breath of spring in the air, still weak but already life-giving, unfettering the waters from their winter chains. Finally in Rochester we beheld the blue waters of huge Lake Ontario. I thought that I had returned to the ocean and was once more gazing at its shoreless expanse. The tracks followed the shoreline, at times so closely that the water lapped against the railroad embankment. To the passengers it seemed almost as though the train were running on the lake itself. Sometimes a white sail could be seen against the blue background of water and sky. Sometimes in the distance drifted a grey ribbon of smoke from an unseen steamer. In places the water receded from the embankment and merged with flat beaches along the lake shore. Close to the water's edge stood small homes; not far from shore boats moored to stakes rocked back and forth, tugging impatiently at their ropes as though eager to break loose and to escape beyond the distant horizon. Wet fishing nets glittering in the sunshine were hung out in front of the houses. Heaps of seaweed lay piled under them. The odor of fish scales and sweet flag filled the air. A flock of birds floated in the sky like small crosses suspended in the blue, alternately vanishing and reappearing.

At last we reached the Suspension Bridge where we stopped to view Niagara and its famous waterfall. The train proceeded with our baggage in the direction of Lake Huron. My companion and I, however, together with a young Englishman whose name I do not recall, hired a carriage and set out across the bridge to the falls. This bridge joins the United States and Canada. At one end, therefore, is the American customs house; at the other, the English. Since the great falls are unapproachable from the American side, it is necessary to cross over into the possessions of Queen Victoria. The whole breadth of both falls can be seen from the bridge, but whether because of the misty and rainy weather, or because of the spray created by the force of the water falling from such height, I saw only what appeared to be tremendous clouds of mist, rising heavenward from the abyss. But the terrifying roar issuing from the mist indicated clearly what was happening behind the white curtain.

Having crossed the bridge, we stopped at last in front of a row of houses situated on an extremely high embankment adjacent to the falls. From here I had an excellent view of them. Truly, the very recollection of this sight stuns my mind and causes my pen to drop from my hand. Lake Erie's tremendous volume of water, flowing through a mighty throat into Lake Ontario, is suddenly deprived of its river bed and falls in two places into the abyss. At first glance it seems that the earth will be unable to withstand the weight and impact of the wild, raging waters which themselves appear terror-stricken. In this sight there is a kind of antedeluvian barbarity, an incomprehensible power, and at the same time an indefinable horror which strikes the senses with a frightening force. Involuntarily the thought comes to mind that something terrible has happened, some cataclysm of nature, and you refuse to believe that this upheaval will continue endlessly. The sky here is dark and ragged. The wind-driven clouds gather and scatter like a herd of wild horses. All around are black, scowling cliffs, chiseled in diabolical shapes. The roar of the water is deafening. The sharp wind stings your face with spray. Sometimes a mist suddenly bursts from the foot of the falls and hides everything from view. Then again it disappears and you see a mass of foam and the entire falls as clearly as an object in the palm of your hand.

But such moments are brief. Usually the mist, foam, water, and air, all mixed together, create such chaos that in it you lose sight and hearing and even consciousness of what is happening. Everything seems seized by a madness. After five minutes you feel exhausted; beads of perspiration, chilled by the icy breath from the abyss, cover your brow. You would like to call out: "Enough, enough!" But still the falls roar and snarl, the yawning gulf spits foam, groaning voices plead for mercy, wild laughter changes suddenly into the roar of madness—all hell seems let loose in a terrible orgy amidst this chaos.

Such is the impression, or rather the half-conscious feeling, evoked by Niagara. In this feeling there is a sense of anguish, but there is elation, too, caused by the momentary abandonment of self and total surrender to nature. Then, having conquered the first confusion of your oppressed thoughts, you find it difficult to tear your eyes away from this sight. The abyss begins to fascinate and entice you. Some kind of irresistible force draws you to the very brink of the precipice. You crave to be closer, to be one with it. You want to lean over and remain suspended, if only for a moment, between life and death. And there below, the awful vortex of foaming waters seems to be opening to devour a victim, while the spray reaches out like arms ready to embrace and carry you away. The precipice whispers, "Come to me!"—but instinct replies, "Very well, but with all due precaution."

Incredible as it many seem, it is possible "with all due precaution" to descend under the cascade, for the water falls with such force and speed that it curves and creates an arch between whose concave side and the cliff is an open space filled only with foam and ice. But in order to get there, you have to dress appropriately; therefore we went to the little house of the Negro guide who hires out himself and his costumes. In the Negro's cabin we encountered an English couple who were putting on waterfall costumes. The elderly, unattractive, gaunt spinster, dressed in the unflattering coat and hood made of fish bladders from under which could be seen the tip of her nose and her gold spectacles, looked like a scarecrow. We dressed in similar cloaks and hoods and then our caravan set out.

The Negro led us to a small, wooden building in the floor of which was a dark opening with descending stairs. At the top of the stairs we were at once enveloped by the darkness and icy air of the gorge. The Negro, resembling a gorilla more than a human being, led the way, calling from time to time "Ho! Ho!" to guide us in the darkness. At last, after descending a score of steps, our eyes were struck by a pale light coming from below. We entered a small passageway leading directly under the falls. Here the guide called a halt and proceeded to tie soles studded with sharp iron nails to our boots. Our English spinster appeared to regard this as quite "shocking," but in the end was persuaded and, lowering her eyes (or was it her spectacles?), she modestly held out her legs to the Negro, or rather something resembling broomsticks. Then we entered under the falls.

I do not know why but the roar inside seems less deafening than outside. The grey daylight penetrates the curtain of water,

filling the whole cavern with a gloomy twilight. The rock of
the rear wall is black and fissured. The ground is covered with
great slabs of ice. All seems primitive and deathlike. Narrow
ribbons of water, detached from the main waterfall, cascade
noisily upon the ice. The air is permeated with mist and
droplets of water. The wind (I cannot imagine how it gets
here), blows as in the devil's forge. The cold pierces our fish-
bladder coats and hoods. In spite of the lessened roar, it is
impossible to hear and understand each other. Over the tremendous blocks of ice, slippery as glass, I managed to approach
very close to the falls for the sharp thorns of my boots
precluded all danger. The guide began to call out something,
but I saw only his gestures and the movement of his lips; his
voice was lost amidst the thunder.

Nothing is more beautiful than this inside view of the waterfall. As I looked upward, the curtain of water seemed motionless, like a single colossal pane of ice, and were it not for
the boiling cauldron below, I would have thought it actually
was frozen. But the clouds of mist which occasionally came
through from outside dispelled all illusions. Then I looked
down. What an unfathomable chasm these waters must have
cut out of the earth, falling for centuries with such tremendous
force! Everything below boils, seethes, crashes and foams—in
short, a veritable inferno. Moving back from the icy edge, I
took a deep breath as if after excessive exertion. The interior
of the cave seemed peaceful. The small ribbons of dripping
water burst gracefully into delicate rainbow spray against the
ice, in drastic contrast to the demonic monster roaring only
a few feet away. My eyes were now so accustomed to the twilight
that I could clearly see every crack and crevice in the black rock
as well as the tufts of moss glittering with moisture in the
crevices.

It was time to return for the cold and dampness became ever
more penetrating but our English companions delayed the
return, stuffing their every pocket with pieces of rock. I suspect·

that had it been possible they would have hidden the whole of Niagara in their pockets in order to transfer it to the British Museum as they had done with the Greek Acropolis. At last we emerged.

Along the way my companion began to argue with the young Englishman who stoutly insisted that the falls were in England since Canada is England. But when finally we informed him that England, by relinquishing fishing rights on the lakes to the Americans, had thereby relinquished her rights to the lakes, he became silent, evidently angry, whether with the Yankees or with us I do not know.

Upon reaching the surface we were unable to see the waterfall for everything was concealed by a white cloud of mist. We now visited the house along the bank. One of them is a museum containing Niagara curiosities which are hardly unique as, for example, shells, petrified objects, skeletons of animals swept away by the speed of the water, photographs of local scenes, and the like. In reality these houses are traps for the tourists to whom are sold here all kinds of souvenir trifles at outrageous prices. To top it off, they are sold by so young and pretty a miss that it is practically impossible to resist the temptation; therefore, everyone buys ten times as much as he had intended. Next the tourists are led to the rooftop of the museum where there is a small turret or observatory from which the entire neighborhood can be clearly seen. The walls and the balustrade of the turret are covered with thousands of inscriptions in English, French, Italian, and other languages. I saw also Polish and Russian inscriptions, for everyone regards it as a duty to leave his signature here, as well as the date of his visit. As for me, like a good scout I bequeathed to ever memorable immortality on the wall not only my own name, but the names of all my acquaintances that I could recall at the moment, of all my cousins, and even of their progeny. The young Englishman beside his own name "Henry" wrote also the name "Mary"; then encircling both with a very complicated scroll, stepped back a few paces and admired his artistry with satisfaction. When we descended, we were seized, seated upon a log, and within the space of five minutes photographed in our fish-bladder costumes—for which service we were required to pay a handsome sum.

Meanwhile it had grown dark. An almost impenetrable curtain of mist obscured the falls. A slight drizzle began. We entered our carriage and drove back to the Suspension Bridge. At the end of the bridge the American customs officials pounced upon us, demanding duty on all the old rubbish we had purchased. But a dollar slipped into the hand of the chief customs official appeased his republican concern for the revenues of the United States and we were allowed to proceed in peace. From the Suspension Bridge we took one last glance in the direction of the waterfall which could now only be heard, but no longer seen.

The American train soon arrived and we moved across Canadian territory to Hamilton, from where we traveled throughout the night to the extreme western corner of Ontario to Detroit, situated on the very edge of Lake Erie. The elevation of the countryside rose slowly but steadily, for Lake Erie lies almost two hundred feet above Lake Ontario. Niagara is really only the outflow of waters from Lake Erie into Ontario. The outflow, coming across a rock which is suddenly cut off, creates the waterfall. From Ontario the land again declines with a gentle slope toward the ocean with which the lakes are joined by the magnificent St. Lawrence River, perhaps the widest river in the world.

The next morning we arrived in Detroit, a city located in Michigan on a river connecting the waters of Lake Huron with Lake Erie. All I knew about Detroit from my geography was that it existed—nothing more. Therefore, you can imagine my surprise when, upon emerging from the railroad station, I beheld an enormous city, exceptionally clean and more attractive than any I had thus far seen in America. As the hour was very early, everyone was still asleep. We went along a wide street where there were many churches which appared to be of the Catholic denomination. Both sides of the street were lined, not with ordinary red brick houses, but with beautiful, small-scale palaces, separated from the street by gilded fences. Behind these fences could be seen flower beds, shrubbery already turning green, and pyramid-shaped spruce trees through which the graceful outlines of the white walls and the large, rose-tinted windows of the small mansions shone attractively. Here and there in the yards Negroes were putting things in order, singing quietly and smoking pipes. We came out upon a spacious square which was the municipal market. In the middle of it stood a handsome statue of some general of the recent war with the South. Surrounding the square were the inevitable brick buildings, but these were stately and ornate in design and housed immense stores whose show windows were open to view, unprotected by shutters. Already the market place was teeming with life. Wagons drawn by mules and piled high with lumber rumbled over the pavement.

At last we returned to the station. The train was to leave in half an hour. We just had time for breakfast at which we were served an excellent oyster stew by a métis waiter.[2] It was the first time I had seen a person in whose veins flowed Indian blood. IIe was a man of excellent physique, with copper colored skin, thick straight hair so black that it seemed almost blue, and a good-natured face. He had a narrow brow and somewhat protruding cheekbones; otherwise his features were quite regular, reminding me of the faces of our wandering tinkers. With each order given to him he would reply with a dignified "Yes, sir!" and he served us expertly and quickly. After breakfast when, contrary to American custom, I slipped a tip into his hand, he looked at it and then exclaimed, "Oh! yes, indeed, sir!" smiling with satisfaction, and voluntarily carried our fur coats and travel bags to the train.

[2] A métis is a person of mixed blood.

We proceeded across the state of Michigan toward the lake by this name on whose southwestern shore lies Chicago. The countryside through which I was traveling closely resembles Polish Prussia. It has a multitude of large and small lakes, rivers, and streams, an unusual abundance of water. In a word, it is evident everywhere that this is one great former lake region over which waves once flowed ages ago. Everywhere the forests are quite extensive. The proximity of great bodies of water has evidently a moderating effect upon the climate for we saw practically no snow anywhere, while the trees in the forests were sprouting spring buds and the grass was turning green in the low meadows. From time to time I closely scrutinized the passing landscape, curious to know if I might spot a redskin. Numerous tribes of them formerly lived around the lake and one such tribe left in the name Huron a permanent monument to their memory. Now all trace of them has disappeared not only in Michigan, but also in Ohio, Indiana, and Illinois. The Indian, wild boar, bear, coyote, and jaguar are constantly retreating farther and farther West before the advancing whites or are being destroyed in the desperate struggle with them.

Twenty-four hours after leaving Detroit we finally reached Chicago. This immense city lies on the southwestern shore of Lake Michigan and serves as a port for all ships sailing between Canada and the United States. Only a few years ago it was almost completely destroyed by fire,[3] but it is being rebuilt with inconceivable speed. Here and there traces of the conflagration can still be seen.

It was already twilight when we arrived; nevertheless, I left the hotel for the street. After my disenchantment with New York and with the dirt and disorder of the famous Empire City, Chicago made a favorable and even majestic impression. The city has an imposing appearance. The streets are unusually wide, the homes are immense, dignified, and magnificently

[3] The great Chicago fire occurred in 1871.

laid out. The sidewalks are elevated above the level of the streets and astonish one by their width and the tremendous stone slabs from which they are constructed. In short, everything is enormous here. One might say the city was built by giants and for giants. It has its own unique characteristics. It is evident that the city is new, built in accordance with the needs of modern living. I had read somewhere a fantastic description of such cities and how they would look in the twentieth century. Chicago reminded me of this description. Everything here is just as that description had said it should be; everything is symmetrically laid out—perpendicular, rectangular. Everywhere are innovations which are not even known elsewhere. Along all the streets stand rows of telegraph poles supporting a vast number of wires. On other wires stretched across the street from one house to another hang signs with all kinds of inscriptions. In the evening twilight which obscures the sight of the wires, the signs appear to be suspended in mid-air without support. As you look down the street, you see entire rows of large and small signs in various colors, almost as if the town were decorated with flags for some celebration.

On the sidewalks there is tremendous movement. Crowds of people, both white and colored, hurry in all directions with that typical American haste characteristic of business determination. The streets are full of carriages and cabs; the bells of the streetcars clang; cab men shout; everywhere are crowds and tumult, evidence of the great exuberance of life in this young city. Evening has finally fallen, yet it remains as bright as day from the thousands of gas lights. The display windows in the gigantic stores are so brilliantly illuminated by gas flames that they almost have the appearance of real fireplaces. Having selected a street at random, I walked where my eyes led me. In some places the rows of houses broke off suddenly and in their place were empty areas covered with crumbled brick and debris, evidences of the recent fire. In other localities it appeared that a new, gigantic city was being erected. As far as

the eye could see I beheld scaffolding after scaffolding, unfinished houses staring out through their empty window frames,
storey rising upon storey, heaps of bricks and lime. Then comes
a street already built up and completed, filled with the clamor
and clatter of people, and the glitter of gas lamps—in short,
a city reborn like the phoenix from the ashes.

What strikes one most in these American towns is their
vitality and also the almost incredible energy of their inhabitants. A fire of dimensions unheard of in modern times occurred that burned out the city like a cartridge of powder. Its
inhabitants were dispersed; commerce and industry ceased;
fortunes were ruined; its people were left homeless and without
food. Several years elapsed and the city stands again on its
former site; four hundred thousand inhabitants find work and
livelihood in it; homes, mansions, churches, factories, hotels,
stores are being erected. Within a few years no traces of the
fire will remain—and if the town should burn again, it will
once more be rebuilt. It will be rebuilt twice or even ten times,
for the energy of these people surmounts all misfortunes and
all disasters.

The extraordinary growth of Chicago must be attributed not
only to the energy of its inhabitants but also to its extremely
favorable commercial location. Situated on the shores of Lake
Michigan, this "Queen of the Lakes" reigns over the entire
waterway system connecting Canada with the United States.
All of the trade of these inland lakes lies directly in this city's
hands. Thus, Chicago might be called a port in the middle of
a continent, profiting simultaneously from its inland as well as
its port location. Furthermore, as the greatest city on the western
route of the transcontinental railroad connecting New York
with San Francisco, it unites civilization with the Far West.
The East sends out the products of its industry, the West its
agricultural products and natural resources, and Chicago is the
great market place where the exchange takes place.

Walking aimlessly along the streets, I entered a district which was empty and quiet. Here the town ended abruptly as though cut off, and before me I beheld Lake Michigan. Waves made silvery by the light of the moon broke against the low retaining wall directly at my feet. I could scarcely hear the noise of the city in the distance. Here were no crowds; the air was fresh and all was quiet and peaceful. Only the lapping of the water and an occasional whistle from a far away steamer broke the solemn, poetic silence.

At last I returned to my hotel, the Palmer House, an edifice built of huge slabs of marble in true Babylonian magnificence. Everything within it simply drips with gold, silk, and velvet. My eyes, accustomed but a moment ago to a dim, empty, watery expanse, now blinked under the brilliant lights and the opulence spilling over the brim like the bubbles in a glass of champagne. Indeed, this hotel is the most remarkable sight in town. But in Chicago, too, as in all American cities, there are no stone or marble ruins, no churches or museums to conjure up memories of a historic past. Everything is new and contemporary. Everywhere people look to "tomorrow." "Yesterday" to them means only deserts, primeval forests, and the vast silence of the prairies.

The following day we visited other parts of the city. Since, however, only a few hours are sufficient to become acquainted with most American cities, we saw little that was new. But the day passed quickly and next morning at the break of dawn we resumed our journey westward.

The state of Illinois through whose northern extremity we traveled the entire day is a well-cultivated and densely populated state. Its main difference from the states I have previously described is its general lack of forests and trees, which gives the region a rather melancholy appearance. On both sides of the railroad track, however, can be seen cultivated fields and numerous farms one after the other.

In Illinois, as in Wisconsin to the north, there are many

Polish settlements, inhabited primarily by peasants under the leadership of their parish priests. These settlements, although adequately populated, are more or less poor. Their inhabitants lack many necessities of life and long for their homeland in spite of the fact that the settlements are provided with all the conditions necessary to promote prosperity and development with fertile soil and excellent communication facilities. The reason for this is their inability to speak the English language and their unfamiliarity with American customs and local conditions in general.[4]

After twelve hours of travel we reached the border between Illinois and Iowa at the settlement of Clinton, situated right on the banks of the Mississippi. The sun was setting. The magnificent "Father of the Waters," although not yet very wide at this particular point, glittered in its immense turns and bends like a colossal, golden ribbon, disappearing amidst the dark forests. Its banks are covered with a wild and picturesque undergrowth. It has been only a few years since the white man placed his iron hand over this region. In Clinton itself the wooden houses have not yet turned black from the sun and wind. The settlement seems as if it had been established only yesterday. The few houses stand on black mud. Here and there glisten large pools of water. Piles of wood chips still lie near the houses. Further on are to be seen houses under construction and stacks of boards and logs cut from the neighboring forests. Curved axes are stuck in some of the tree stumps. Everywhere are chaos and disorder as one would expect in a settlement that is just being established. This disorder is made all the greater by the roving cattle and the pigs which wallow in the black mud and raise their grunting snouts out of the mud puddles as the train approaches. This was the first settlement where I witnessed real pioneer life, but who knows—in a few years

[4] For a more detailed description of Polish settlements in this country, see Letter XIII.

this place may be transformed into an important city, thanks to its favorable location where the great railroad crosses the Mississippi.[5]

Everywhere on the waters of the "Great Father" there was teeming activity. I saw barges, rafts, and steamboats loaded with all kinds of merchandise being floated down to St. Louis and perhaps even farther. The tall strong raftsmen and crewmen, dressed in flannel shirts and tattered hats, represent typical American frontiersmen who live on the edge of civilization and on the prairie and about whom I had read so much in the novels of Cooper, Bret Harte, and others. Their heavily bearded chins and alert faces and the revolvers protruding from their hip pockets—all of this gives them a storybook, romantic, half-brigandish appearance. They come mostly from Wisconsin and from the tributaries of the "Great Father of the Waters" along whose banks life is still as wild and primitive as on the steppes. Their life may be described as follows: they drink heavily and fight at the slightest provocation; their uninhibited passions explode at almost any cause; but otherwise, they are honest and upright men, although their sense of justice, in the application of the law, often borders on cruelty.

Iowa, however, already belongs to the civilized states, and the Great West really begins only beyond the Missouri, beyond the rather large city of Omaha through which the transcontinental railroad also runs. Not wishing to anticipate geography in my narrative, however, I return to Clinton. After a half-hour's stop the train again proceeds. The road now runs through territory utterly devoid of trees and rises constantly, for we are now approaching the great plateau which comprises the center of the United States and which constitutes the steppes, or, as they are called here, the prairies. On both sides of the railway track farms can still be seen, but much less frequently than in Illinois.

[5] In 1876 Clinton had a population of about 7,000. According to the 1950 Census its population was 30,400.

Here and there by the light of the moon I see fields of corn whose tall, black stalks, now wilted and dejected, are still standing from last year. As we speed westward, the country becomes more and more desolate. Although crisscrossed in every direction by railroads, Iowa forms a kind of vestibule to the immense prairies embracing the entire expanse of territory from the Missouri as far as the Sierra Nevadas. The country is generally level and flat and only occasionally is it broken by small hills and valleys. Of trees there is not even a trace. The eyes lose themselves in the distance, finding no object on which to rest.

That this is the frontier of civilization is evident even from the kind of people who fill the trains. They are not elegant, carefully dressed gentlemen, but bearded and mustached individuals dressed in ragged garments, carrying dirty bundles, and with revolvers stuck in their belts. Their talk is loud and stormy and filled with profanity. Clouds of tobacco smoke rise to the ceiling of the coaches. Doors slam as they are opened and closed by strong hands. References to the Sioux and Pawnees, Indian tribes inhabiting Nebraska and the Dakotas, are frequently heard in the conversation.

I had thought the train would stop less frequently as we moved westward and was therefore surprised to find large crowds waiting at every station. It finally became so crowded in the coaches that one could scarcely move. From an European's point of view this was the worst sort of company. As before, bearded men with revolvers sticking out of their back pockets continued to board the train, but now their faces seemed more savage. I began to suspect that there must be some special reason for this large number of strange men who were crowding into the train. Therefore, when I heard a nearby fellow traveler speak French, I asked him about the meaning of all this. He replied that all of these people were headed for Omaha and from there through Sioux City to the Black Hills where gold had just been discovered. Thus they were miners, or rather adventurers of all kinds who had abandoned their other occupations in the expectation of making fabulous fortunes in the hills. The French traveler informed me that many such groups had already gone to the Black Hills, and more people were being attracted there daily. Even women with babes at their breasts were not lacking. Sometimes they traveled alone; sometimes they accompanied their husbands. A similar movement is taking place along the branch lines in Iowa. In short, throughout all the frontier states you hear only the cry, "To the Black Hills! To the Black Hills!"

And yet this dream of paradise becomes a grave for many, because the entire surrounding country, as well as the Black Hills, belong to the Sioux, the largest Indian tribe in the north, who are able to put ten thousand warriors into the field. The United States government long ago recognized their possession of the Black Hills and guaranteed this territory to them. Therefore, the tomahawk of war has long remained buried between the reds and the whites. But now crowds of white adventurers, disregarding government treaties, were rushing into the hills. To be sure, under such circumstances the government gives them no protection, nor does it send armies to their defence. But the adventurers, armed and accustomed to warfare with the Indians, care even less for protection than they do for treaties, and seize what they please. Such a state of affairs, which is common to all the States, has driven the Indians to desperation.

In vain the Indians send emissaries who prove their ownership with parchments, seals, and signatures. The government does not have the power to restrain the adventurers. Moreover, when a region becomes occupied, when farms and towns begin to rise, the government has no choice but to sanction the seizure and to add one more territory to the States. So it is happening in the Dakotas, in Nebraska, in Kansas, and in the Indian Territory—in a word, everywhere. The government allots land to the savages, but the white men take it from them, and once the Indians are driven out, new states are set up. In the face of this, what can the redskins do? They wage a continuous war, a war to the death without hope of victory. Today the red warriors are already aware that they will not survive the struggle with the "Long Knives," as they call the white men. They are therefore anxious not to perish without avenging themselves and in the next world to place at the feet of the "Great Spirit" as many bloody scalps as possible torn from the heads of the invaders. Briefly stated, this valiant though savage race is being relentlessly exterminated throughout the United States. The Indians cannot reconcile themselves with a civilization which, of course, is being presented to them in its worst possible form, and therefore this civilization is wiping them off the face of the earth, inexorably and brutally.

Now the turn of the Sioux has come. Their warriors have painted themselves with ochre and stand ready for the battle which, in fact, has already begun. The newspapers are full of descriptions of dramatic events in the Black Hills, and these descriptions, often purposely exaggerated, only foment the hatred of the white men, and instead of frightening them away, only incite all restless souls to seek bloody adventures and vengeance upon the redskins. Some of the tales actually sound like the plot of a novel. Thus, I have heard tell of a certain well-to-do young woman, beautiful as a lily, who married a poor immigrant in spite of the opposition of her parents. The parents gave her no dowry, so the young couple lived in poverty. Beautiful Nelly scrubbed clothes with her delicate white hands, while her young husband worked as a pedlar, that is, he carried and sold merchandise from house to house. They did this until news reached them of the gold mines in the Black Hills. Without further ado the young man and his beloved Nelly went off to the hills. One day with his gun over his shoulder he left the encampment to shoot something for dinner. He did not return. Nelly was left alone among adventurers of the worst type, without protection or means of subsistence. Fortunately, close to the camp shone each evening the fires of trappers, that is, prairie hunters who throughout their lives roam the plains, hunting and fighting with the Indians. Thus, one night ashen-faced Nelly appeared at the fireside of the trappers.

"I am alone, forelorn, and exhausted," she said to them. "The Redskins have seized from me my beloved. I have come to beg you to take me in, for I am alone in the world and need help in my misfortune."

The hearts of the old trappers were moved with compassion. Not only did they receive unfortunate Nelly, but loved her like a daughter and took her under their protection. On the following day they set out to search for the lost bridegroom. They learned that he was being held prisoner in the camp of the Sioux where he was lying ill, beaten and on the point of death. Before the wigwam of the chief a torture stake had already been erected for him. That night the trappers crept up to the tents and raising a war cry, struck at the redskins. With the help of their repeating rifles they soon disposed of the Indians. The bridegroom was rescued, but during the skirmish brave Nelly received a fatal arrow in her breast from the hands of a fleeing Indian. With her dying breath she bid farewell to her bridegroom and to her adopted fathers. Henceforth the bridegroom stopped prospecting for gold and the trappers gave up hunting; the rest of their lives they devoted to seeking revenge. The wind has already dispersed the ashes of many an Indian camp; many warriors have gone to the happy hunting grounds of the Great Spirit; many squaws and children have also perished. But the vengeful trappers have not yet abandoned their bloody work and to this day they still prowl at night around Indian wigwams in the form of wolves and evil spirits.

Such is the story of Nelly, worthy of the pen of Cooper or Gabriel Ferry.[6] Probably there is little truth in it—perhaps

[6] Gabriel Ferry (1809–1852) was a French author who made a visit to the United States and wrote many novels based on life in the New World.

none at all. Only this much is certain that with my own eyes
I have witnessed those embittered relations between Indians
and whites which could indeed have produced such incidents.

In the train speeding towards Omaha and from there through
Sioux City to the Black Hills I encountered many stouthearted
hunters like those mentioned in the story of Nelly. Several of
them sat quietly in the smoking car, puffing at their pipes or
dozing. They were wearing fur caps, belts of buffalo skin and
fur jackets. Close by a long-haired *gambusino* strummed a
guitar.[7] At times I thought I must be dreaming or reading a
novel.

Suddenly my sense of smell received a violent stimulus which
convinced me beyond a doubt that my surroundings were real.
It happened at night while we were approaching the western
border of Iowa. Whether the train ran over a skunk or whether
there were many of these animals in the vicinity, suffice it to
say that such a terrific stench filled the coach that it was scarcely
possible to breathe. Although we covered our noses with our
handkerchiefs, we seemed even to taste this loathsome smell
in our mouths. I opened the window but that made it all the
worse. As compensation for this unpleasant experience I wanted
at least to catch sight of one of these animals, but through
the window of the coach I saw only the prairie overgrown
with grass and flooded with moonlight, otherwise not a living
creature. The Frenchman assured me that at the next station
they would surely have live skunks, or at least their skins, and
that I would therefore have a chance to see them. At this point
we engaged in conversation on the subject of these animals.
Skunks, or as they are appropriately called in Polish, American
stinkers, are rather large carniverous members of the marten
family. They feed upon birds and eggs and destroy a large
number of rats, hamsters, ground squirrels and prairie dogs,
and from this point of view they are even useful for these small

[7] *Gambusino:* a Spanish-Americanism meaning adventurer or soldier of
fortune.

creatures do enormous damage in the fields. Some varieties, namely the so-called black skunks, provide expensive and beautiful fur pelts which are well known in Warsaw. But Iowa skunks are black with a white stripe on their backs and on their bellies. Because of their motley appearance the skins are of no value; therefore no one hunts skunks and they multiply as much as they please. Among animals they have no dangerous enemies, or, more accurately, they have a perfect defensive weapon in that ghastly odor and in the ease with which they can poison the air at the slightest commotion. The Frenchman who had spent much time among the Indians and who was thoroughly familiar with their customs, assured me that Indians eat skunks with great appetite. At first I refused to believe this, but now I am convinced that Indians and Chinese eat everything which is soft enough to be chewed.

It took a half hour to pass through the area contaminated by the skunks. Clean cool prairie air now began to flow in through the windows of the coach. The night began to pale. On the eastern horizon appeared the dim light of dawn. Though not yet bright, nor golden, nor rose-colored, it already seemed to proclaim to the prairies and the heavens *"Fiat lux!"* I walked out on the coach platform. The long lonely iron rails and the cross-shaped telegraph posts were gradually emerging from out of the shadows and could be seen stretching far into the distance. Here the dawn was not greeted by the song of birds nor by the rustle of leaves glistening with morning dew. The landscape was lifeless, barren, without trees or water. The stillness was broken only by the feverish snorting of the locomotive which seemed to devour the miles with a relentless anger.

For a long time I continued to gaze at the tracks which I could see distinctly as far as the horizon. There is nothing more depressing than such a road across the prairie. At the top of the telegraph poles were attached horizontal crossbars, giving the appearance of crucifixes. All around stretched a grey, endless plain covered with sweetbroom and occasional patches

of snow, and the long row of crosses, sad and funereal, as far
as the eye could see. They seemed to mark the path leading
into the valley of death, or to represent monuments upon the
graves of wanderers.

They really are monuments. They mark the graves of the
original inhabitants of this land. Wherever such a cross appears, there people, forests, buffaloes will perish; there will
perish the virginity of the soil. Today's vast silence will be
transformed into the hubbub of men selling, buying, cheating,
and being cheated. On the graves of the Indians a learned
professor will discourse upon the rights of nations. Over the
lair of the fox a lawyer will set up his office. Yonder where
the wolf roamed, a priest will tend his flock. Alas! the chase
of humanity after what seems to be happiness will be no more
successful than the chase of a dog after his own tail.

By the time all of these Schopenhauer and Hartmann reflec-
tions had passed through my mind it was practically broad daylight.[8] The lights in the coaches grew dim and finally went
out. The villainous faces of the adventurers appeared wan and
tired. Meanwhile the train stopped; we had reached Ketchum,
a small station on the Iowa border not far from Omaha. And
here, too, waited new crowds of gold seekers and it was therefore
necessary to attach additional coaches to the train, causing considerable delay. For me this was a real joy and surprise as in
Ketchum I beheld my first wild Indians.

Upon leaving the coach, I noticed close to the station a small
group of people standing in a circle around something which
attracted their curiosity. When I inquired what this might
mean, I was told that an embassy of the Sioux was traveling
east to see President Grant, or, what was more likely, to the
governor of Iowa, or to a certain general who was in command
of the troops in the Black Hills region. Others maintained
that these were Indians who had been invited to the Exhibi-

---

[8] Karl Hartmann (1842–1906), like Arthur Schopenhauer (1788–1860),
was a German philosopher of pessimism.

tion in Philadelphia. I hunted out my Frenchman who knew not only English but also the language of the Sioux, and God knows how many other tongues, and together we scurried over to the Indians. Six warriors, no longer young, were squatting around a fire built of dry twigs. They were dressed partly in skins, partly in shabby European clothes, or wrapped in horse blankets stamped with the letters U.S. which the government distributes to them. Some had their hair hanging down unadorned—straight, black, and coarse. Others had stuck feathers and pieces of ribbon or other brightly colored ornaments into their hair. The majority were armed with Kentucky rifles; all of them carried knives and small hatchets called tomahawks. At the belts of some of them hung scalps, that is, hair together with the skin torn from the heads of their enemies; human hair also decorated the seams of their garments. They sat quiet and motionless, without uttering a word, exactly like bronze statues. The surrounding crowd was obviously very hostile toward them. "God damn you!" "Pest on you!" and other typically American profanities were constantly hurled at them. The unruly conduct of the white men was in striking contrast to the stolidity of the red warriors. They looked at no one, wondered at nothing. Their faces were expressionless as though they were deeply absorbed in thought, and the look in their eyes was one of complete indifference, even of apathy.

Nevertheless, Indians possess the same violent passions common to all children of nature, but according to Indian standards, only a woman, or a man unworthy of the name, reveals what is happening within her soul. The true warrior is master of his emotions. While his soul seethes with an insane rage, he can look upon his victim with that impassive expression which makes one's blood curdle. On the other hand, when he has been captured by enemies and tied to the torture stake, he will not betray his pain by even the slightest twitch of his muscles. On the contrary, he will incite the fury of his captors

with his insults and with his recital of the bloody wrongs which
he had inflicted upon them during his lifetime.

Such is the Indian code. Of course, there must be very few
warriors who possess the strength of will necessary to uphold
the above ideal honorably in every instance. Yet the Apaches
and the Comanches who live in the South are reputed to be
even more valiant than the Sioux.[9] Be that as it may, the Sioux
are trying to preserve at least the appearance of that stoicism
which constitutes a strange yet admirable trait of this half-
savage race, a race which has produced certain conceptions and
ideals which belong only to peoples of a high intellectual development.

Despite all of this, the Sioux warriors did not correspond
entirely to the mental picture of Indians which I had acquired
from my reading of the novels of Cooper, Bellemare, and others.
Upon closer inspection, they appeared shabby, extremely dirty,
and slovenly. An odor emanated from them which was hardly
better than that from the skunks; fortunately, it was somewhat mitigated by the smoke of the burning heather. When
the Frenchman and I sat down beside the fire without any
greeting or ceremony, the faces of the warriors remained immobile. They did not favor us even with a single glance. When,
however, I produced a large package of cigars and chocolates,
and when the Frenchman told them (as he explained to me
later) that I was a young warrior from the North who belonged
to another race of whites friendly to the redskins and who
had come to make the acquaintance of his red brothers and
bring them gifts—the stoicism of the warriors vanished like
the fog. Their eyes and faces remained expressionless, but a
muffled, hoarse "hello" could now be heard among them. Enormous bronze paws stretched greedily in the direction of the

[9] Sienkiewicz's footnote: During the war which broke out shortly after,
the Sioux gave the lie to this opinion, for their leader, Sitting Bull, in a
bloody battle defeated an American army under the command of General
Custer who was himself killed. Ultimately the Sioux were conquered and
Sitting Bull fled to Canada.

gifts and both chocolates and cigars disappeared immediately into the jaws of my new allies. For a while could be heard only the crunching of the unfortunate tablets of chocolate given to me by beautiful, delicate hands in Warsaw,[10] and then a solemn silence ensued.

The ice was now broken. I could converse with them to my heart's content. But before I had time to ask the names of my brothers and invent an effective one for myself, the locomotive whistled and we had to return to the train. The Frenchman, however, managed to learn that heavy snows had fallen in the plateaus and that the "great wagons of the whites" would be unable to proceed. I wanted to find out how long "my red brethren" had been in Ketchum and where they were going, but time did not permit, for we had wasted much of it sitting by the fire in the obligatory ceremonial silence.

As we were returning to the coaches, the adventurers began to reproach the Frenchman and me for having talked to "those scoundrels, red devils, murderers" as though they were human beings. We replied, or rather the Frenchman replied, that they should mind their own business, whereupon we entered our coach. In the coaches everyone was talking about the redskins. It is difficult to comprehend the extent of the hatred and contempt of the American frontiersman for the Indian. It is true that a battle to the death was raging and that pillage and murder severely strain relations. But it is also true that the white frontiersmen do not regard the Indians as human beings and look upon their extermination as a service to humanity. According to the philosophy of the frontier, the white man has the same right to exterminate Indians as he would rattlesnakes, grizzly bears, and other harmful creatures. While New York curbstone philanthropists from time to time arrange charity balls at which Indians are exhibited, out on the frontier a merciless and dreadful war rages incessantly.

[10] Sienkiewicz had received these chocolates upon his departure from Warsaw from Stefania Leo, the wife of *Gazeta Polska's* editor.

One must understand that the frontiersmen, although loyal and even honest in their relations with each other, are no less savage than the redskins themselves when dealing with the latter. It is true that the Indian knows no mercy. A victim who falls into his hands would find all human prayer and pleading to no avail. The red warrior looks upon his victim with impassive eyes and supplications merely tickle his ears pleasantly. The suffering of his victim gives him pleasure, he feasts upon it, and for a while he is happy. And the whites treat the Indians in exactly the same manner. The Indian tears off the scalp of his captive as a war trophy; the whites have adopted this custom from the redskins and they likewise scalp their prisoners. In view of all this, if someone should ask me on whose side justice lies, I should answer that, judging in accordance with simple principles based not on sophistry but on the heart and a consciousness of justice, it lies on the side of the Indians.

Let us look at this vaunted civilization and see how it appears to the Indians who are declared incapable of adopting it. First of all, the government of the United States guarantees land to them, but the citizens from whose bosom the government sprang take the land from them in spite of the government. Thus, at the very outset, the Indian meets with deception and perjury and, as a simple child of nature, he is unable to differentiate between the government and the people. The Indian's sole impression from all this is that he has been deeply wronged. Moreover, the Indian sees in such a civilization only the destruction of everything which has served as a means of livelihood for him and his forefathers. First, the wide open prairies are taken from him and he is given a piece of land which he does not know how to cultivate. A horse blanket is given to him, but his liberty is taken from him. What an excellent exchange! The savage warrior astride the bare back of his mustang roams across the prairie. He hunts, fights, and fills his lungs with the fresh air. The wild, prairie life is as necessary to him as are the wide open heavens to the birds. Without it he cannot exist; he withers away and dies. Let us consider what he gains and what he loses by accepting so-called civilization. Above all, he suffers from hunger on his small piece of land. Those same "brothers" who preached to him of civilization, now look upon him with contempt, as we in Europe do upon the gypsies. Ultimately nothing remains for him but to lead the life of a gypsy: begging and thieving, living from hand to mouth, and steadily becoming more and more degraded.

Finally, who are these apostles of civilization with whom he comes in contact? First, there is the merchant who cheats him, then the adventurer who scalps him, next, the trapper who hunts buffaloes right in front of his wigwam—the buffaloes that are the redskin's main source of livelihood, finally, the American government commissioner with his documents which contain, hidden between the lines, the motto *Mane, tekel, fares!* for the entire race.[11]

Later at many of the railroad stations on the prairies of Nebraska and Wyoming, I met so-called civilized Indians. They present a uniform picture of misery and despair. The men are shabby, dirty, and degraded; the women stretch their emaciated hands toward the coaches, begging for handouts. You may inquire: why don't they work? They do not know how to work, and no one is concerned about teaching them. They have renounced their wars with the whites, and given up their raids and hunting. In return, they have received . . . horse blankets . . . and contempt.

Finally, the immediate benefits which all savages received as the direct result of civilization were whiskey, smallpox, and syphilis. Is it at all surprising, therefore, that upon viewing civilization from their experience of these first benefits, they do not yearn for it, but rather fight against it to the death?

[11] The mysterious Aramaic handwriting on the wall at Belshazzar's feast, prophesying doom and destruction, Daniel 5:25.

Most of them perish. Entire tribes, whether they accept
civilization or continue to lead a wild life, are vanishing from
the face of the earth with frightening speed. They can neither
resist civilization nor support its heavy burden upon their weak
shoulders. This same phenomenon has been experienced by
many savage peoples. Our learned countryman, Strzelecki,[12]
having proved this phenomenon, has transformed it into a
scientific law to which the English have given the name
"Strzelecki's law," and which is still today regarded as an axiom
by the anthropologists. As for the Indians, or at least certain
of their tribes (for there are great differences among them),
if instead of coming in contact with the worst aspects of civilization, they had met with its better, gentler, and protective
rather than destructive side, perhaps in the end they would
have adapted themselves to it and would have been spared
extinction. Civilization ought to be an extremely gentle teacher,
however, and ought to bend a people gradually rather than
break them suddenly. Permanent settlement and cultivation
of the soil, which appear to be a necessity in the face of today's
conditions, are a change in the Indian mode of life which is
being forced upon tribes who are unprepared for it, instead of
coming slowly as a natural consequence of gradual evolution.

It even seems to me that the scientific law concerning the
inevitable extinction of peoples who resist civilization may be
explained, not by the absolute incapacity of such peoples, but
by the fact that they do not have the time to civilize themselves
as did the European peoples, that is, by means of continuous
and gradual development. Living in a state of complete primitive-
ness, sometimes even in cannibalism, savage tribes suddenly
are confronted with a highly developed and advanced civilization—in short, with a civilization which is absolutely too complex for their comprehension. Therefore, it is not at all

[12] Paul Edmund Strzelecki (1796–1873) was a world-wide Polish traveler
and explorer who settled in England. In 1845 he published a book dealing
with his explorations in Australia.

surprising that, instead of being elevated and enlightened under its influence, they become bewildered and frantic, and end by dashing their heads against this civilization which is too tough for them to digest.

I return once again to the Indians. I have heard from experienced people and have become personally convinced that the Indian tribes possess a relatively high intellectual development. They are by no means inferior, for example, to the Kalmuks, Bashkirs, and other tribes who roam the steppes of Russia and Asia. They have their own traditions, their own mythology, and even their own poetry consisting of war songs, funeral songs, and the like. Some of their legends are even very cleverly composed and give evidence of a certain ingeniousness in making use of external observations of man and nature. According to one legend, when the Great Manitou decided to create man, he took clay, molded it in human form, and decided to bake it in the fire. But the first time he burned it to a coal-black color. Nevertheless, he allowed his creation to live and thus originated the Negro. His second attempt was baked inadequately and the result was a white man. Only after the third attempt, taught by experience, was he able to strike the happy medium. He neither underbaked nor overbaked, and the result was a perfect creation, a truly beautiful red man.

In this legend there is a certain logic based upon an adroit utilization of the three colors of the human race. Furthermore, the speech of the Indians, full of comparisons and metaphors in the most ordinary conversation, is highly poetic and gives proof of a certain degree of mental maturity. In some individuals native intelligence is truly astounding and, generally speaking, all of them are very astute and are able to distinguish between truth and falsehood, even though sweetened to the highest degree. On the other hand, it is true that these traits are mingled with a naïveté that is practically childlike.

In conclusion, whatever may be said of these tribes, they have created a certain civilization of their own. They might progress even further and, with intelligent assistance, reach our own level of development—were it not for the fact that *our* civilization has discovered a much shorter road to progress: instead of encouraging and strengthening the weak, it exterminates them.

Such were my thoughts when I arrived at Omaha on the border between Iowa and Nebraska, that is, at the half-way point on the railroad connecting the two oceans. I shall defer describing the remainder of my trip, that is, from Omaha to San Francisco, until my next letter.

Letter III

ABOARD THE TRANSCONTINENTAL: OMAHA TO SAN FRANCISCO

I HAD often read of the many dangers to which transcontinental passengers traveling from New York to San Francisco were exposed. About two years ago our newspapers carried a story about Indians setting fire to a forest through which the train passes. The engineer not only did not stop the train but charged at top speed into the ocean of flames which were rent asunder by the strong current of air. The train emerged undamaged and the passengers were saved, albeit a little scorched. What's more, in French and German magazines I had even seen pictures to support this fantastic tale. Now that I have traversed the whole length of the railroad, I realize that both the story and the pictures merely serve to illustrate what humbugs and lies are reproduced in our own newspapers from the American press or derived from the narratives of those travelers who, upon reaching some Atlantic port, describe the entire United States with accuracy and detail as though the complete length and breadth of this land could be viewed with the naked eye from any church steeple.

To refute the above report about the forest fire it will be sufficient for me to cite the following simple facts: while in the Eastern states there are extensive forests, there are no Indians; on the other hand, in the Western states beginning with Iowa, a traveler literally does not see a single tree until he reaches the wooded borders of California and Nevada, a distance more or less comparable to that separating Warsaw from Madrid. The central portions of Iowa, Nebraska, Wyoming, Utah, and Nevada are one tremendous, treeless prairie, covered only with grass and sweetbroom, and here and there with scrawny willow bushes along the river beds.

The best example of a prairie is found in Nebraska. Here the traveler, weary with the Eastern states so densely populated and checkered with farms, and yearning to see the prairie, finds what he had been searching for. Occasionally, the small hut of a stray settler can be seen nestled close to the railroad tracks. Otherwise, all is emptiness, one limitless, silent plain. The human eye, like a bird hovering over an endless ocean, cannot detect a single object on which to alight and finally falls with exhaustion. At times, when the train stopped for longer intervals, I would run out into the prairie which began immediately beyond the enclosure of the miserable, wooden house that substituted for a railroad station. The snow crunched under my feet; the wind swayed the tips of the heather and the thistle burrs protruding through the snow. A deep silence reigned. Nowhere could a bird, animal, or any living creature be seen.

But this silence and wilderness have a peculiar charm. Not only one's sight but even one's soul and thoughts lose themselves in the prairie. The soul abandons familiar paths, forgets its own identity, merges with the environment, and soon ceases to be a thing apart, having been absorbed by the powerful presence of the prairie like a drop of water in the sea. It is from such feelings and impressions as these that all systems of pantheism have originated.

But I return to the prairies of Nebraska, or rather to those of the Middle West. They make an unusually striking impression because of their wildness and their magnitude. They extend thousands of miles in every direction, embracing practically every state west of the Mississippi with the exception of California. Truly miraculous tales are told about the harvests in Nebraska, Kansas, the Indian Territory, and Texas. And yet these lands are almost unoccupied, being inhabited only by various Indian tribes and all kinds of wild animals. Immense forests are said to be located between the Missouri and Mississippi Rivers, but in the prairies along the whole length of the railroad I scarcely saw a single tree, with the exception of the few planted in the vicinity of the railroad stations. In all directions stretches nothing but prairie overgrown with a species of heather, bitter apple, and a plant whose burrs resemble our henbane. It makes a somber and depressing sight.

True, I first saw the prairies in the middle of March at a time when everything was still numb from winter's sleep. Although the prairies of Iowa, Nebraska, Wyoming, Utah, and Nevada are situated at forty-two degrees north latitude, that is, more or less at the same latitude as Portugal, Spain, and southern Italy, they have a long and severe winter. The reason for the severe climate of the prairies is their elevation above sea level. Beginning with the Great Lakes, or more accurately with the Mississippi, the prairie plateau rises constantly until in Wyoming and Utah it reaches several thousand feet above sea level, that is, the line of perpetual snows. And yet the rise is so imperceptible and gradual that a traveler, suddenly finding himself at an altitude equivalent to that of Mt. Blanc or St. Gotthard, has not even been aware of the ascent. The train appears to be speeding steadily across level plains and only the snow drifts and the snow sheds through which the train passes reveal the changing elevation.

Although Nebraska is situated at a much lower level, even here, especially in the western portion, winter lasts to the middle of April. In summer, however, the heat exceeds 100° Fahrenheit. The sun's rays, falling almost perpendicularly on the treeless, shadeless prairie, raise its heat to that of a smelting furnace. Grass, weeds, bitter apple, and thistles become dry as peppercorn and having fallen to the ground, they are blended together in one matted, yellowed litter. The smaller rivers or so-called "creeks," and even the larger ones, dry up completely. The leaves of the willows blacken, curl around their stems, and crumble to dust in one's hands. There is not the slightest breeze to cool the air. The skies are cloudless, somewhat grayish, and seem to exhale a fiery breath upon the earth. The ground begins to crack. The prairies become as deserted and silent as death itself. Not even an insect crawls about, no bird is on the wing, and the wild animal rests in its lair throughout the day.

Even the jaguar and the cougar, the tawny lion of the prairies, seldom dare to roam during the midday hours when the heat reaches its greatest intensity. The large grey bears, the most terrible marauders of the prairies, take to the hills where the snow never melts, or follow lazily in the tracks of the buffalo, seeking shelter in river beds which the heat has not succeeded in drying up entirely. Even the buffaloes suffer from the torturing effect of the heat. From time to time they lower their huge curly heads, covered several inches thick with dust, clay, and tangled prairie weeds, and with their horns plow the hard prairie land as though in search of water. The big old bulls, the leaders of the herds, impatiently paw the soil with their hoofs or raise their snorting nostrils first in one direction and then another in the hope of scenting a cool, moist breeze from some river or lake. Their bleary, bloodshot eyes and hanging tongues reveal their raging thirst.

Only in the evening when the great red orb of the sun begins to vanish below the horizon does the prairie come to life. Here and there are heard the angry, throaty screams of the jaguars. Sometimes an old grey bear roars in reply. Then for a moment everything falls silent. Later the breeze carries the plaintive whine of the coyotes, the small prairie wolves that follow in the tracks of the great marauders and live off the remnants of their feasts.

Most of the animal life is found near the rivers and lakes whose waters do not dry up despite the heat. Hidden in the reeds and rushes along the shores is a whole menagerie of animals. Against the red rays of the setting sun are outlined with strange clarity the immense, black silhouettes of the buffaloes. They are coming at a trot over the high prairies toward the water. Into it they plunge joyously head and all. With light, graceful leaps, small herds of picturesque antelope approach and after them crawl stealthily the beasts of prey. Occasionally the grass and bushes are parted and for a moment an Indian's head, decorated with feathers, appears. Squatting low on his horse and armed with a javelin, the red warrior scans with glowing eyes these creatures soon to become his victims.

During the hours of intense heat when everything on the prairie is silent and asleep and when even the Indian seeks refuge in the shade of his tepee, only one creature dares to expose his head to the sun's rays and that creature is the white man. Often when the temperature is at its highest and the air is filled with dust, you will see huge wagons, here called "prairie schooners," drawn by three, four, and even six pairs of mules. The ring and clatter of such a caravan can be heard from afar, for to each mule's collar four bells are attached whose sound urges the animals on and gives them added strength. The tops of the wagons are covered with striped canvas, and inside are the women, children, and household belongings. Behind the caravan trail herds of cattle and sheep, often driven by Negroes or Mestizos who crack their long whips and shout "Ho! ho!" or curse the heat and each other. Alongside of each team a man walks slowly, dressed in a flannel shirt, wearing a huge sombrero to protect him from the sun, and carrying a rifle across his shoulder.

Who are these people? They are settlers headed for the Far West, together with their wives, children, and all of their possessions. Frequently they themselves do not know where they are going. Sometimes they are able to cite a state or territory. "We are going to Kansas, Colorado, or Nebraska," they say, "or else into the silent prairie. When we find land, some trees and water, there we shall settle."

I need not describe the dangers of such a journey. It is true that a score of well-armed, courageous men need not fear a hundred Sioux, Pawnees, or Hurons, providing they are on guard and do not allow themselves to be ambushed. An Indian never attacks if he believes he will have to pay dearly for small loot and few scalps. Moreover, under present-day conditions and in the face of the whites' readiness to avenge each other, the red warriors have little inclination to attack even lone travelers. On the other hand, they steal whenever they can. Horses and mules especially are easy prey for them. These they steal with such adroitness that prairie travelers must guard their animals day and night.

If, however, the pioneers create a prairie settlement in the vicinity of an Indian village, their watchfulness never ceases. The new settler usually announces that he will shoot like a dog every Indian whom he sees within a certain radius of his farm, without inquiring whether the redskin is guilty or innocent. But even this helps little and he must be on constant guard against attacks, robbery, and even arson, for the Indians frequently burn the grain of the whites simply to cause damage. Such conditions exist particularly in the Indian Territory where the land set aside for the Indians is becoming increasingly populated with white settlers in spite of existing government restrictions.

But the greatest danger of a wagon journey across the prairie are the grass fires that occur frequently during the summer. Sometimes the Indians start them intentionally. Often they are the result of neglected campfires of the travelers, or they originate spontaneously from the intense heat of the sun. Nothing is more incredible than the speed with which the flames spread, being driven across the plains by the wind. The dry undergrowth of grass, here called "blue grass," burns like sulphur. No sooner is the flame started by a spark in one place than it greedily consumes the thistle, the leaves of the bitter apple, and the resinous torch weed. It leaps across barren stretches, scatters its golden sparks in all directions, roars and runs as if possessed with madness. It overtakes the animals that are attempting in vain to flee. Half-suffocated from smoke and heat, they collapse with lolling tongues before the flame embraces them and moves on over their charred carcasses.

Woe to the traveler who at night sees a red band of light on the horizon resembling the first rays of dawn and who does not immediately set fire to the grass before him. If he perceives the danger too late and has no freshly burned space on which to take refuge, the roaring, red wave will reach him as if on wings, and then there is no hope for him. Even if the flames do not consume him, smoke, heat, and lack of air will suffocate him. However, this simple method of salvation, that of setting fire to the prairie in front of him, has its evil aspect: it starts a new fire that in turn engulfs vast stretches. There is nothing more dismal than the sight of a burned prairie. The land is transformed into a layer of ashes. An absolute stillness descends upon it, and the hot rays of the sun beating down upon the blackened earth create such intense heat that to breathe is virtually impossible.

On the other hand, fires have the effect of fertilizing the prairies. After the winter rains when the moist earth dons its first spring apparel, the verdure is most luxuriant upon the burned areas. I was often shown broad belts that had been swept by fire the previous summer. They were easily distinguishable by their deep green color and their tall grass—grass so high that it hid all but the head and shoulders of a horseman.

It is almost impossible to describe the full charm of the prairies in springtime. When the snows have been melted by the sun and the earth has become saturated with moisture, all the creeks overflow their beds, flooding wide areas with glistening, shallow waters. Then new growth rises before your very eyes and buds burst into blossom. The plain takes on the appearance of a multicolored carpet. A myriad of bright flowers is entangled amidst the grass, pushing and pressing upward, bloom upon bloom, in a joyful, loving delirium. Green and variegated waves are formed by the veritable deluge of plants, known and unknown, of a thousand names and varieties. A thousand fragrances scent the air, now honeyed and intoxicating as of lilies and heliotrope, now strong and spicy. Then the refreshing odor of grass predominates, only to yield once more to the perfume of the flowers.

In the midst of this flora there exists still another world —the world of animals. From time to time a narrow band of grass begins to tremble and suddenly the threatening head of a buffalo appears. Or perhaps the beautiful head of an antelope with sorrowful eyes and piercing horns shows itself momentarily and then disappears. Underfoot constantly scamper prairie dogs and small, noxious gophers. And sometimes, where the grass is short, a young rabbit sits on its haunches, its eyes protruding and ears pricked up. Having threateningly twitched its whiskers, it scuttles away as if convinced that it has thoroughly frightened the intruder. Finally, the sinister dry rattle of the rattlesnake is heard as it waves its tail ominously, but it glides away as quickly as possible, knowing full well that the human enemy kills without mercy.

There are places on the prairie visible even from the passing train where the prairie dogs have founded whole camps consisting of small, adjacent mounds with openings leading to spacious, subterranean burrows. Amongst the mounds their little inhabitants scamper incessantly, now fighting, now frolicking, now gathering grass and roots. Some of them sit upon their haunches at the entrance of their hillocks, overseeing with dignity everything that is happening in the camp, just like a farmer's wife standing in the doorway of her home. A short distance from the camp sentinels stand on guard, "ne quid republica detrimenti capiat." [1] In a word, everything is just like an orderly and organized human society.

I have seen many such camps and for that very reason I advise the traveler to approach them cautiously. Several yards

[1] That the state suffer no harm.

away dark, elongated objects can be seen lying in the sunshine, now and then moving indolently. These are the rattlesnakes that abound in every camp. Apparently these dangerous neighbors live in the best of harmony with the little republicans. But men versed in prairie lore have told me that the snakes eat the little creatures and the latter must tolerate what they cannot remedy. Perhaps they look upon the rattlers as their priests or gods.

In spring the prairies become populated with a multitude of birds which come here from the forest regions and usually remain close to the rivers whose banks are overgrown with willows. Sometimes small grey owls are to be seen, sitting with eyes closed as though stupefied by the daylight. These birds live on mice, rats, and gophers, and for this reason they are highly respected by the settlers. Besides the owls, mighty eagles, small hawks, and falcons hover in the air upon outspread wings. With head hanging down and eyes glued to the prairie, they remain immobile for long periods as though hypnotized by their own shadows cast upon the ground by the sun.

But much more numerous than the birds of prey are the songbirds. In the early hours the whole prairie resounds with whistling, singing, chirping—in a word, one great concert of these self-educated artists. The most beautiful singer of all is the mockingbird, also known as the joker thrush. This is an extraordinary bird. Since it is often kept in cages, I therefore had an opportunity to observe it closely. In shape resembling our lark, it is not distinguished by beautiful feathers, but is entirely grey with small, white specks on the wings. Its talents, however, amply compensate for the absence of exterior beauty. Not only does it sing melodiously, but it imitates whatever sound it hears.

On hearing the mew of a cat, it immediately begins to mew like a cat; on hearing the bark of a dog, it begins to bark like a dog. As if this were not enough, such a bird kept in the home even imitates human voices. Once, when visiting a farmer friend in California, I noticed a cage containing a mockingbird suspended above the door. I stopped before the cage and began to make a murmuring sound. The little bird jumped to a lower perch, and cocking his head to one side, he poked it through the wire bars. Then he closed one of his beady, black eyes, and seemed to listen attentively. After a little while, as if he now understood what it was all about, he jumped to an upper rung, and puffing up his feathers, he began to murmur very distinctly. When I burst into laughter, the bird followed my example as if he had just heard a most amusing joke. His natural song closely resembles that of the nightingale, although not as clear, sweet, and melodious. On the prairies he flies from one plant to another and, rocking on a thistle, he sings or mocks in his own fashion the voices of the other birds and animals.

All this prairie life, so colorful and vocal, lasts but a short time. From the moment that the heat begins, everything flees, or hides itself and becomes mute until the following spring. The autumn season is almost as beautiful as the spring, but it, too, is brief and is soon followed by a deathlike silence that embraces the whole region. The air is filled with snowflakes, the prairie grows numb and dies, and the pervading stillness is interrupted only by the rustling of the dry thistles under the touch of the wind, or by the violent, panting breath of the locomotives thundering westward.

The prairies of the southern states are an exception. Those of the Indian Territory, for example, enjoy eternal spring, while those of lower Texas suffer unremitting heat. Nebraska has clearly demarcated seasons with severe winters and oppressive summer heat.

This prairie country, although almost devoid of population as yet, has a great future before it. The enterprising Americans are already planning to establish enormous cattle ranches like those of the pampas of South America in Argentina, Paraguay, and Uruguay. The railroad companies distribute even the lands close to the stations at a very low price to be paid over a ten-year period. Beyond the railroads' right-of-way one may settle without asking permission of anybody and without making any payment.

On March 11 (1876) I finally reached Sidney, a large station on the western border of Nebraska. The station here is adorned with the heads of buffaloes shot from the train since Sidney is located on the trail followed by tens of thousands of these animals as they trek southward during certain seasons of the year. Not far away the train passes through a region where antelope are so numerous that they can easily be seen from the windows of the train. This is also the country of the Pawnee Indians who occasionally come to the railroad station to exchange furs and to purchase various small articles.

The elevation of the prairie continues to rise. We are already several thousand feet above sea level and yet the train's upward climb is scarcely noticeable. Outside the ground is covered with frost and snow. In the coaches the stoves are burning furiously. Everything indicates we are nearing the Rocky Mountains.

That same evening we reach Pine Bluffs on the border between Nebraska and Wyoming. The character of the landscape changes completely as the prairies give way to mountains. The train continues at the same level, but on both sides can now be seen snow-capped mountains or rocks of fantastic shapes reminding one of the ruins of castles along the Rhine. The region is wild and gloomy. From the windows of the train we again see antelope and colonies of prairie dogs. We are approaching Cheyenne, a station in Wyoming, but before we arrive there, we pass through the first snowshed more than a mile in length. These snowsheds are very long galleries with a roof over them, protecting the railroad tracks from snow slides and drifts. I had heard many strange tales about them, but I was completely disenchanted when I saw them. It is true that these galleries are extremely long, but they are constructed most primitively from boards and rafters and their roofs are full of holes. In short, they are built like our own peasant huts of many years ago. These structures may be entirely adequate for the purpose they serve, but in no case should they be regarded as the eighth wonder of the world.

As we emerged from the snowshed, we beheld a magnificent panorama before us. To the right of the train clearly stood out the Black Hills, the destination of so many people passing through Omaha and Sioux City. They are a separate mountain group isolated from other ranges just like our Tatras.[2] In the midst of a snow-covered landscape and against the background of a lead-colored sky, these hills really appear as black as the night—gloomy, mysterious, and ominous. Only the peaks of the highest crests are covered with snow. Otherwise, their black hue has not the slightest trace of that bluish haze usually associated with mountains. At this moment they are the scene of a terrible drama being enacted by redskins and whites.[3]

At last we reach Cheyenne. Everybody at the station is in a state of feverish excitement. One person after another tells us of the battle that took place the previous day between the gold miners and the Sioux and in which the former were defeated. Eight of their number were killed and a score wounded. In addition, they lost all of their horses, oxen, and food supplies. Apparently, they will be suffering from misery and hunger before new provisions reach them through Omaha and Sioux City. Supplies cannot be brought them through Cheyenne, for although this is the shortest route, the road is inaccessible.

In Cheyenne the train halted for a quarter of an hour. For a few minutes I listened to the descriptions of the battle. Then

[2] The Tatras are the principal mountain group of the central Carpathians.
[3] Sienkiewicz's footnote: Even as I am writing (the latter part of July) war is raging in the Black Hills and vicinity, not between miners and Indians, but between the United States Government and the Indians. According to latest dispatches, the troops under General Custer's command have suffered a disastrous defeat.

I stared with amazement at the huge grizzly bear that had ventured too close to the station and had been killed by the local residents, or rather drilled full of holes with all the available rifles. He was a monster with a head more than a foot wide and so tall that men of average height reached only to his shoulders. It is said that there are many of these bears in the neighborhood of Cheyenne.

Cheyenne is located in the midst of the Rocky Mountains, 6,041 feet above sea level, or at about the same altitude as our Lomnica.[4] Beyond this point snowsheds continue almost without interruption, for the snows here are very heavy. Small stations like Hazard, Otto, Granite Canon, and Buford, are situated at still higher elevations. Finally we arrive at Sherman, the highest point on the whole line, being 9,000 feet above sea level. Nothing is more desolate than the view from here. On the small, bald plateau stands a house with its roof heavily covered with snow. The air is rare and the cold so penetrating that we all shiver despite our fur coats. Snow falls here almost continuously; the wind howls and whirls amidst clouds of snowflakes; here and there protrude bare, black rocks, swept clear by the wind, but soon to be covered once more by the snow. I cannot understand how people can live permanently in such places where the lungs gasp for air, the ears ring, and blood flecks the lips of the weak.

On March 12 we begin to descend slowly down the west side of the mountains, but even here the slope is scarcely noticeable. We are still several thousand feet above sea level. At last we reach the western border of Wyoming. At noon of that day we cross the Green River that has its source in the nearby hills. The whole region is full of rock formations of such fantastic shapes as to make this part of the journey most interesting. Some resemble obelisks, others pyramids; and yonder stands a castle that you would swear was built by human hands, for it lacks neither towers, turrets, nor even an encircling wall.

---

[4] Lomnica Peak, the second highest summit in the High Tatras, rises to a height of 8,642 ft.

The scene suddenly changes. The rocks are much smaller and as far as the eye can see, they form a long, straight wall that is as regular as if built by rule and compass.

The most unusual formations are found in Utah not far from Echo station. Here are the so-called Devil's Gate and Devil's Path, parallel cliffs of rock forming two deep corridors so wild and demoniacal that surely nowhere else on earth could the devil find for himself a more appropriate residence.

Finally, after crossing one more tributary of the Green River, we arrived at Ogden, a city in the state of Utah. Not far from Ogden, but on a branch of the main line, are Salt Lake and Salt Lake City, the capital of the Mormons. Unfortunately, a few hours before our arrival, a telegram had been received stating that the road to Salt Lake City was closed by snow drifts and would not be open until the following day. Undisturbed by this news, I was resolved to visit this unique city. But new telegrams arrived, indicating that within a few days communication even along the main line might be cut off as unprecedented snows were continuing to fall in the mountains. There was no alternative. I had to abandon my visit to the Mormons and hurry on to San Francisco, but I promised myself to stop among them if only for a few days on my return trip.

As matters turned out, however, I would have done better to have remained in Ogden. We had scarcely traveled one day and reached the miserable, little station of Toano, where the train usually makes a three-minute stop, when word came that the road ahead was impassable, being covered over a stretch of many miles with snow several yards deep.

"What shall we do?" asked my companions.

"It's very simple! We shall return to Ogden and from there go on to Salt Lake City."

Cheered by this happy idea, we went to the ticket agent and inquired about the next train for Ogden.

"There is no local between here and Ogden, only the through train from San Francisco to New York," was his reply.

"And when does the train arrive from San Francisco?"

"When the road is open."

We hung our heads in dejection, for we would have to remain in Toano and await God's mercy. Nothing could be more tiresome than Toano. Five or six shanties, slapped together with a few boards, stand isolated in the snow. Having to sit there, while beautiful California lay just ahead of us, was equivalent to death itself. Nor could anyone tell us how long we would have to do penance. "Perhaps a week," "perhaps a couple of days," "perhaps ten"—these were the conflicting replies we received to our queries.

We did, indeed, hear that six engines were coming from the direction of San Francisco. Four others, which we ourselves saw passing through Toano, arrived from Ogden. Armed with immense plows, they set out to clear the snow drifts. But it was entirely possible that what the plows cleared might again be covered with snow.

To overcome the monotony of the first day we practiced revolver shooting for four hours. Towards evening, having borrowed rifles from the Toano residents, we went hunting for bears which we were told were in the nearby mountains. We returned late at night from our hunting expedition without having seen even the tracks of a bear. We were exhausted and chilled to the bone, for more than once we had sunk to our necks in the snow.

Thus the day passed. We struck up acquaintance with the people in our sleeping car, some of them very distinguished individuals. It is difficult not to become acquainted when you live and sleep in the same car. But the ladies of our salon were hardly alluring since the youngest of their number had already passed forty.

The Americans began to make preparations as though we were going to settle down here for a permanent stay. And, indeed, it was beginning to appear that our quarantine might not be a short one. One day followed another and each evening we retired with one thought: "Tomorrow, perhaps, we shall awake in Nevada." And each morning we awoke . . . in Toano.

It was not long before great intimacy reigned among the occupants of our car. We all went to dinner together; in the evening we sipped tea in our car; and then usually until 11 p.m. we sang in unison American patriotic songs, especially "Marching through Georgia." At last Charles, the Negro porter, made up our berths and we retired.

During the day we likewise had a prearranged program. In the morning: a revolver shooting competition; the prize from the ladies: an orange. I succeeded in winning the prize on the second day. After the shooting, a promenade around the train and a ladies' tournament consisting of walking on the rails. The lady who managed to balance herself longest on the track and who traversed the greatest distance received the prize from the gentlemen: an orange. You should have seen the ladies competing with one another as, with their skirts girded up, they kept sliding off the rails every few steps.

At last, the evening of the fourth day, someone spread the news that we were to leave that night. We were so happy that we arranged a picnic which took place in grand style at the baker's. Then, filled with the highest hope, we retired and next morning we awoke . . . in Toano.

By this time our spirits began to fall, for we were threatened by still another danger. The food supply in Toano was running low. There were still plenty of crackers, sugar, coffee, tea, and California apples, but meat was becoming scarce. Nor could it be brought from Ogden since the road to Ogden was also closed by snowdrifts. Fortunately, definite news reached us that evening by telegram that the locomotives with the snow plows had cleared the snow and that they would soon be in Toano.

Never shall I forget the moment when the locomotives arrived. Twilight was already upon us and only the reflection of the snow relieved the darkness. Suddenly we heard the engines in the distance and soon sighted them in the dusk. It was, in fact, an entire train of locomotives. The first, armed with an enormous plow, bore the earmarks of hard labor, for it was completely covered with snow. They approached with clanging bells, roaring, whistling, spraying sparks from their smokestacks, and belching clouds of smoke. It seemed as though these black monsters were with this uproar celebrating their triumph, that these were sounds of joy after a difficult battle and ultimate victory. Although the locomotives appeared to be panting with exhaustion, they were still filled with the fury of the fight, and happy and intoxicated with their own power. They resembled living creatures and their sounds of triumph strengthened this illusion still further. An indescribable force emanated from this black procession of engines and smoke stacks passing us and melting into the darkness like gigantic nocturnal phantoms. Only the hissing, the roaring, and the ringing of bells continued to echo in our ears from the distance.

Then our coaches quivered, knocked against each other, and slowly moved forward. Soon we were in Nevada through which we traveled the entire day and the following night.

Had Gustav Doré been born in America, I would say that he took the models for his landscapes of the inferno from the region through which we were now passing.[5] Nothing oppresses the soul so heavily, nothing fills one with so much doubt and discouragement as these ridges of bare, black rocks. I imagine that this is the appearance of the dead fields of the moon. Here, too, everything is dead. Nowhere is there a sign of vegetation; nowhere a single, living creature. The rocks resemble tombstones; the plain, one vast cemetery. This entire region seems to have fallen into a benumbed sleep as though bewitched by the spell of an evil spirit. A sense of fatigue adds to your depression and you feel that you, too, will succumb to sleep.

Even the names in this strange region are rather ominous.

---

[5] Gustave Doré (1833–1883), French illustrator, painter, and sculptor, who achieved great popularity for his illustrations of numerous books, including Dante's *Inferno*.

Thus to the right of the train these scowling hills are called Battle Mountains. And this plain itself has been an endless field of battles fought between whites and Indians not so long ago. Some sad memory is connected with each and every place. "Here a whole caravan of pioneers was massacred," you are told by the traveler who is familiar with the locality. Over yonder some two hundred Indians perished at one time; they were smoked to death in the caves. And what is this? A grave surrounded by a black railing and a cross bearing the inscription "Jenny . . ."

Who was this unfortunate girl? Some years ago, before the existence of the railroad, a caravan of travelers became snowbound in this place. Everyone fell into despair; women and children became ill with typhus; starvation reached serious proportions. It was then that Jenny, going from one tent to another, cared for the sick and comforted the weak. During the night she tended the fires; during the day she dug moss from under the snow and boiled it for food. In short, she was the guardian angel of the camp. But later she collapsed under the burden, became ill, and died. The others recovered, for help arrived on the very same day that Jenny passed away. The grateful pioneers erected a mound and placed the cross upon it. Today the cross stands close to the railroad embankment and the inscription upon it can be read from the coach window. There you have the story of Jenny whose grave we passed at noon.

In the evening we arrived at the great salt lakes on the western borders of Nevada. Close to their shores the soil was completely covered with salt and practically without vegetation. The scenery differed very little from what we had seen previously, for these grey, motionless, barely translucent waters likewise appeared to have fallen into an enchanted sleep. The winter here is apparently long and severe. Patches of snow still lay on the plain, while the crests of the hills were completely white. A sharp, penetrating wind blew continuously, forcing its way even into the coaches and causing the flames in the lamps to flicker. Having walked out momentarily on the platform, I returned chilled to the bone and completely dejected. If California resembles Nevada, I thought to myself, why am I hurrying toward it night and day? Will I arrive there only to freeze and be disillusioned?

With this thought, weary both in body and soul, I retired for the night. I dreamed that we were still marooned in Toano and for that reason I kept waking every moment. Finally, when the first rays of the sun peeked through the green curtain of the sleeping car, I dressed and strolled out to the front of the coach.

At first, it seemed to me that I was still dreaming. Nevada with its Dantian scenes, with its winter and its biting wind . . . disappeared. I was in the midst of a forest, a beautiful, fragrant, pine forest nestled among the hills. The woods seemed gay as though they were smiling in the rose-colored rays of the sunrise. A warm spring breeze gently caressed my face. Clear blue skies filled the heavens above me. Thousands of streamlets murmured in the hills and the forest resounded with the song of birds. The red cliffs on both sides of the train were covered with flowers glistening with morning dew. In short, spring was everywhere, with its resurrection, life, and gaiety. We were in California.

The train sped rapidly down the steep western slopes of the Sierra Nevadas. Soon, all who were awake scrambled out on the coach platforms. Joy and rapture beamed from every face. The people smiled at nature and nature smiled at them. The scenery became more and more attractive. Nowhere have I ever seen such a wealth of colors, yet blended so harmoniously. The Italian-blue sky, the dark green forest, the grassy, light green valleys, the red cliffs—all of these shimmered and danced in the rays of the sun like a rainbow. In the deep, precipitous ravines could be heard the gushing waters of spring. Here and there stretched mile-long wooden sluices used for washing gold.

Groups of Chinese in long, black pig-tails were scurrying about, shoveling gold-bearing sand and earth into these sluices. In the valleys white farm houses stood in the shadow of the forests. Herds of cattle and sheep were scattered in picturesque fashion on the hillsides, feeding amidst the grass and flowers. Occasionally, a horseman galloped by, seated in a high saddle with a lasso wound around the pommel, and disappeared in the winding forest road.

As we continued the descent, the countryside became more and more beautiful and at the same time assumed a tropical appearance. In front of the small houses standing close to the railroad tracks were enormous cacti and trees already in full bloom. Many large plants of species unknown to me wound themselves around the tracks or attached themselves to the sluices, covering the latter in some places almost completely. Finally the mountains gave way to meadows where tremendous oak trees grew. Some of these pastures were inundated with water. Others were so completely carpeted with poppies that you could scarcely see the grass. Thousands of wild ducks, teals, and grebes soared above the water. In the fields I saw whole droves of rabbits which scampered away at the approach of the train or hid themselves in the grass, leaving only their ears and whiskers protruding above it. Multicolored birds flitted from tree to tree, filling the air with joyful songs.

At eleven o'clock in the morning we reached Sacramento, the capital of California. Large crowds were waiting at the station, anxious to see the train that had recently escaped from a snowy captivity. In the throng swarmed many flat-nosed Chinamen with long queues reaching almost to the ground and braided with black silk. Leaving the coach, I looked at them with curiosity. This seemed to amuse them and they began to laugh, no doubt recognizing me as a foreigner who was seeing Chinamen for the first time in his life. After a fifteen-minute stop we moved on.

For several minutes the road followed the banks of the gold-bearing Sacramento River. Swollen with the flood waters of spring, it tossed its red waves with force, inundating its banks and even the small houses not far from its shores. After a while, however, the river disappeared from view. The countryside became ever more populous, the farm houses closer to one another, and the cultivation more intensive. Only the hot rays of the sun and the sight of the tropical flora dispelled the momentary illusion that this could be Saxony or Belgium.

At last, after a journey of several hours, I beheld glistening, blue ocean waves at the edge of the horizon. I assumed that this must be the Pacific Ocean, but it was only the bay on which San Francisco and its suburb, Oakland, are situated. The train did not stop at Oakland but sped furiously on. You can easily imagine my surprise when, looking out the window, I saw ocean waves, wild ducks, and sea gulls on both sides of the train. Although the train seemed to be traveling upon the ocean, it was, in fact, upon a wooden trestle about two miles long whose end I could not see even from the platform. I must confess that this mode of travel struck me as being somewhat too American, especially since I did not know how long we would continue in this manner. At last, however, the bridge terminated in about the middle of the bay and the train stopped. Our journey likewise was at an end. We had only to board the ferry and cross the other half of the bay on whose opposite shore the city of San Francisco could be seen dimly through the ocean mist.

SIENKIEWICZ arrived at the Golden Gate City about the middle of March, 1876. Although he remained in San Francisco several weeks, he did little writing, for he was much too occupied exploring this fascinating metropolis and its vicinity, cultivating acquaintance with the handful of Polish political refugees living there, asking questions of them about the more puzzling aspects of American life, and, above all, making inquiries as to a suitable location for the proposed colony.

Beginning June 20, 1876, Sienkiewicz took up his residence in Anaheim, which had been selected as the site of the colony, and remained in southern California until the end of the year. The four months that he awaited the arrival of the colonists were filled with a variety of activities. He made side trips to Los Angeles, Anaheim Landing, the canyons, and the mountains. He studied Spanish and English, making considerable progress in both languages. Thanks to his knowledge of French and Latin, he did not find Spanish at all difficult. His Polish newspaper friend in San Francisco, Julian Horain, assisted by sending him Spanish books and a French-Spanish dictionary. Of still greater assistance were his new friends among the senoritas, who provided the necessary incentive for learning the language and instruction in it. While at Anaheim he did some hunting for small game and birds. He captured a young badger of whom he made a household pet.

None of these activities, however, distracted Sienkiewicz from his literary work. Here he found the atmosphere conducive to writing and the time for it. He himself remarked that he accomplished more in a few months in southern California than he did in two years in Warsaw. He finished several short stories and a play and began to send a steady stream of reports to his newspaper.

When he completed the account of the transcontinental railroad, Sienkiewicz fully intended to write about San Francisco. Instead, however, he broke off the sequence of his personal narrative in order to deal with a subject close to his heart. In Warsaw he had been a publicist. In his column "The Present Moment" he had analyzed and criticized practically every aspect of Polish society. Now, during the peaceful interlude in southern California, he had time to reflect and to write on the essential differences between Europe and America. Sienkiewicz was at first repelled by much of what he had observed, but as he became better acquainted with American customs and institutions, he soon learned to respect them and reached the conclusion that American democracy was the nearest approach to an ideal society.

That Sienkiewicz should have turned his attention to the subject of American women is not at all surprising. The whole topic of female emancipation was at this time arousing considerable public debate in Europe where exaggerated reports had been received of the movement's progress in America. Sienkiewicz tried to set the record straight. Further, as an alert young bachelor, he could not resist the opportunity of passing personal judgment on American womenfolk as compared with the product back home. Although his remarks on the women of this country were generally uncomplimentary, Sienkiewicz was by no means a misogynist; he was strongly attracted by the charms of two young Spanish women during his stay in Anaheim.

Letter IV

AMERICAN DEMOCRACY

IN this letter I shall comment further on the differences between American and European society. These differences are so striking and so fundamental that not only the social structure of the United States but also the whole mode of life and the customs of its people are incomprehensible to the newly arrived European. Let us compare, for example, the American and European concepts of democracy. They differ from each other as practice differs from theory. In Europe, every country which possesses equality of suffrage, and in which a percentage of one's income constitutes the basis of taxation, regards itself as democratic. According to this definition, the majority of the European states, especially those in the west, are democratic. But the distinction between American and European democracy does not rest solely on institutional differences, and in order that I may show this distinction in its proper light, let me begin by saying that a democratic government by no means implies a democratic society; whereas the former is frequently found in Europe, the latter is practically nonexistent there.

No one will deny that the French system of government, for example, has been democratic since the Great Revolution. And yet everyone will agree that, despite the inscription of "Liberty, Equality, Fraternity" on all churches, equality in a social sense is pure myth. Where is the social equality of doctor, merchant, civil servant, common laborer, farmer, soldier, teacher, and banker? Is it not true that in France, as everywhere in Europe for that matter, there exist side by side two distinct worlds as closed to each other as the castes of India: the world of the common man in his blouse or jerkin, and the arrogant, cultured, aristocratic world of the educated man? And is it not true that the latter world considers itself superior to the former? The truth cannot be denied. What is more, such conditions have developed because of historical and economic necessity. They are a natural development because they accurately reflect existing social distinctions.

In America the situation is entirely different. Democracy here is not only political but also social: it exists not only as an institution and a theory but also in men's relations with one another. Here the people of various walks of life whom I listed above are truly each other's equals. They may live together, befriend each other, belong to the same club, eat at the same table. In a word, they do not stand on different rungs of the social ladder, for the simple reason that there is no ladder here at all. Everybody here stands on the same social level, with no one towering above another. The division into a world of common people and a world of their betters does not and cannot exist in the United States for reasons which I shall state directly.

One of the great principles of social democracy is respect for labor. Where each type of work is equally respected and equally sacred, there is no justification for dividing workers into social classes. We Europeans do not have and cannot have the slightest conception of the respect shown to every kind of labor in America. In this regard Americans are unquestionably far ahead of every European society. Let us concede the truth that with us theories about the equality of labor are so many empty phrases which have no meaning in practice. In our country a person belonging to the upper stratum of society who is compelled by circumstances to engage in manual labor as the only means of earning a living becomes degraded both in his own and in popular opinion—despite everything we say and write to the contrary. To be frank, he loses caste, severs all ties which united him with his previous estate, and sinks into the so-called lower classes of society. This does not happen in America.

Here, in fact, social classes in the European sense do not exist. There are simply various types of "businesses," and a gentleman engaged in the manufacture of shoes is as highly esteemed as a gentleman engaged in the practice of law, merely because public opinion makes no distinction in its regard for both professions. Let Europe learn this respect for labor and its people will acquire political and social equality more quickly than through any institutional changes.

This unique respect for labor is the principal reason for the absence of any division of society into two worlds. At the same time it serves as the key to understanding American democracy, which at first seems so incomprehensible. The high regard for labor can be explained historically and economically. The historical explanation lies in the fact that American society sprang from lower-class immigrants who were chiefly artisans and who had always earned their livelihood through manual labor. They were accustomed to judge a man by his work, which they regarded as his most effective weapon and his greatest asset.

The economic cause is equally clear and unmistakable. The sparse population in relation to the vast expanse of the country, and the great number of needs which could not be satisfied because of the scarcity of labor, have placed a premium on every type of work. These factors have given labor and the laboring classes greater recognition than can be found anywhere else. To speak in economic terms, the demand for labor has been ten times greater than its supply. The direct result has been the high value placed on labor, not only from a material but also from a moral point of view. This disproportionate relationship between the demand and supply of labor continues to exist in most states and the high value of labor therefore remains constant. Consciously upheld by public opinion and upbringing, respect for labor has become an important national trait.

Furthermore, since local self-government enables the character of society to be immediately reflected in political life, it has been possible to establish strictly democratic institutions which conform in spirit to this respect for labor. This is especially true of the public schools. Although in Europe the need for educating the lower classes has long been recognized, attention has been devoted chiefly to the institutions of higher learning instead of to the elementary schools. Needless to say these higher institutions are practically closed to the so-called common people, for European public education is designed not for the entire population but primarily for the upper classes. This creates such differences in the intellectual development of the people that social equality becomes impossible.

In America, on the other hand, the situation is quite different. The schools are more concerned with general education than with the arts and sciences. Institutions of higher learning do, of course, exist, but society is more interested in the elementary schools, which are attended by the entire population. For this reason the arts and sciences in the United States are on a lower plane than in Europe; but general education unquestionably is of higher quality, is more widely diffused, and is available to everyone without exception. It should be added that the scope of primary instruction here is much broader than in Europe. The elementary schools teach more than mere reading and writing. Every American acquires not only a knowledge of reading and writing but also a certain acquaintance with mathematics, geography, natural sciences, and civics. Social experiences and newspapers are instrumental in continuing his education. One can easily understand how a citizen—who is a voter, who belongs to one of the parties, and whose interests are tied directly to the fate of the party—simply through contact with politics or by direct participation in them not only acquires certain information and attitudes but also a wider knowledge and understanding of his environment. Consequently, to find a person as ignorant as the "common man" of Europe, as, for example, the Polish or French peasant, you would have to search among the recently emancipated Negroes. In this country you can discuss with almost any farmer, craftsman, coachman, or sailor the various forms of government, foreign policy, paper money and specie (a question which at present is being hotly debated)—in a word, anything you wish except literature and the fine arts. He has heard about all of these things in school and read about them in the newspapers. He has had to think about them as a voter. He has heard a thousand political speeches, Republican and Democratic, in which everything was explained from all angles and virtually crammed into his head. His views may not always be profound; at times they may even betray an innate stupidity, but they will never reveal an absolute ignorance. There is not the slightest exaggeration in what I am saying. The average American is not a learned person, but his native shrewdness has been developed by experience. The tremendous intellectual gulf between individuals, so common in Europe, can be found nowhere in America.

In short, general education is more widespread and more evenly distributed here than in Europe. The mental development of the people is more uniform, and mutual understanding is therefore more easily achieved. Professional training, under these circumstances, is no justification for one individual to consider himself superior to another. For example, though a doctor has specialized knowledge which a shoemaker does not possess, a doctor cannot make shoes. Both doctor and shoemaker are, however, mentally mature individuals. Their specializations are simply two different types of "business" which cannot have any effect on their mutual relations. This, then, is the second factor which accounts for social equality among the Americans.

Let us now turn to the third factor. In Europe the upper classes differ from the lower not only in their pursuit of more intellectual occupations, in their wealth, in their education, but also in their manners. The last necessarily stems from the others. In fact, refined manners can take root and develop only on suitably prepared soil. Refinement is like a delicate plant which requires careful cultivation to enable one to make the subtle distinction between all that is aesthetic, appropriate, and gracious and what is boorish and uncouth. Among the upper classes of Europe, where favorable conditions exist, social manners have attained a height as yet undreamed of in America. For this reason the newcomer from Europe regards Americans with their peculiar habits—chewing tobacco and putting their feet on window sills—as an uncivilized people.

Social intercourse has attained a higher degree of perfection in Europe than in America. But what an abyss separates the manners of the upper classes in the Old World from those of the lower! Place a nobleman beside a peasant and the contrast is so great that you have the impression that these individuals come from different planets. If we were to regard the behavior of the lower classes as the criterion, we could say that social refinement in Europe is on a lower plane than in America. Thus, if we take everything into consideration, we reach the same conclusion as in the case of education. In Europe the development of good manners among the various classes of society has been extremely uneven; some have made great progress; others, none at all. Just as conditions in Europe have created these differences, conditions in America have destroyed them. While manners here are not so refined as among the upper classes in Europe, neither are they so primitive and undeveloped as among our lower classes. This is the third reason for the existence of social equality in America.

When one understands these three factors, that is: 1) respect for labor; 2) absence of great differences in education; 3) lack of marked disparity in manners—only then can one understand American democracy and American life in general. I remember that some months ago we hired a coachman to drive us to the home of a millionaire rancher. On our arrival, instead of remaining with his horses, the coachman entered the living room with us. Here he sat on the sofa and began

to entertain our host's daughter. This incident refused to penetrate my European skull—the more so because I did not yet
know English and I could not judge the nature of his conversation. And yet the incident appeared perfectly natural to our
hosts. The liveryman to them was a gentleman engaged in his
own business, that of keeping horses for hire, and a social equal
of all other citizens of the United States. Today even I would
no longer be surprised by such an episode. I know now that if
the American millionaire ranks below the European millionaire
in refinement of manners, the American coachman ranks ten
times higher than his European counterpart.

This same principle of more or less social and intellectual
equality explains thousands of incidents in daily life which
make European newcomers stare with amazement. The servants
here dine at the same table as their employers and do not
form a separate class. At the country dances the well-dressed
farmers' daughters dance with their fathers' farm hands as with
gentlemen who are their exact social equals. Railroad conductors
during their free moments entertain genteel lady travelers.
Waiters in restaurants chat with the guests on terms of complete equality. In short, practically no distinctions exist anywhere; the entire populace forms but one community, one large
friendly fellowship. All these practices lead one to believe that
the Americans are determined to do everything exactly opposite
from the way it is done in Europe.

The respect for labor which I mentioned earlier permits an
individual to engage in any kind of work without injury to his
dignity or his social position. Many high public officials are
engaged in commerce, industry, or a craft—only to the extent,
of course, that time permits. After leaving public office, they
enter some type of business, unperturbed by the fact that they
had previously been important government officials. I am myself
acquainted with a former brigadier-general and wartime governor of Georgia who at present is the owner of a huge saloon

and who himself frequently serves beer and whiskey to his
guests.[1] Of course, according to European standards, this is
something incredible. But the only thing that would arouse
curiosity here would be a European's surprise at things so
simple and natural. Such generals, governors, etc., are very
numerous, all the more so because public life in America usually
lasts but a few years, resulting in a great number of ex-officials.

I mention these facts for still another reason—in order to
indicate to my readers that the willingness of all kinds of people
to engage in various types of occupations contributes greatly
to the maintenance of equality in public and private life. Indeed, how can one look down upon a tavern-keeper, a grocer,
or a craftsman who only yesterday was a governor or a senator
and who tomorrow, if his party secures a majority and takes
over the government, will again occupy an equally important
or more important office? Thus everywhere and under all circumstances respect for labor gives birth to equality; social and
intellectual equality in turn destroys class distinctions. Briefly,
in speaking of the United States and its democracy, it would
be entirely accurate to change the Latin proverb "Abyssus
abyssum provocat" into "Equalitas equalitatem provocat." [2]

In view of all this, if I were asked which society has produced
the better civilization, I should without hesitation concede
superiority to the American. In Europe civilization is the attribute only of certain social classes, or rather only of one,
which controls and devours everything. Everything exists only
within and for that class; science and knowledge belong to it
alone, as do poetry, the arts, and intellectual activity. In short,
everything that makes life really beautiful, noble, and spiritual,
that represents the truly human, aesthetic, and intellectual
side of life, finds expression only in the one class and exists

[1] The reference is to Wlodzimierz Krzyzanowski (1824–1887), who distinguished himself in the Civil War and became military governor not of
Georgia but of Alabama. As a participant in the Polish insurrection of 1846,
he was forced to flee his native land.
[2] Abyss begets abyss and equality begets equality.

for its benefit alone. Outside of this class no one knows or does anything of consequence. It is the upper stratum of society which writes, judges, makes speeches, creates public opinion, publishes newspapers, fills the art galleries, libraries, theaters; in a word, this class constitutes the whole of civilization, outside of which is the huge confused mass of people, leading a purely physical existence, uncultured, ignorant, crass.

If millions of people—a half, a fourth, an eighth, or even a tenth of the total populace—belonged to the upper class of European society, one could at least say that its confines were not too narrow. But we shall see that such is not the case. Of course, it is difficult to determine with accuracy to which class an individual belongs. Yet one can cite approximate figures by classifying persons on the basis of their income. Such classification is entirely logical, for it is clear that only those who have the means can afford to cultivate aesthetic and scholarly instincts. I have at hand this very moment an unusually interesting book which contains the official report of Prussia for 1851, compiled in connection with the establishment of the income tax in that country. This report shows that out of a population of seventeen millions only 44,408 persons had an annual income of more than one thousand thalers. Taking 50,000 as a round number, does the reader know what this figure means? It means that science, literature, the fine arts, informed opinion, refined manners—in short, the very essence of that high civilization of which Prussia is so proud and which is regarded as the civilization of the entire nation—belonged in 1851 only to 200,000 Prussians. This figure may now easily be excessive, for although the population has increased, the number of wealthy families has decreased. Thus, the remaining millions who comprise the common people are separated by a huge gap from the privileged class and its civilization, despite the great development of elementary education in Prussia.

In the democratic United States the situation is entirely different. Knowledge may not be so profound nor good manners so refined here as in Europe, but both are certainly more widely diffused. This is the essence of American democracy. And now I should like to make the following observation: If civilization does not ensure man's happiness, then it should be rejected and man should return to the era when human beings ran around on all fours. If, as is universally believed, civilization promotes happiness, then we must admit that the opportunities for happiness are incomparably greater in America than anywhere in Europe. American democracy approaches nearest that ideal society for which we have striven through the ages.

Enough about American democracy. In fact, I have already said too much, for this letter is not intended to be a definitive social study. From what has been said, the reader should be able to form some conception not only of American democracy but also of the conditions which made its development possible.

Now let us speak briefly of the morals of this society. I have already mentioned in previous letters the large amount of graft in government. I have explained this by the fact that a politician remains in office only so long as his party is in the majority; whenever the party changes, the public officials likewise change. Thus, when an official leaves his business, that is, his means of livelihood, to assume the duties of public office, he knows that within a few years he will lose this office. Consequently, the politician has but one recourse: to steal—and he steals as zealously as he knows how. This is the fault of the machinery of government. For this very reason, these abuses must not be taken as an indication of the morality of the entire nation, especially since the officials here are neither so powerful nor so numerous as under other forms of government in Europe.

For an appraisal of the average morality of the nation one must search for another standard. One of the soundest principles of sociology is that extension of education leads to the development of a higher morality. Those who doubt this principle should consult the criminal statistics of any society and discover how many crimes are committed by the illiterate, how many by those who can read and write, and how many by those who are well educated. Since general education is so widespread in America, morality has attained a very high level. I am not speaking of the port cities where newly arrived immigrants, pressed by poverty, commit numerous crimes. Clearly, American society should not be charged with these offenses. Nor do I speak of conditions on the Indian frontier, that is, the borderlands. Society is not yet organized on the frontier; there are no towns, institutions, or laws. In short, these are wild territories where the individual does not live as a social being but is dependent solely upon himself and his gun. His independence and his passions are in no way restricted by considerations of public welfare or public order. Continuous warfare, constant dangers, attacks, reprisals, and the whole wild, raw environment sharpen individual passions which grow to dangerous proportions. But it cannot be otherwise. Let us recall only our own Cossacks, settled along the routes and borderlands of the Tartars, and we shall have an analogous picture. Despite the predominance of humane tendencies among these courageous men, they loved war and the spilling of blood; they were cruel, tempestuous, and always in search of adventure. Here in America the same conditions prevail but to an even greater degree. The people on the frontier consist of the scum of society. Either they could not live under the law, or they had to escape from it into the desert where no eyes other than the stars of heaven would look down upon them. There they form not a society, but a social leaven which ferments because it must ferment.

How often we have read in history that brigandage was the basic principle of existence in primitive societies. Thus Livy wrote concerning the origin of Rome that the original population was "pastorum convenarumque plebs transfuga ex suis populis." [3] Likewise, the German people and the Gallic tribes were merely bands whose means of livelihood was robbery. The same can be said for the Normans. Thus the American frontiersman, those "knights of the plains," those "cowboys,"

---

[3] A group of shepherds and herdsmen, exiles from their own people.

likewise constitute the roots from which a society springs. As soon as a borderland is freed of its wild tribes and deprived of its savage nature, as soon as its people become more numerous and social relationships increase, law and order are immediately established. At first order is maintained through the terrible courts of the vigilantes and by lynch law. Gradually, however, as population increases, the courts of the vigilantes and lynch law become illegal; passions, like stormy seas, subside; conditions become more orderly and legal and more compatible with the demands of a higher civilization. In the end, the only trace of the former stormy era can be found in some name, as for example *Bloody* Arkansas, or in the fireplace tales of old settlers, or in some sensational, romantic novel, depicting through hundreds of pages a struggle between Indians and white men over a beautiful maiden who, despite long days and nights of captivity, somehow manages to remain virtuous for her happy hero.

Such is the manner in which most of the states here have originated. It is an unusually instructive phenomenon, for this is the very same process through which the European states have passed in the creation of their own organized societies. In Europe, however, this process lasted thousands of years. Here it is evolving before our very eyes. Moreover, this picture is encouraging because it proves that progress, which is inherent in human nature, has within itself that irrepressible power which inevitably will overcome and destroy all obstacles. Universal peace, respect for human law, and an order of society under which every man receives his due will be established. Consequently, all unlawful actions, all preponderance of physical force can be considered only as transitory, as a violent fluctuation of the political and social scale, seeking an equilibrium in the eternal laws of nature.

But I return to the subject at hand. Speaking of public morality, it would be unfair to take into account those territories of the United States which are not yet organized politically. I shall only speak of those states which already possess constitutions and where normal conditions prevail. Thus I can say that I know of no people who are more law-abiding than the Americans. Public safety is greater here than anywhere else. Believing the rumors about the United States which I had heard in Europe, I used to go about at first with a revolver at my belt, brass knuckles in my pocket, and a sword concealed in my walking cane. I was armed like some bandit in an opera. But people who were familiar with conditions here laughed at me: They inquired whether in the company of ladies I would likewise go about with my finger on the trigger. I have now been in the United States for more than six months. I have been in all kinds of regions and have brushed shoulders with all kinds of people. I have had occasion to sleep in lonely farm houses located scores of miles from inhabited communities and in the huts of herdsmen and fishermen. Nowhere have I had the slightest quarrel with anyone; never did I feel that either my person or my wallet was in danger, at least not from any Americans.

I cannot say the same, though, about the Mexicans who live in the southern part of California, nor about the half-civilized Indians. Both are very apt to wring your neck in some dark corner and to make off with your purse. But within the bounds of the United States this happens only rarely. Such disorders are prevented not only by the vigilance of the police, but also by the energy of practically all the inhabitants, who know how to be their own policemen. One seldom hears of robberies or of organized bands of criminals. Indians and Mexicans do commit crimes along the border, but within the duly constituted states order is preserved. On the other hand, take at random any issue of our *Warsaw Courier*. There you will invariably find more or less dramatic descriptions of house-breakings or burglaries which occurred within the city. The same incidents occur in Paris, Berlin, and in all the more important European centers. Here such crimes are much less frequent. They are so rare that when they do take place they are considered great events. They are described in the daily newspapers and illustrated in the weeklies, all of which are on such occasions unsparing in their criticism of the police and the government. In fact, even the President is attacked, for he is held responsible for practically everything. "The rooster is to blame, therefore up and at him," says the old fable.

And if you ask our rural inhabitants what is happening in the villages, you will invariably hear many tales about the stealing of rye and wheat, of night grazing in meadows and clover fields, of the breaking of fences and the cutting of trees, of nocturnal raids on orchards, etc. Here private property is regarded with the utmost respect. In California, for example, because of the warm climate no one locks up his horses, sheeps, cows, or fowl. Orchards are not enclosed by picket fences. There are practically no barns or granaries. And yet I have heard no one complain that anything has been stolen from him. Private property here is so sacred that one might practically leave it on the public highway and yet it would not be disturbed.

This highly moral character is typical of American society. Nor is it confined to the upper classes, for democratic general education, extending to the entire people, promotes morality among all classes. Yet in addition to education, another factor conducive to this honesty is the widespread economic prosperity.

Let me emphasize that I am not speaking of the port cities, where immigrants lead a miserable existence until they find employment, but of the country as a whole. That the people are more prosperous here than anywhere in Europe is explained by the simple fact that the amount of land available to each individual is at least 100 times greater than in Europe. Everyone is still entitled to 160 acres practically without charge, for he is given ten years to pay at $1.50 per acre.[4] As I mentioned

[4] None of the land laws provided for payment over a ten-year period at $1.50 per acre. The Preemption Act of 1841 required payment at the end of about fourteen months of residence at $1.25 per acre. According to the Homestead Act of 1862, the land was granted free after five years of residence.

earlier, it is the small number of people in relation to the abundance of land that results in the high cost of labor and the low cost of the necessities of life. Therefore one cannot speak here of poverty in the same sense as one does in Europe, where it is synonymous with hunger. In Anaheim I was told, for example, that Brown or Harrison or Down was extremely poor. But what does that mean? Let us visit one of these poverty-stricken individuals. Before us stands a respectable house, surrounded by tamaracks, pepperwood, peach trees, and grape vines. In the corral near the house there are a cow and one or two horses. In the fields stand shocks of corn, barley, etc. Finally the door opens and the American pauper comes out to meet us. True, he is wearing only boots, a pair of trousers, and a shirt, but here no one dresses otherwise. "Hello, gentlemen," says our host as he invites us in. "Hello," we reply as we enter. Inside the house there are several rooms. One of them, I notice, has its floor completely carpeted, as is the custom in America, and contains a table, rocking chairs, and other furniture. Another room contains cooking utensils. In still another, a huge bed, large enough to accommodate the entire family, occupies half the room. Somehow this kind of poverty is not hard on one's eyes. Is this person on the point of starvation? Far from it! He eats meat three times per day and has wine with his meals, for this is the least expensive drink here. Why, then, is he considered poor? Simply because he does not have on hand a hundred dollars in cash! Good heavens! How many literary figures, lawyers, and doctors do I know in Warsaw, and how many respectable citizens in the country, none of whom has on hand a hundred dollars in cash! But we do not call *this* poverty, and certainly not destitution. Destitution skulks in cellars, eats but once or twice per day, never sees meat except through the show window of a butcher shop. Destitution in Poland makes teeth chatter from cold, bloats bodies from hunger; it begs, steals, and murders. This is the kind of poverty one finds in Europe.

In America such extreme poverty is unknown. Mr. Brown,

Harrison, or Down is poor, but he is not in absolute want. It is correct, however, to call him poor, for he has no cash on hand and he may even have debts, in payment of which all may be taken from him. But "all" has a special meaning in America: creditors cannot take his agricultural implements or his household effects. Nor can they prevent him on the eve of the sheriff's auction from selling his cow, horses, sheep, and chickens and pocketing the money. Thus in the end, they may take only his land, providing it is not protected by homestead law.[5] But suppose all of his land should be taken from him. What then? Fifteen, twenty, or fifty miles away lie thousands of acres merely awaiting settlers. He has only to take his family there, cut a clearing in the forest, build a cabin, and his new home is complete. I need not add that his former debts cannot be attached to the new homestead.

But if a bankrupt farmer should not wish to stake out a new claim, he may choose any one of a thousand occupations. He may become a laborer either on a farm or in the city. He does not have to seek a job; the job will seek him. And his wages will no doubt be sufficient to cover the needs of himself and his family. It is true that the Western states, among them California, have especially favorable conditions in this respect. In the East, poverty does perhaps resemble more closely the European variety. But it is never so severe, simply for the same obvious reason—the small population as compared with the vast amount of land.

Now then, how can you expect a person who possesses education, average intelligence, and the rights of citizenship, who considers himself secure and the equal of any man, who has enough to eat, to drink, and to wear—how can you expect such a person to abandon voluntarily his comfortable position

[5] In a footnote Sienkiewicz explained homestead law as follows: "In Polish this principle might be rendered as 'the inviolability of the hearth.' In accordance with this law, property is jointly owned by wife and children; in the event of the bankruptcy of the husband, it cannot be taken from the family nor sold for debts." Most states had laws protecting homesteaders against complete financial ruin.

and to embark upon the thorny, uncertain path of crime? He would have to be a villain by nature, such as we see on the stage. But such evildoers are not found in large numbers anywhere. I do not wish to imply that transgressions and crimes do not occur in the United States. Of course they are committed here as elsewhere. But whereas in Europe they are for the most part the result of unfortunate social conditions, here they stem almost exclusively from individual passions, not from ignorance or extreme poverty. Surely I need not point out that poverty and ignorance are the cause of twice as many crimes as passion. In view of these factors, statistics could easily be compiled to show that the morality of American society is on a much higher plane than that of any European society.

Finally, just a word concerning the purity of personal moral standards. In the cities morality in this sense is on the average not much higher than in Europe; and where there are large Chinese populations, perhaps even lower. In general, however, the naturally unemotional temperament of the people makes for few excesses, and the life of the young people, full of activity and physical work and exercise, is a powerful restraint on immorality.

Such are the traits and attributes of this society which at first repelled me, but which, now that I understand it, I have learned to respect. In my descriptions I have tried to be objective and accurate. They are neither the result of optimism, of which I have never been accused, nor of predisposed sympathy for American institutions. I understand clearly that there are no institutions which are good in the absolute sense and which therefore would be equally appropriate under all conditions. Only those institutions are desirable which best suit the temperament of a nation, its customs, and traditions, and which insure its greatest progress. They are undesirable if they retard a nation's growth, if they tend to remain permanent and unalterable when new conditions require their discard or their reform.

These, then, are my views on the subject. Furthermore, I believe that by closely examining American institutions and by perceiving their true character one will profit and learn much and in the process will discard old prejudices and unwarranted pretensions of superiority. Finally, one will acquire those characteristics so representative of the nineteenth century—love of mankind and a tolerant outlook upon the world.

Incidentally, I have observed that letters written from here to our newspapers, although frequently written with great talent, must, because of their limited timeliness, deal with transitory events, superficial details, and political situations of the moment. They deal with those *silvae rerum*[6] which are the outward manifestations of life, but not its governing principle. Since I am not bound by any deadlines in sending my own letters, I am able to make my observations with greater care, passing over superficialities and inquiring into basic causes. In a word, I am able to study the essence of things, *das Ding an sich,* as old Kant would say, and to share my observations from time to time with my readers, even though I do so only through the medium of a newspaper *feuilleton* and in a fleeting and incomplete manner.

[6] Forests of things.

Letter V

AMERICAN WOMEN

I SHALL discuss literature and fine arts with my readers later, for it is worth devoting a separate letter to this subject.[1] In passing, however, I should like to say that literature and the fine arts in the United States are not yet so highly developed as they are in Europe. Henry Thomas Buckle[2] in his *History of Civilization in England* makes the statement that literature (poetry excepted) and the fine arts begin to appear and to flourish in a particular society only after that society begins to accumulate wealth. Or to put it another way, they begin to flourish only when, first, civilization has fought with nature and has subjugated it; and, secondly, when it begins to feel a certain surfeit of life and of the world of reality. Since these conditions do not yet exist in America, the aesthetic needs of the people, taken as a whole, are small indeed. These needs are satisfied in part by native but mostly by English literature. But more on this subject later.

Let us now turn to a question which in recent years has been given much attention both in literature and in journalism, namely, the emancipation of women in America. It is universally believed in Europe that the emancipation of women has nowhere been as fully realized as in the United States. I was certain that I would find a large number of women doctors, lawyers, and even clergy. I was sure that I would at least find many women devoting their lives to serious scientific research.

[1] Despite his intention, Sienkiewicz fails to return to this subject in any of his letters.
[2] Henry Thomas Buckle (1821–1862), English historian, planned to write a many-volume history of world civilization, but completed only the first two. These were published in 1857–61 as *History of Civilization in England*.

They might only be toying with the outward trappings of emancipation which, despite all of their amusing and eccentric forms, nevertheless would indicate a certain general trend. Curiously enough, the situation is quite different. It is true that elementary education here is largely in the hands of women, who in this regard perform an invaluable service to society. But if by emancipation we are to understand higher, specialized education for women and their participation in public affairs, then in this respect less has been accomplished here than in Europe.[3]

Emancipation here does have great potentialities. The Americans have one inestimable attribute: they have the courage to try any theory which would appear to promote human progress. If the theory is not obviously foolish, if it attracts supporters, if it evokes academic discussion and appears to possess at least some merit, the way will be opened for putting it into practice.

In Europe, where public opinion is created in the salons, such an outcry and alarm are immediately aroused by the appearance of a new idea from abroad that to attempt its application or to suggest any kind of reform requires courage bordering on foolhardiness. In America the steed of progress is not an unbroken colt which cannot be mounted. If you wish to experiment with a new theory, you are free to do so.

So it was with the emancipation of women. Public opinion approved it from the very outset and official sanction was not necessary. The government may forbid certain practices if they contravene morality, public safety, etc., but permission for their inception is never required. Thus the movement for the emancipation of women began spontaneously and gradually took hold of the minds of the people. It gathered strength—the mountain labored and brought forth—a mouse. In short, emancipation in the sense that I have described it did not become a reality.

[3] It is well to bear in mind that Sienkiewicz was least familiar with the East Coast where the emancipation movement was furthest advanced.

In New York there is a woman colonel whose name, I believe, is Miss MacCleftan.[4] In the state of Wyoming there is a woman preacher. Undoubtedly, there are some women lawyers. Here and there at the universities one comes across a female student.[5] Yet the very publicity attending these persons and reaching as far as Europe indicates that these women are exceptions. For the most part they are individuals endowed with a vivid imagination, whom most women refuse to follow and whom public opinion, despite prevailing tolerance, ridicules.

I ask you, what would you say about a woman clergyman who heard the confession of her own husband? Or better still, what about a female colonel? Suppose, in case of war, it suddenly became necessary for such a colonel to request an armistice because of an expected, innocent addition to the staff. Such an embarrassing situation among the military leaders would perhaps be more effective in mitigating the brutalities of war then the Brussels Conference.[6] But perhaps not. Those who know about these matters say that the sight of a colonel, issuing orders in a soprano voice and possessing an attractive figure (accentuated by the close-fitting military uniform), has an unusually effective influence on the enthusiasm of the soldiers.

But enough of jest. What I wish to say is that emancipation has not really become a part of the American scene and that in general women here do not take an active part in the industrial and public life of the nation. Someone will, of course, be quick to point out that women work in the factories of New England. That is true, but so do many women, and even

---

[4] A Negro battalion of the New York National Guard selected Tennessee Claflin (1846–1923) as its colonel in 1872. She and her more famous sister, Victoria Claflin Woodhull, were leaders in the suffragist movement.

[5] Oberlin College had in 1834 admitted women on an equal basis with men. By the time Sienkiewicz was writing, most of the state universities of the Middle West had followed Oberlin's example.

[6] Called by Tsar Alexander II, the Brussels Conference met in 1874 to draft an "international convention concerning the laws and customs of war."

children, work in the factories of Europe. In Great Britain, for example, the government had to limit the working hours of women and children in the factories; the same has happened in other countries, as the reader can learn from any economist. Thus it is apparent that in this respect the position of women here is by no means exceptional. In fact, women here play a less important role in industrial life than in the Old World.

To continue, women have deluged the Exposition here with their handicrafts which are displayed in a separate "Women's Pavilion." [7] European expositions have had no separate women's pavilions, but that does not mean that thousands of articles on display have not been made by women. Whose work are the many laces so universally admired, the large variety of ornaments, the embroidery and the gobelin tapestries, the porcelains, silks, apparel, etc.? All of these are either exclusively or in large part the handiwork of women. It would be difficult to deny that there is an incomparably greater proportion of women factory workers in Europe than in America. But, of course, working in the factories cannot be attributed to emancipation. In Europe we find women serving in post and telegraph offices and in national and private banks; such is rarely the case here. The number of women typesetters in Europe is likewise greater. In short, nowhere do I find a significant number of women engaged in masculine occupations. The emancipation movement does not deserve either the clamor or the glowing accounts which appear in our books, newspapers, and pamphlets. [8]

There remains only the teaching profession, in which women play a most commendable role. But their role in teaching is neither a result nor a part of the emancipation movement. Yet even if it should be regarded as evidence of emancipation,

[7] The reference is to the Centennial Exposition of 1876 in Philadelphia.

[8] Sienkiewicz's views on emancipation do not accord with those writers who have made a more careful study of the subject. Compare, for example, the work of the English suffragist, Emily Faithfull, *Three Visits to America* (London, 1884).

it is but a single phase of the movement, only the first step on the long road to complete equality with men in work and responsibilities. But Europeans believe that complete equality is already an accomplished fact in America.

Finally a word about specialized education for women. They can obtain such training since the institutions of higher learning are open to them. No obstacles preclude the admission of women into the law and medical schools. But very few take advantage of these opportunities. The reports circulating in Europe about women's colleges are greatly exaggerated. Such institutions as, for example, the so-called Vassar Academy, and other colleges in New York, Washington, Boston, and Philadelphia, are regarded throughout Europe as universities, the equivalent of those in Germany. This is what the Americans would call so much "humbug." As soon as I have gathered a sufficient amount of material, I shall devote a separate letter to these female academies.[9] For the present I shall say only this: that as far as I have been able to ascertain they are merely advanced boarding schools whose curriculum is much more comprehensive on paper than it is in reality.

It is true that men and women here receive the same education, but only in the elementary and secondary schools which provide a general education instead of specialized training in preparation for a profession. Most men learn their professions later, either in special schools or, as is frequently the case, through actual experience. On the other hand, most women do not continue their education and gradually forget even what they have learned in the schools.

In my opinion this is quite natural. Women do not pursue professional training nor do they take part in the public and business life of the country simply because general conditions do not encourage them to do so. Theories become realities not merely because the government places no obstacles in their way, but because they satisfy urgent needs which are funda-

---

[9] Sienkiewicz does not devote a separate letter to women's colleges.

mental to life itself. Where women outnumber men, where thousands of them remain unmarried and therefore must support themselves, the pressure of women in search of new means of livelihood is so great that no power can resist it, and emancipation is inevitable. But in America conditions are reversed. Although the country is as yet only sparsely populated, it is extremely wealthy. I have already referred to the great average wealth of this nation. Land and the basic necessities of life are cheap, while labor is dear. Every man who works six hours a day easily earns enough to support not only himself but also his family. As with the Israelites, children are considered blessings from heaven, for, upon growing up, they constitute a valuable labor force.

On the other hand, this nation which is so wealthy in every other respect is poor only in women. I do not have at hand the population statistics of the states. However, I am sure that with the exception of several of the Eastern states, the number of men in the United States as a whole is several times greater than the number of women. And in some of the Southern and Western states the ratio is five to one.[10] Consequently, the odds are at least five to one that a woman will marry and that she will find the earnings of her husband sufficient to purchase not only the necessities of life but even a few luxuries.

There have been instances where Polish, Russian, and Czech families, fairly numerous in California, could not accustom themselves to the absolute equality with servants which prevails here and have therefore brought plain, rural servant girls from their homelands. Their joy at having such servants was great but of short duration. Within a few months some "gentleman" would appear—a tradesman, laborer, or farmer—who would propose to Miss Katy or Miss Aggie and promptly marry her.

---

[10] The 1880 census reveals that there were almost as many females in the United States as males (24,636,963 to 25,518,820). In the Western states and territories the men did outnumber the women, but only in a few of them, such as Nevada, Colorado, Arizona, and Idaho, was the ratio even as high as two to one.

He would then proceed to buy her silks and velvets. Lady Kate, who in Europe used to carry buckets of water, here rocks back and forth in her rocking chair. She quickly becomes accustomed to her new station and soon differs not a whit from other "ladies." I have met a few of these persons; some had already begun to forget their native tongue but were moved to tears when they heard it spoken again. As a result of all this, a woman realizes that even if she does not work, she will not die of hunger but may exist quite comfortably. These factors explain the slow progress of women's emancipation.

In general, people tend to seek education or employment not because of some abstract ideal but because of necessity. Such necessity does not confront the women of America. After all, sitting in a rocking chair and leading a carefree life is more pleasant than exerting one's mind and muscles. Small wonder then that women here choose the former!

Speaking only of California, I must confess that women here abstain from many occupations which elsewhere are performed exclusively by women. In the country, for instance, the men are the ones who milk the cows; on many farms I have seen men sweeping the floors. Where a family is sufficiently well off to employ a Chinese servant, all household chores rest upon his shoulders. The honest and inexhaustibly patient "John" serves as nurse, cook, and gardener, while the lady of the house sits in her rocking chair, receives guests, decks herself out in finery, and pampers her spoiled "baby." That is the whole of her activity.

I should like to conclude my few remarks concerning emancipation with this statement: The possibility of emancipation does exist, but since there is no real need for it, it has not been put into practice. In Europe, however, they mistake "possibility" for "reality" and therefore have an erroneous conception of the American woman.

A few more words to complete the picture. Perhaps nowhere else is a woman's life so comfortable as in America.

Legislation coddles her, custom gives her freedom, public opinion protects her even when she misbehaves, and men pamper
her. This regard for women is a characteristic common to the
Anglo-Saxon race, but in America it is carried even further
than in England. Perhaps that is why a woman here is rather
like a spoiled child.

But if someone were to suggest that I compare her in terms
of native intelligence, intellectual development, and refinement of manners with the European woman, I should have
to inquire first of all: with what kind of European woman
should I make the comparison? Such striking differences
as are found among European women do not exist here.
Take Poland, for example. A lady and a farmer's wife, or
a society girl and a peasant lass, belong to two different worlds,
or at least stand leagues apart. One might ask why do I
compare such extremes? My reply would be: simply because
I have no choice. It is not I who creates these extremes; they
already exist in society.

The society girl in Poland speaks heaven knows how many
tongues besides Polish, for ever since childhood she has had
a governess versed in languages. She plays the piano and is
able to converse about literature and the fine arts in a fascinating manner. To be charming is her chief concern. Her mind
is mature and nimble. If she wishes to pose as a woman of
pleasing disposition, she skillfully masks her true nature. She
knows also how to weave meaningful phrases into a seemingly
trivial conversation. In the dense forest of subtly shaded
words and sentiments, she moves about as freely as in her
own home. At first glance and without even the aid of a
lorgnette, she appraises the character, strength and adroitness of her adversary. It was not for idle pastime but for experience that she enticed her cousins and the tutors of her
younger brothers to fall in love with her. She is acute, keen
as a razor sharpened on the strop of social life. To be sure,
she is not a learned person, but psychologically and aestheti-

cally she has reached maturity. She may be good or bad, noble
or mean, depending upon her upbringing and her conscience.
In any case, she is a highly intelligent person. In sketch-
ing her thus, I admit my indebtedness to many of my old
and new acquaintances. It is immaterial to me whether my
portrait is a source of pleasure or embarrassment to them.

I now turn to the other extreme, the peasant girl. Chloe
walks barefoot over the fields of stubble.[11] She drinks vodka,
wraps herself in a shawl, and to all questions gives the same
answer, "I am too shy to speak." Yet this idyllic bashfulness
is no obstacle to certain equally idyllic incidents in the newly
gathered hay. It is all a matter of how one is brought up. Chloe
cannot read or write; she has absolutely no comprehension
of what is happening in the world about her. Her eyes merely
reflect the world, as water reflects the sky. Nothing penetrates
her mind.

Now then, with which type shall I compare the American
woman? You may say, with the average one. But such a
woman is a nonexistent type in Europe. Perhaps you would
be good enough to create one, for I find myself unable to do
so. When it comes to finding an average woman in the United
States, however, that is another matter. Excluding intellectual
females and the several hundred who, having traveled abroad,
have acquired the characteristics of European women, I can
select one at random and say that she is typical. What I have
already written about American education would apply here
as well; the great distinctions found in Europe are absent in
America. Intellectual development and good breeding are
not the monopoly of a single class. Every woman knows how
to read and write; they all read the newspapers; and all possess some maturity of mind. They all dress alike, at least in
the same fashion. There are no great differences among them
in their manners. From the point of view of their intellectual

[11] The name Chloe has often been used for idyllic heroines. It comes
from the Greek idyll, *Daphnis and Chloe*, written in the third century A.D.

development, their aesthetic appreciation, and their behavior, they are inferior to a few of our women, but superior to the great majority. And yet American women generally make an unfavorable impression upon European travelers, who all too frequently compare them with the women of only one class in Europe. That is the reason Christine Narbutt painted such a dismal picture of American women. I can fully understand how they must have appeared to her—rather ignorant, plain, and in general of a *mauvais genre*. If Horain in his comparison had likewise considered only the women of our upper class, he too would not have found American women to his taste. But Horain will write nothing unfavorable about them, for he is a connoisseur and indefatigable admirer of the fair sex.[12]

As for me, having given full credit to the better distribution of general education among American women, I do not wish by any means to set them up as an example for the educated European women. I am even prepared to say that they have many of the faults but few of the virtues of European women. Taken as a whole, they are less industrious, less concerned about the home, about household duties and cooking. As a result, American cooking is in a very deplorable state. Furthermore, they seem everlastingly to be concerned about their clothes. Even on the boulevards of Paris, one does not see so many fashionable gowns as on Broadway in New York or on Kearney Street in San Francisco. The styles, as I have already indicated, are identical for everyone and the dress of a servant or a country girl differs from that of the wife of a wealthy merchant or the wife of a high public official only in the price and quality of material, but not in its pattern.

These elaborately attired women look strange indeed beside the men, who pay no attention to their clothes. Gloves and full dress are practically unknown in America. You no doubt

---

[12] In her memoirs Helena Modjeska tells that Horain was nicknamed Mr. "I Lofe You" since these were the only English words he knew and that he delighted in embarrassing young ladies by addressing them with this phrase.

know that President Grant appeared at the ceremonies connected with the opening of the exposition in a business suit and without gloves. During my stay in Anaheim, in southern California, a French circus came to town.[13] Naturally, the entire countryside came to witness the celebration. You should have seen the town and country ladies, dressed like fashion plates, with low-cut gowns, hair in ringlets, powdered and begloved. They attended the evening performances on the arms of their sunburned husbands, who were dressed only in boots, trousers and cotton shirts, without vests or coats. But that is the custom here. A man completely gratifies his aesthetic instincts by decking his wife in finery.

Knowledge of French is considered by American women, as by our own, a particular mark of distinction and refinement. It is not, however, widely known. Whenever the French language is being discussed, every woman will invariably express the stereotype phrase: "It is a very sweet language." Since it is the fashionable thing to do, practically all of them undertake the study of French, but lose their desire and energy when they encounter their first difficulties. Nevertheless, they pass themselves off as being very fluent in the language whenever they are among those who are ignorant of it. Yet as soon as a foreigner appears and begins to converse with them, it develops that they know very little French—"very little" usually being equivalent to exactly none at all.

Women here have very little appreciation of literature, poetry, and the fine arts, and their ignorance of foreign languages impedes their study of foreign literatures. In the education of women less attention is paid here to cultivating whatever talents they may possess. I have never met a woman who could draw or paint. Knowledge of music is more widespread, but it is, unfortunately, extremely superficial. Americans lack perseverance, musical talent, and artistic perception. Looking

---

[13] The visit of this circus provided the theme of Sienkiewicz's short story entitled "Orso" in which the circus strong man was the hero.

over the music in various private homes, not once have I come across the compositions of Handel, Mozart, Beethoven, Chopin, Liszt, or any of the French or Italian masters. Everywhere I found only waltzes, polkas, "Marching through Georgia," and —"quousque tandem, Catalina!" [14]—"The Maiden's Prayer" by Badarzewska. When playing "The Prayer," girls here sway back and forth on the piano bench, up and down the keyboard, sighing and rolling their eyes—exactly as do our own. All of this is supposed to denote their innocence, their idealism, their maidenly yearnings, and other tender feelings.

In social intercourse and conversation there is here a strange mixture of puritan strictness and freedom—a freedom of which we can have no conception. In this respect, nowhere on earth can be found two such totally different societies as the American and the Spanish, i.e., Mexican. I had the opportunity to meet many Mexicans in southern California. In Spanish society, practically the first question which a gentleman will ask in all seriousness of a lady whom he has just met is, "Esta Usted enamorada?" ("Are you in love?"). If she replies, "Si, caballero!"—then politeness requires that he exclaim, "I am lost!" This poetic race, like all the Latin peoples, regards love as a good genie without whom life would not be worth a single *real*. To the Spanish, love is a basic and indispensable need, as essential as daily bread. Is it any wonder that they talk mostly of love?

In American society such conversation would be frowned upon. And yet very frequently a young lady without intentional boldness speaks so freely that her remarks might be completely misconstrued, at least by a European. While on an excursion, for example, I had the pleasure of meeting two very distinguished ladies: the aunt, apparently a writer of some poetry, and her niece, a beautiful girl with a snow-white complexion,

[14] "How long, pray, Catilina!" Taken from Cicero's oration against the Roman conspirator, Catilina, the full quotation is, "How long, pray, will you abuse our patience?"

blue eyes, and auburn hair. I spoke with the niece through an interpreter, for at that time I hardly knew a word of English. After a few moments I ventured to say:

"I regret very much that I do not know your language and therefore cannot speak directly to you."

"That doesn't matter," replied the young lady, "If you wish, I shall be your teacher."

"You are very kind indeed and I am grateful to you."

"But I shall be your teacher only on one condition."

"I agree in advance to everything; but pray, what is your condition?"

"Well, providing that during the lessons you let me squeeze your hand from time to time."

I confess, I was completely flabbergasted! Had we been alone, I am sure that my innate conceit would have found a wide field for speculation. But this was said through the intermediary of a third person, known to us both. And it was said out loud, in the presence of everyone, as an ordinary pleasantry, *sans conséquence*. Had I been an old man of sixty, I should have heard the same. Such remarks are entirely permissible.

Likewise, only such informality in social intercourse, existing side by side with puritanical conventionality, can explain the relationship which is here called a "flirtation." The Polish equivalent would be "wooing" or "courting." A "flirtation" is by no means a clandestine relationship. The young man and woman may see each other alone and as often as they wish. They take walks by themselves and even go together on trips. In a word, they are together constantly and become thoroughly acquainted. If their personalities are congenial, then the "flirtation" changes into marriage. If not, they part and each goes his own way.

Such a relationship in Europe would invariably evoke a multitude of scandalous rumors, but not in the United States. In the first place, the unemotional temperament of the American woman, whose reason prevails over feeling, serves to allay such rumors. Besides, public opinion places complete responsibility upon the young man, and he alone is subjected to public opprobrium. Finally, the law, by threatening heavy financial penalties, requires him to marry at once. It considers the young woman to be in the right, even in those instances when the facts appear to indicate otherwise.

With these remarks I close my present sketch. Because of space limitations, it must, I'm sure, contain inaccuracies and deficiencies. I have tried, however, to avoid giving false impressions and to be as objective as possible. Let the reader regard my observations as premises from which he may draw his own conclusions. I can only repeat, that while not shutting my eyes to the darker aspects of American society, the longer and more closely I observe it, the brighter it appears to me.

✳✳✳✳✳✳✳✳✳✳✳✳✳✳✳✳✳✳✳✳✳✳✳✳✳

ONE beautiful morning, having become restless in Anaheim, Sienkiewicz gathered up his menagerie (his dog, his tame badger, and a young eagle with an injured wing) and set out for Anaheim Landing. Fifteen miles away, the Landing was a small fishing village consisting of "six huts, a tavern, and that's all." He had come here for the ocean swimming which he enjoyed and which he regarded as conducive to better health.

The tavern keeper at the Landing was a German by the name of Max Neblung whose wanderlust had taken him to the four corners of the earth. The language he spoke, according to Sienkiewicz, was "a mixture of all the European tongues." The author stayed with Neblung, in fact, shared a room with him next to the bar. It was in this room that he did his writing and even conceived plots for some of his future novels. He admitted, however, that he was at times disturbed in his labors by the profanity which reached his ears from the adjoining barroom where the fishermen played cards all day long.

At Anaheim Landing Sienkiewicz stayed but a short time. His host was a garrulous individual and Sienkiewicz found he had little in common with the fishermen. Then, too, food was scarce at the Landing, so he was often compelled to eat ocean fish for breakfast, lunch, and dinner. Though he entertained no doubt that turbot, flounder, and the like were an "elegant dish," after eating ocean fish "three times per day for a couple of weeks, a man finally reaches the point where he would prefer a piece of beef." He began to look yearningly eastward toward those mountains which surrounded the Anaheim valley. The attraction of the mountains became even greater when one day he learned from Neblung that there were Indians in them, "as well as mountain lions, bears, deer, and God knows what." "It was then," reveals Sienkiewicz, "that in my book of intentions I folded down the corner of a page and wrote upon it the words, 'Some day I shall go there.'"

The opportunity to visit the mountains soon presented itself. Sienkiewicz was awakened one morning before daybreak by a rustling sound close to his bed. Max Neblung was taking down the Mexican saddles hanging on the wall nearby. When Sienkiewicz learned that Neblung was preparing to visit a friend in the Santa Ana Mountains, he jumped out of bed, lit a candle, and began at once to pack. The awaited moment had arrived.

Letter VI

IDYLL IN THE SANTA ANA MOUNTAINS

THE Santa Ana Mountains, from which I am sending this letter, constitute the southern part of the enormous range that stretches in scattered masses and under various names from Oregon all the way to southern California and to Mexican Sonora.[1] I came here from Anaheim Landing together with my host Max Neblung. We arrived late at night, but this night, being my first spent in a wild and completely uninhabited region, left an unforgettable impression upon me.

We had stopped with a certain squatter, Jack Harrison by name, who reminded me of Robinson Crusoe, for he lives all alone in a tent with a dog and rifle as his sole companions. My neo-Robinson was a gentleman no longer young, about fifty years of age, whose appearance was such that if I had met him on one of my expeditions, I should have reached for my revolver without hesitation. He was dressed in a flannel shirt, trousers made of the skin of fallow deer, and a tattered Mexican hat whose ragged brim covered a bearded and threatening face. As soon as Max introduced us to one another, the squatter shook my hand firmly and, uttering the usual "Hello," he departed immediately for the ravine to light the fire and to prepare our supper. Max and I proceeded to unsaddle our mustangs, which we had tied to a tree with long lassos. The horses started to munch clover that was growing luxuriantly under the oaks, while we, having lighted our pipes, sat in the tents waiting for supper.

I began to examine my surroundings. Black, piled-up masses

---

[1] Sonora is a state in northwestern Mexico, bordering on the United States.

of mountains enclosed the valley whose only outlet to the north and south was the bed of a deep mountain stream. The region seemed to me extremely wild and gloomy. Rocky cliffs hung over the valley in huge, titanic blocks, thrown up as if with confused fury one upon another. It seemed to me that at any moment these blocks might break loose and crash to the bottom of the valley. The bright night increased still further the wild extravagance of all these forms. The moon's beams threw a silver ribbon around the edges of the rocks whose black, motionless silhouettes were etched against the illuminated background with strangely severe clarity. The sounds of night heightened still more the grim spell of the environment. In the rock crevices covered with trees, wildcats wailed threateningly and hoarsely; now and again an owl hooted; at times the horses neighed. My dog, unaccustomed to such commotion, raised his muzzle towards the moon and began to howl. My tame badger clambered up determinedly on my knees as if from fright. As for me, I was intoxicated by all this and in a state of complete ecstasy. Although I had galloped about thirty miles on a wretched nag and felt as though not a bone in my body was left intact, nothing in the world would have induced me to follow the example of Max. He had spread a blanket in front of the tent, lain down on it, and fallen asleep.

I had lost my interest in food and rest, and instead began to meditate that the earliest dreams of my childhood years had been transformed into realities. I had always dreamed that I might some day behold those still uninhabited lands where nature's powerful forces, unchecked by human hands, remain unruly, do whatever they please, and are absolutely sovereign. To confront primitive nature face to face and eye to eye, to plunge into the depths of the virgin forests and prairies described by Cooper, this was the epitome of happiness for which I had long yearned in secret. Now unspoiled nature lay before my eyes, surrounding me on all sides, enfolding me completely, overwhelming my mind and senses. I felt myself becoming one with her and disappearing like a mere drop of rain in the ocean.

Today it seems to me that my journey really began only from the moment I arrived in these mountains. After all, does sailing across the seas in splendid ships, traversing the prairies in comfortable Pullman cars, stopping at hotels, sight-seeing in cities and the like, deserve to be called a journey? Does such a traveler-explorer from civilized parts perform any real function? He is transported just like any old trunk and that's all. The only active role which is left for him is to spend money. But in these almost uninhabited mountains lying beyond the pale of civilization, the role of the traveler is entirely different and it is above all an active one. The only passport and ticket required for the journey is your own rifle; the only means of transporting yourself from place to place are your own two feet, or your half-broken mustang. But as soon as you approach your mount, he rolls his terrified, bloodshot eyes. You must first of all half strangle him with your lasso before you can ride him. Nor does he neglect any opportunity to throw you or to snap at you with his teeth.

In addition, your only guide here is your own instinct. You sleep under the stars in a rocky crevice, which you must first clear of scorpions and snakes; you keep warm only if you yourself kindle a fire; you eat what you kill in the hunt; you sleep with one eye shut; with the other you probe the dangerous depths of the darkness; you jump to your feet with every rustle; you snatch up your rifle when the dog growls and bristles. In short, you travel like a real man. All the elements of your courage not spoiled by city life come into play against danger. Everything that happens, happens because of you, because of your manliness, energy, and foresight. You cannot relax for a moment. And there is one final difference: you are not merely a sight-seer, but a discoverer. You must admit that only this kind of journey, active and creative, is worthy of the name.

I now had whole days and months of such travel conditions

before me inasmuch as the Temescal, Santa Ana, and San Bernardino Mountains, which I penetrated after considerable effort, lie beyond the civilized California range. This range stretches from north to south along the seashore, from Oregon all the way to the city of San Diego. This city is located almost on the border between California proper and what is called Lower California, a peninsula belonging to Mexico. In the north, especially around San Francisco, the civilized belt is wide and embraces the whole area from the Pacific all the way to the peaks of the Sierra Nevadas that mark the border of gold-bearing, gloomy, barren Nevada. The territory here is as densely populated as the kingdom of Poland. The beautiful valleys between the middle mountains, like the mountains themselves, are thronged with human settlements.

A few months ago at sunrise I gazed from the peak of Mt. Diablo at the countryside lying at my feet. From the rosy morning mist emerged on one side the emerald depth of the ocean with numerous masts, sails, and multicolored flags. On the other side the whole land was awakening from its sleep and looked so beguiling that surely Satan at the top of the precipice could not have tempted Christ with anything more beautiful. In the green valleys glittered the gold and silver ribbons of winding streams. Here too nestled cities filled with spires whose pinnacles and globes were kissed by the first rays from the east: enormous San Francisco, smaller Oakland, Haywards, Benicia, California's New York, Brooklyn,[2] San Leandro, San Mateo, Vallejo, Martinez, San Pablo, and on the other side the capital Sacramento, washed by the red waves of the river of the same name.

From the number of the above mentioned cities lying in the radius of your vision around Mt. Diablo, you can perceive how densely populated is this area. Were it not for the strangely blue skies overhead, for the too warm breath of the morning

[2] A "New York" and a "Brooklyn" did exist in California at the time Sienkiewicz was writing, but they have since disappeared.

breeze, for the hummingbirds and the large golden butterflies circling about, for the scorching, radiant sun—all of which betrayed a semi-equatorial clime, I could have believed that I was looking from the tower of St. Gudule over the environs of Brussels so densely populated, so thoroughly cultivated, and so similar to an enormous garden was the scene before me. Between the cities the countryside was dotted with farms, watermills, windmills, mile-long sluices; and all this was embraced by the greenness of myrtles, cypresses, and gum trees; submerged in tendrils of ivy, liana, and wild grape; or adorned with palms that stretched their wide leaves like protecting arms over a human abode.

Southwards from San Francisco down to San Diego, this civilized, populated, and cultivated belt of land becomes more and more narrow. It is not that the soil is less productive, for, on the contrary, the populated seacoast is less fertile than the uninhabited mountain canyons. The population is concentrated along the coast because settlers seek to live in the proximity of towns, especially seaports, where they can easily dispose of the fruits of their toil. But the main reason is the small, total population of California. There are only seven hundred thousand people in an area of six thousand square miles. Therefore, it is neither unnatural nor strange that the hinterland, though extremely rich and fruitful, has not yet been occupied.

When you travel eastwards from Anaheim in the direction of the mountains and your horse crosses the wide, sandy bed of the Santa Ana River, you recognize that you have left the pale of civilization where land is divided up and constitutes private property, where society is governed by the laws of the United States, and where all relationships are regularized. Government lands begin on the other side of this river. They are only sparsely inhabited by squatters and Indians, and for the most part are still unoccupied and awaiting the pioneer. The only law in this territory is the terrifying lynch law which can best be defined in these words: not merely a tooth for a tooth, an eye for an eye, but for every assault against an individual or his property, there is but one penalty—the rope. But owing to the integrity and decency of the squatters, it is never applied.

These lands are divided into so-called claims, that is, square sections of 160 acres. Actually this division is not exact, for no surveyor ever set foot on the remote, mountainous wastelands. The law allows each American or candidate for naturalization to take this set amount of land for his use, on condition that he pay the government $1.50 per acre within a ten-year period. After the expiration of this period of use, the land becomes unconditionally his own property which he may sell, bequeath, or rent; in a word, he may do with it what he pleases. The obligation to pay the government exists only on paper, for, in reality, a squatter who occupied unowned land, cultivated it, and erected buildings upon it, although he has not paid a cent, cannot be ousted by any law.

In view of such liberal terms and the ease of taking up land without legal obstacles, and in view of the almost fabulous fertility of these valleys covered for the most part with age-old forests of oak, platan, and laurel, one might expect that squatters would come swarming and teeming in; but such is not the case. I have already mentioned the main cause—lack of people! Undoubtedly a large penniless mob of immigrants with nothing to lose would descend upon the place were it not for the enormous distance between the Eastern states and California. Furthermore, the cost of the journey from New York, Philadelphia, Washington, or Boston, not to mention Europe, is the equivalent of more than two claims.

As for the Americans living in towns, they are all businessmen, that is, people engaged in industrial or commercial affairs, who see no material gain from settling in the mountains and on empty wastelands. Aesthetic reasons such as picturesque scenery, solitude, undisturbed peace, and life in the bosom of nature, these are things for which a true Yankee will never pay a nickel. What's more, there are no roads leading into these beautiful mountain valleys.

The Spanish name *cañón* means, speaking precisely, a gorge. When such a gorge widens abruptly or gradually so that it forms a spacious dale surrounded by an amphitheater of mountains, enough space is thus made for cattle raising, beekeeping, and even farming. But most often such clearings lie deep in the mountain chain and only the bed of a stream serves as an entrance. It is simply a large crack, or as it is called in the Ukraine, a *yar*, at whose base water roars over stones. Its sides consist of cliffs rising perpendicularly sometimes two or three hundred feet.

Nothing is more grim than the gullies of such streams. At the bottom reigns eternal twilight since the fertile tops of the cliffs are covered with trees whose branches often meet each other over these streams and hide the sky from the traveler's eye. In places wild hops, wild grapes, or liana reach out from bank to bank, join together, become entangled, strangle each other with their arms, forming such thick festoons of greenery that daylight passes through them with difficulty. Sometimes the traveler is under the impression that he is moving along some underground passage. Wherever blue sky can be seen through a chink above, the cheering sight is disturbed by the whir of the wings of vultures, ravens, and eagles, and by their gloomy cawing that fills one with sadness and foreboding.

From the depths of such crevices after sunset there resound those ominous cries and roars which are unbearable to nerves unaccustomed to them. When the sun is extinguished on the peaks, all the wild beasts come down to drink water from the streams. First come the deer, antelopes, then Rocky Mountain sheep with sickle-like horns almost touching their backs, and small white-flecked mountain goats. Behind them come the rapacious animals of the mountains. The silver and red cougar crawls quietly in the twilight like a greyish snake. From a rocky crevice the lynx raises his head and rolls his fiery eyes. In the trees sneak grey wildcats. Now and again there comes a distant sound of stones falling down the steep rock face. It is the grim tyrant of the mountains, the grey bear, plodding along with heavy steps as he goes to plunge in the stream, his huge frame fatigued by the heat of the day.

In many places the stream beds are so blocked with various size rocks that it is impossible to cross either by wagon or on horseback, especially since the stones are always covered with wet and slippery moss. In winter during the rainy season and in spring during the general flooding of the waters, the streams become bursting torrents, and at that time the inhabitants of the canyons are completely cut off from the rest of the world. As a result, they are compelled to live a rough life in the canyons and not even to dream of the comforts of civilized life.

To be sure, where the canyons widen, the valleys are beautiful and fertile. It is easy to reach and to occupy them, to find a spot as yet unvisited by man, and to say to oneself: this is mine! As on a desert island, no one will dispute your right to ownership. While it is simple enough to take up the land, it is not easy to live upon it. A squatter is usually a poor man, without a wife or children, a lonely individual. Such a person comes to the mountains, chooses the canyon that pleases him most, and says to himself: "I will settle here." But to settle, you must build a house. The squatter does not ordinarily own any tools other than an ax, a saw, and a drill. There is plenty of timber for a cabin, but how do you commence when all around you whispers a virgin forest of century-old trees whose trunks are several feet in diameter and whose tops are lost somewhere in the clouds? A huge, black oak grows next to a white-barked plane tree; next, a grey oak; then again, a hickory with such a hard grain that the ax rebounds from it as from a stone; further on grows a laurel. Everything is so tied in snakelike knots of liana, so intertwined, so crowded, that the forest seems to be one solid, indestructible mass. Imagine what hardships the settler must endure to clear a place for a cabin and a yard, to cut down and drag away the gigantic trees. Later, in building the cabin, what enormous strength is required for one person without help from anyone else to lift into place one log after another, one rafter after another. For thinner trees it is sometimes necessary to walk a mile or two and then to drag them along the spiteful bed of the stream. At the same time you must carry on your back a heavy rifle without which you dare not move, first of all for protection, and secondly to kill something to eat. It is obvious that the mere construction of a cabin is almost too much for human strength. Therefore, it is not at all surprising that squatters are very few in number. Those embarked upon such a life are either wanderers from abroad who, having arrived without a knowledge of the language or any financial means, and unwilling to be dependent, have no other alternative; or they may be shipwrecks from life pursued by the law, or unhappy souls seeking solitude, or finally, nature's exceptional adventurers who value such rugged independence above all earthly treasures.

But just as a shepherd sorts out his sheep and removes the weaker ones from the flock, so in similar circumstances does life sort out the squatters. Weaker individuals fall in the unequal battle. Thus, squatters are generally men of great physical strength and of uncommonly tough spirit. It could be said that civilization has sent out her most robust members to clear the way for her in the virgin forests. Stronger yet are the qualities of those squatters in the territories inhabited by wild Indians, but their attributes are outweighed by their faults which make pioneers of progress extremely dangerous men. Bloody conflicts with the redskins and the need to use a knife or a revolver at any moment develop wild passions and cruelties in them, as well as coarseness verging on brutality, while the uncertainties of tomorrow give rise to recklessness. To be accurate, a squatter from New Mexico, Arizona, or the Indian Territory is not a settler, but a lumberjack. Gathered into groups of a few dozen men, these squatters search out virgin forests untouched by the ax, and not really caring whether the timber belongs to the Indians, or to the government, or even to private companies, they cut it down, form it into rafts on the waters of the Red River, Rio Colorado, or Rio Grande, and float it to the nearest towns. After selling the timber, a squatter with his pockets loaded with twenty-dollar gold pieces abandons himself to drunkenness and absolute idleness in the town or the nearest tavern until he has lost his last penny, and then, poor as a churchmouse, he goes back to the wilderness. I need not add that this life is often full of very bloody incidents.

The wilderness is not so unpeopled as it seems at first glance. Besides squatters, in it roam trappers, namely, people who make hunting and brawling their trade; *vaqueros*,[3] that is, guards of herds or merchants' caravans; simple rogues, occasional miners, and finally, during the season when the buffaloes migrate, various bands of Indians, hunting for these animals and, wherever they can, for scalps.

The squatters encounter these people constantly. Sometimes they make friends with them and drink together in taverns located along the trails. But at other times, because of the hot-blooded temperaments and readiness to fight of both sides, it comes to real battles fought with Indian shrewdness and with a fierceness reminiscent of the Middle Ages. Moreover, feeling strong, free as a bird, in short, king of the wilderness, this squatter generally scorns other people and, on coming in contact with them, is a bully and a brute with whom it is impossible not to fight. He calls everyone names, he is afraid of no one and nothing, and trembles before only one person in the world —"Uncle Lynch," as this terrifying law is commonly called in the wilderness.

The very name "Uncle" is proof that the squatters have personified this concept with humor, almost in the same way as

---

[3] The Spanish word for cowherd, *vaquero* is commonly used in the Southwest.

the Hindus did with the destroying force in the person of Shiva.[4] Even the most daring squatter feels that "Lynch," as though some kind of god, is definitely stronger than he. Curiously enough, this most terrible uncle of all uncles is simultaneously indulgent and inexorable. He allows a squatter to shoot every Indian on the "battle field"; to kill anyone with impunity in a quarrel which becomes a brawl; to murder in revenge for a brother, best friend, or relative. He allows a squatter to consider any forest as God's gift from which everyone is entitled to reap equal benefit, and permits great leeway in a squatter's personal behavior. But for any treacherous assault on a man's person or on his property for personal gain, he punishes ruthlessly by a death all too cruel.

But although this law is a savage one, it has emerged from the feeling of solidarity amongst the whites and their recognition of the need for justice, two fundamental prerequisites for a society to pass from a primitive to a civilized state. I have already mentioned that when the wilderness becomes inhabited and more complex conditions require in turn more complex criminal and civil laws, lynch law readily gives way to the United States code. However, the inclination to help oneself seems almost inherent in the American people and is so strong that even in well-organized states the government and the police find it difficult to restrain the people from taking the law into their own hands in more important cases. Every citizen here is so much devoted to the public good that he personally considers himself its guardian, and therefore judge, policeman, and executor of justice.

I could give many examples of this. A few years ago the Mexican bandit Joachim was ravaging the length and breadth of California at the head of a band of robbers. It was not the police, in those days neither too numerous nor too efficient, who hunted him down, but the entire people. Mounting their

---

[4] One of the triad of Hindu Gods, Shiva represents the principle of destruction.

horses, they pursued him with such tenacity across plains, through inaccessible wilderness, in wild mountain gorges, that in spite of such natural hideouts which could have given refuge to thousands, Joachim was captured and hanged, and his followers exterminated in the forest like wolves.

We often read about wars with small Indian tribes which are conducted in such an inefficient way that they last for years. But these wars are conducted and purposely prolonged by generals for their own profit. But when the populace exhausts its patience and goes for its guns, woe to the redskinned robbers: their hiding places are found, their wigwams destroyed, their people exterminated, and the war is finished in a few days.

I have heard of very recent cases in which the local population managed its own affairs with no help from the government. Two years ago in Anaheim itself two Indians dragged into a vineyard the young wife of one of the citizens and killed her. Next morning the whole town was out on horseback. The tradition of lynching awoke like a lion from its slumbers and roared over the Indians' heads like a storm. It is true that some of the innocent were killed too, but such fear fell upon the rest that they themselves found the guilty men and handed them over to the posse. But why look for such examples when any theft by Mexicans of a cow, sheep, or horse will be a sufficient cause for all a farmer's neighbors to leave the most urgent work and affairs, thus losing time and money, and not to drop their revolvers until the stolen property is recovered and returned.

In the face of the energy displayed by Americans in occupying new territories previously inhabited by brawling Mexican-Indians, the turmoil usually lasts only a few years, that is, only until the original inhabitants have had their fingers badly burned in their marauding, thieving undertakings. Later follows a peace, the like of which you could never find in Europe. You can travel everywhere not only without a revolver, but carrying a sack of money on your back. However, this does not exclude brawls which inherited hot blood and energy make more frequent here than anywhere else. But this is a different thing. When two men agree that it is proper to blacken each other's eyes with their fists, or to hunt for each other with rifles in a duel, the citizens generally do not interfere at all, saying that it is none of their business. Furthermore, in some states the fanaticism of religious sects gives rise to abuses.[5] In other states long contested by reds and whites, people conditioned to bloodshed do not readily renounce lynching, nor do they easily submit to the authority of the law. Finally, political passions burn more ardently here than elsewhere. But these phenomena are transitory: this same energy which calls forth these outbursts, later quells them, and leads the swollen stream back to its natural river bed.

Nevertheless, I recall, for example, how the French provinces, led on a leash by their mayors, panicked when they were cut off from Paris during the war.[6] I recall how often our own little country has had well-organized bands of horse thieves, and how our sluggish people would show themselves incapable of any initiative or of undertaking any remedial action, and merely would await God's mercy. Then I am overwhelmed by a deep melancholy, and I prefer this Yankee republican energy, even with all its abuses. In my analysis of our helplessness I am not concerned with specific deeds and acts of injustice, but rather with the conclusions that may be drawn from them: that exuberance of spirit and self-reliance have withered woefully in old Europe, and that it is difficult there to take any kind of action without being restrained in one way or another.

In America it is the opposite; self-reliance and energy are flourishing and growing ever stronger. It cannot be said that freedom and decentralization, the basis of the organization of

[5] An excellent example of what Sienkiewicz had in mind is the mob murder of the Mormon leader, Joseph Smith, at Carthage, Illinois, in 1844.
[6] Paris was completely surrounded for several months by the German armies during the Franco-Prussian War (1870–1871).

the United States, account for this growth, although they certainly contribute substantially to it. But, at the same time, they are themselves possible because of American self-reliance and energy. This same political organization elsewhere might have borne entirely different fruit. Thus, the real reason lies in the continual occupation of wild territories, or those inhabited only by primitive people. Of course, men do not come to these regions with a ready-made social order, but must be their own government, court, and police. They must be everything for themselves, and, in addition, they must fight with the forces of nature and with bloodthirsty tribes. Through these Herculean battles the talent for self-government, freedom, and decentralization is most powerfully developed.

I pull up the reins of my thoughts and return to the squatters. Thus the squatters of New Mexico, Arizona, and the Indian Territory are tough, hardened, stormy men, but they always keep their word, stick together, and abhor any treachery. A California squatter possesses their virtues but not their faults. The former are lumberjacks and wanderers; the latter is a settler. The former must live continuously as though on the brink of war, but in California peace reigns. This different mode of life imparts to the California squatter characteristics that readily distinguish him from his counterpart on the other side of the Sierra Nevadas.

The total number of squatter-settlers is, however, very small. In the course of two months after my arrival in the mountains, I met several score of them, including Indians and Mexicans, but scattered over an area so vast that it could comfortably accommodate half of the population of the province of Warsaw. Having nothing else to do, and having a mustang raised in the mountains and able to climb like a goat, I roamed from settlement to settlement. It often happened that I had to sleep by the fire under the stars as it was impossible to cover the distances in a single day.

The Indians, who live in small groups, and the Mexicans

are chiefly engaged in cattle raising; the Americans, in beekeeping. Probably there are no other places in the world where beekeeping could grow and flourish so well as in these mountains. The canyons themselves, extensive yet enclosed on all sides by mountain peaks, form a sort of natural bee pasture from which the workers cannot fly away, scatter, and disappear. The bees find here both water and enough nourishment everywhere, especially since the mountain slopes are covered with masses of the most luxuriant flowers the year round. The squatters protect their property from the heat by placing the beehives under the shade of the black oaks. In all these ideal conditions the honey-giving swarm multiplies and grows with unheard-of speed. Starting with five or six beehives, a squatter can within a few years acquire an enormous apiary. Accordingly, not only the sale of honey and wax, but principally the sale of beehives constitute the squatters' source of income. The beehives are bought by farmers living throughout the area between the mountains and the ocean. To be sure, these beehives must sometimes be transported one by one on a man's back, but a squatter is not afraid of any type of work.

In general, the more remote squatters living in the inaccessible canyons have far more honey than money, that is, they sometimes have ten times as much as they can sell. On the other hand, the needs of a squatter are so limited that money is required by him chiefly to buy powder and lead.

I return to the narration of my personal adventures. I was sitting by my tent that first night of our arrival, admiring mighty nature in silence, when suddenly the voice of our host emanating from the depths of the ravine pulled me out of my musings. Both Neblung and I arose and went down into the ravine. A fire of laurel branches glittered there and Jack was busy roasting, or rather raking out from the ashes, a haunch of venison which he had roasted for our reception and whose splendid fragrance filled the air. The rest of the deer, or rather the whole animal lacking only its haunches, was hanging on a tree close by, and the flame of the fire was reflected in its glassy, open eyes. Besides this, water for Japan tea, which is generally drunk by the poorer people in California, was boiling in a tin container on the coals. When the roast was taken out from the ashes and its burnt surface cut away with a knife, pink, steaming meat was disclosed and we sat down to a truly Homeric feast. We took in our hands pieces dripping with blood, cutting them up with only our hunting knives. Known as bowie knives, these account for the nickname "long knives" by which the Indians call the whites. Even the surroundings could remind one of the pre-Homeric gorges of the Pindus and Ata Mountains. Near our feet a brook murmured over the stones; all around stood blocks of rock against which we leaned; in the middle a fire threw a blood-red glow on the nearby oaks growing in the crevices; and further away waited the awesome twilight of the forest depths.

From time to time the squatter threw some dry laurel branches on the fire which started crackling. Its sparks spattered like golden rain, only to be extinguished in the darkness. The replenished flame flared up and lighted up our faces, our rifles, and our dogs who were sitting close by and watching with greedy eyes every morsel of meat that we were putting in our mouths. At times it seemed to me that I was participating in some romantic opera, singing the baritone role of an Alpine brigand. It was truly the beginning of a new life for me, one with which I was to fall in love so madly that if I were ever to give it up for another, I would do so only with sadness and reluctance.

Overhead the moon shone with incredible brilliance: its beams, together with the firelight, gilded the tree tops; nearby the forest was rustling, the streams were grumbling over the stones; animal calls could be heard in the darkness. All of this was so beautiful, so romantic, and so picturesque that my spirits seemed to soar on wings, and I regretted the years of my youth wasted on city streets, in restricted interests, and often among petty people.

At first we sat in silence. The squatter by nature was taciturn; as for me, I could not cope with my own impressions, and talkative Neblung's mouth was so stuffed with venison that the impatient words could not find their way through. I was noticing, however, that the squatter was glancing at us with unconcealed joy. I came to understand the reason when, after he had finished eating, he said:

"I have not seen a human face for two months."

"I told you, Jack, that this gentleman," declared Neblung, pointing at me, "wishes to spend a few weeks here. He is a tourist; he travels all over the world; and what he sees, he writes about in Polish newspapers. Jack! Do you hear? I have already been written up in newspapers. Jack! What a thrill! Take care of this gentleman so that he does not get lost in these mountains and you, too, will be written up. Jack, people on the other side of the world will know about us."

The squatter appeared to be unimpressed by such resounding fame, but extended his hand in which, incidentally, my hand disappeared like a mouse in a trap, and began to thank me for choosing his abode as the starting point for my excursions. I answered, rather too much in the European manner, that I, also, was very pleased to meet such a gallant gentleman, but I feared that perhaps my presence might afford him some troubles and inconveniences.

"What troubles and inconveniences!" exclaimed Neblung with laughter. "Jack, have you heard of troubles and inconveniences? I already have discussed the matter with this gentleman at Anaheim Landing. I said to him plainly: 'I know Jack. You must not even suggest payment to him, for he will consider your stay as a favor.' "

"I would not accept payment from anyone," replied the squatter, "and as for your arrival, sir, I can look upon it only as a lucky break for me. I will tell you why. I am tired of living in a tent. During the rains of the winter a tent isn't very comfortable, so I have decided to build a house. I have almost finished the walls, but this is no small job. Each board takes me several days of work. Moreover, there are no other trees in the vicinity except those of a few feet in diameter, and therefore I must look for thin trunks at a considerable distance from here. I work several hours a day and besides this, I must keep the fire burning, cook for myself and my dog, look after my goats and my horse, and most difficult of all, go hunting. I simply do not have enough time, and if I don't hunt, I don't eat. I can shoot partridges without leaving my tent, but one soon tires of partridge. I also have a stock of dry venison, but this is no better either. Therefore, if you wish to hunt, sir, as do all travelers, you will not only save me time, but you will also keep me supplied with fresh meat."

"In any case, hospitality in the town is one thing," interrupted Neblung, "and it is another in the canyon. In the town I supply a guest with lodging for which I can charge money. I give him breakfast, lunch, and dinner. All this costs money. And here? A guest is two hands and one rifle more, and besides, a man's company is also worth something. Jack, I should go mad, living here all alone. How do you manage, Jack, not to go crazy too?"

"I have become used to it," replied this squatter, "but, of course, sometimes it is very hard, particularly when the rainy season comes and there is nothing to do. What do you say, sir, will you stay in the mountains until the rainy season?" he asked, turning to me.

I answered him that I did not know, as I actually didn't, any more than I know now where I shall be a few months hence. In a year I may be in Warsaw, or perhaps in San Pablo. The mania for traveling is like all other bad habits. The first step is the most difficult and then some strange force pushes one further and further, like the Wandering Jew.

But in the meantime, the squatter and I reached an agreement. We confirmed it by repeatedly shaking hands, and with each handshake I winced. Then we started drinking Japan tea, naturally with honey rather than sugar. I recollected that in my saddlebags amongst sundry odds and ends there were two small kegs, one with brandy, the other with wine. After bringing them to the fire, I invited my comrades to help themselves. We wrapped ourselves in blankets, lit our pipes, and now puffing, now sipping tea with brandy, we lay around the fire and chatted more and more gaily. At last the squatter said,

"Tomorrow at dawn I shall take you deer hunting."

"All right!" we both replied.

Then he started teaching us how we should behave. Although there are very few humans in the canyons to frighten animals, nevertheless such horned creatures as the deer and the antelope are extremely cautious because cougars and wildcats, as well as people, hunt them. Attacks usually occur by the water. It is a well-known fact that once a deer has chosen a path to a water hole, it will always use it. Such a path is easily recognized because not only is the chaparral and chamisal thicket torn asunder along its whole length, but even in places where bushes do not grow, the displaced gravel and larger stones indicate the path clearly. Thus when hunting, one has to discover a deer trail and then at dawn sit in the thicket on the far side of the brook and wait for the game to approach within shooting range. Such hunts may even prove dangerous, as often a two-legged hunter meets a four-legged hunter very jealous of his rights.

The squatter told us of a few such dangerous encounters when he did not know whether he was the hunter or the hunted. And it was hard not to believe these narratives when the various sounds emanating from the forest were providing undeniable evidence of their truth. At one time such an awe-inspiring roar resounded in the darkness that the whole forest was hushed, and we with it. The squatter added a bundle of dry laurel to the fire.

"A curse on your hide and may God plague you!" he exclaimed after a moment.

"Is it close by?" I asked him, hiding my fright with difficulty and involuntarily reaching for my rifle.

"No, about two or three thousand yards away," he replied, "but sound amplifies amid the rocks at night and seems to be close by. I know you, you devil!"

"What kind of beast roars like that"

"A silver lion. My poor Ren!"

I poured a third round of brandy into our tea, and then I questioned him about the episode of the silver lion and Ren.

"Do you see, Jack, how curious these travelers are?" interrupted Neblung. "All of this will be written up, Jack, and your Ren will be in the newspapers!"

"You are a mockingbird, Max," replied the squatter, alluding thus to Neblung's talkativeness. "I repeat: my poor Ren, and I should not be consoled even if the *Herald* printed an article about him. This dog of mine, sir," he said, turning toward me, "came with me here all the way from Louisiana where I was born. He was a worthy dog, courageous and strong! One night two weeks ago this devilish creature that was roaring just now, on becoming tired of venison, came up to the corral where I keep my goats. This hoodlum," he continued, pointing to an enormous mastiff sitting by the fire, "scenting her, hid himself in the moss under the tent; but Ren, although smaller, threw himself upon her like a mad dog. I snatched up my rifle immediately, but before I had run out of my tent, I heard her roar and a short whimper from Ren. I fired into the air to frighten her and then ran to Ren's rescue with my revolver and bowie knife, but it was too late. The silver lion had escaped, and Ren had his innards torn out and a crushed back; his legs were still quivering . . ."

Whether the tea with brandy intensified the squatter's sorrow for Ren, or whether he loved the deceased one so deeply, I do not know, but suddenly he broke off his narrative, clenched his fists, and began repeating quickly, as if in a paroxysm of rage: "God damn you! God damn you! God damn . . ."

"Calm yourself, Jack!" said Neblung.

Soon Jack calmed down, but this usually reticent and grave man, having once become talkative, poured forth a veritable ocean of every kind of tale. Perhaps because he had imbibed a little, or perhaps because for so long he had seen no one and been silent for many months previous, he now astonished even Max with a flood of words so unusual for a squatter. He related that he had fallen in love with this life of a squatter and that he would not give it up for anything in the world in spite of all his troubles. He regarded as his greatest troubles the damage done by wild animals to his property. Sometimes small red bears came at night to his beehives, and real devastation was done by small animals, namely, racoons; he had wanted to keep hens, but during the first night they fell victims to skunks; he had a few pigs: they were choked by lynxes; finally, cougars and coyotes broke at night into the corral where he kept his angora goats. "During the day," he said, "all these animals hide so that there is not a trace of them in the mountains, but at night each one begins its troublesome activity. Sometimes I have to reach for my rifle two and three times a night. That is why I sleep a few hours during the day."

I inquired whether his personal safety was often threatened.

"The silver lion and the grey bear," he answered, "almost never attack a person, unless wounded or suddenly surprised. The silver lion attacks at such a time from fright. But during hunting from an ambush, when you have to remain quiet, it often happens that you meet one of these beasts suddenly and unexpectedly. At such a time presence of mind, a strong hand, and a good bowie knife are your only defense."

"And what about a rifle?" I asked.

"Often there is no time to shoot."

"But with only a bowie knife it is difficult to come off without any injury."

"It can't be helped!" he answered curtly, and rolling up the sleeve of his shirt, he showed me a great number of ragged white marks and scars below the elbow. It was obvious that the muscle there had at one time been terribly torn.

"Did this happen here in California?" I asked.

"No," he answered, "that was still in Texas; it was a jaguar, which is more dangerous than either the silver lion or the red bear."

This mention of Texas led him to reminisce about the distant past. He was born in Louisiana and at one time was a rather well-to-do farmer. But when the war broke out, he quit farming and, together with his sixteen-year-old son, he enlisted in the army of the South. Then misfortunes began to assail him: his son was killed, while he himself fell into the hands of the Northerners. After his captivity he returned home, but meanwhile his wife, having gone bankrupt on the farm, had to leave it and they settled down in the small town of Berwick on Chester Machee Lake in southern Louisiana. Berwick, located in a swampy and humid region, has an even more unhealthy climate than New Orleans; soon both he and his wife became ill with yellow fever. Shortly after, he bought a few wagons and cattle with the remainder of his money and set out for dry Texas, but his wife died on the way. Then Mexicans attacked his caravan and took everything, and he was left practically helpless on the plains. With nothing else to do, he joined some squatters who were clearing the woods along the Brazos, Colorado, and Red Rivers. He led this life for a few years; having saved some money, however, he decided to give up this life and to go to California. There he arrived, again almost penniless because he had spent his money on the way. But by good luck he had met at Anaheim this good fellow, Neblung, who lent him funds and helped him to set up farming as a squatter in the mountains.

"I have been living here since then," he ended, "and I must admit that neither Texas nor Louisiana can equal California."

This man had certainly passed through the storms of life. The wind had tossed him like a leaf, until finally it had cast him into this forest retreat.

When finally the fire began to die out and leaden sleep began to weigh down our eyelids, Jack went to say a prayer, and we decided it was time to go to sleep. The squatter urged me to use his tent, which was simply a piece of canvas hung on some branches with room under it for only one person; but I preferred to spend the night together with Neblung in the unfinished house. Our host brought us a few bundles of moss, I lit a lantern which was among my things, and we went to prepare our beds. The floor of the house was littered with shavings, sawdust, and various pieces of wood. I asked Max to push all this to one side and, leaving him the lantern, I went to the packsaddles for a second blanket because the nights are cool towards morning. I took from the saddles all the provisions which might be eaten at night by coyotes or racoons; next I glanced at the horses to make sure they had not tangled themselves in the lassos, whistled for the dog, and returned to the house.

On arriving, I found Max exclaiming: "God damn! God damn!" and pounding a scorpion with the butt of the rifle. He had found a few of them in the shavings and thrown them out the door, but the last one angered him with its great size. Soon the squatter also arrived, and seeing what was happening, said calmly:

"Oh, they are also under my tent."

And I shuddered.

"And maybe there are some in this moss?" I asked, pointing to the bundles.

"Perhaps," replied the squatter.

"And what if one of them bites?"

"Oh no, he won't bite."

I am not really sure whether these insects are less spiteful or less venomous here than elsewhere, but I do know that people here do not trouble about them. I threw out the rest of the shavings, however, and carefully shook out the moss.

"There are rattlers around here too," the squatter told us by way of good-night, "and this is why I would put a lasso around the house, but since you have a badger with you, there is no danger."

And apparently this is the practice. When it comes to spending a night under the naked sky in regions where snakes are numerous, the squatters spread out a horsehair lasso in a circle on the ground over which a rattler cannot glide. But the presence of our badger made such a precaution superfluous, for the bite of even the most venomous snake does not harm these animals a bit. These unhappy reptiles are persecuted relentlessly by everything that lives.

Finally the squatter left, and we lay down to sleep. Max fell asleep immediately, but I could not. Lying on my back, I looked at the stars, as there was no roof on the house, and I listened intently with a certain apprehension to the voices in the forest. I am no greater coward than the average inhabitant of the banks of the Vistula or Niemen,[7] but this night the wild surroundings and the wailing coming from the forest shattered my nerves. Whoever is tempted to smile ironically at this honest admission, let him spend a night here. I am not one to fear large animals, but every moment it seemed to me, for example, that the moss was moving under me—surely it is a scorpion; then the remains of the shavings in the corners looked somewhat suspicious—surely it is a rattler. Something similar was happening constantly! As for the night sounds, the darkness and quietness bring them closer. It seems to you that these cries and mewings sound no further away than twenty paces, sometimes right behind the wall, sometimes right at your ear, and then, in spite of yourself, you reach for your rifle. Finally come the nervous reasonings. "Why," I

[7] The Vistula, the principal river of Poland, flows through Cracow, Warsaw, and Danzig. The Niemen River is in northeast Poland.

asked myself as I stared at the black top of the wall, "why might I not see at any moment on this framework two eyes shining in the darkness, belonging, perhaps, to a silver lion? This might not happen once in a thousand nights, but who could guarantee that this is not the night?" But then I remembered that the silver lion never attacks first. "And so I will not provoke him. Let him live!" Meditating in this vein, I felt so peacefully inclined towards the whole species of silver lion that momentarily I felt myself their affectionate ally. Also I was cheered by the fact that Max was sleeping right next to me, and there were no good reasons why any rapacious animal should prefer to eat me instead of him. This lack of selfishness on my part raised my spirits so high that I began to imagine in advance how deeply I would mourn Max in such an event.

But joking aside, I do not know myself why I was unnerved most by those animal voices which I did not recognize. One of these voices called constantly "A ha ha!" on the neighboring cliffs. I was almost certain it was some kind of bird, therefore not at all dangerous, and yet this "A ha ha!" annoyed me most. On the following day I found out that the big mountain quail really do scream in this way night and day.

Finally, one who has never heard the howling of coyotes cannot imagine how funereal, how unbelievably sad and mournful is this sound. Even the squatters, accustomed to every commotion in the wilderness, cannot refrain from cursing when they hear these groans and moans as if coming from beyond the grave. I, too, was familiar with them because I had heard them many times at Anaheim Landing, but yet a shudder seized me from head to foot.

At times this entire concert, as if under a conductor's baton, suddenly ceased, even the dogs stopped barking, and the silence of the night was disturbed only by Max's snoring. In such intervals I tried to fall asleep. Fatigue slowly began to get the upper hand. The stars overhead began to mingle together, to quiver, and to bounce about. Hearing dulled; ideas, thoughts, and images blended together in a drowsy disorder. At last I fell asleep.

It was perhaps midnight when I fell asleep, and at five o'clock the violent barking of a dog awakened me. The dawn was already approaching and the stars were fading. In apprehension that a dangerous animal had come close to the horses, I took my rifle and went out to see what was happening. In the morning the nerves are calm, and I was well rested, having slept like a stone, even though very briefly. Thus, full of spirits, I went out to the horses. The dogs were still making a terrible uproar, but the horses were lying quietly under the trees. I turned to go back to the house when suddenly a voice called from under the tree: "Good day, sir!"

It was my squatter, who had likewise come out to look at the horses and the beehives.

"Good morning!" I answered, making for the door.

"Sir, if we want to go deer hunting, now is the time."

"All right! Shall we waken Max?"

"Let him sleep. It is difficult for him to sit quietly in a blind."

I still desperately wanted to sleep, but it would be a shame to miss the hunt because of sleep, so I got my rifle ready and took a bag with ammunition; then we drank some brandy, ate a piece of yesterday's roast, and started on our way.

In these regions the dawn lasts for a shorter time than with us. Thus, it was necessary to hurry so as to be in our places before it became completely light. We walked upstream through a fiendish passageway cluttered with large stones and almost pitch black, since the liana growing on the top of the walls did not let the light through. I had to exert all my strength so as not to fall. Sometimes the stream's water took up the whole space between the walls, and then we waded in the middle. In the first break in the cliff where another smaller brook fell into our stream, there flashed a grey,

elongated shadow, probably a wildcat. Wanting to show my
alertness, I took aim immediately, but the squatter hit the
barrel with the palm of his hand, knocking aside the rifle
almost at the moment I was about to shoot. Later he explained to me that a shot fired near the stand could spoil the
whole hunt.

On the way he continued to instruct me how I should behave, especially recommending the greatest caution, the greatest patience, and warning me not to hurry with my shot even
though the animal might seem to have noticed me and was already scampering off. I made a mental note of all this. Meanwhile we reached an open spot. Instead of rocky cliffs, on one
side of the stream a rather steep incline descended to the
water's edge. On the other side was a small level area completely overgrown with laurels; here we took up our stations behind the two thickest bushes. Now we hardly dared to breathe.
It was growing lighter every minute. At last the first rays of
dawn decorated with a pink ribbon the bush-covered mountain
top. Then I saw clearly a landslide of gravel and stones extending the whole slope of the mountain from its overgrown summit to the stream. I could not conceive that an animal could
descend such a steep incline and not fall down on its head.
But soon I was convinced of this feasibility when suddenly I
saw the head of a deer emerging from the thicket. My heart
began hammering and as slowly as I could, I raised the stock
of the rifle to my cheek. It was not yet time to shoot, but I
wanted to show the squatter that I possessed one of the most
valuable virtues of a hunter—patience. The distance between
me and that head sticking out from the thicket was some three
hundred yards, but the air was so filled with rosy brightness
and was so transparent that I could see the head as though on
the palm of my hand. And only then did I appreciate that
incredible alertness deer and antelope display on approaching
a water hole. The eyes of the animal were wide open, the ears
pricked, the nose twitching rapidly as it analyzed the morning

scents. I thought that it would never emerge from the thicket. Perhaps ten minutes passed and still the deer stood, turning his head from side to side. At last the neck appeared behind the head, the chest below the neck, and then it stood still again.

Finally I saw the splendid animal in all its beauty. It was a buck about four feet in height, with a large head, bulging eyes, and spreading antlers which, when he raised his head, rested on his back. His skin was a uniform yellowish shade, not as dark as our deer, and his belly was covered with white hair. His legs were long and thin, the hind ones even longer than the front. After emerging entirely, he stood still for another moment, catching sounds with his ears and scents with his nostrils; then the gravel and small stones began sliding down with a clatter. The buck was climbing down.

The experienced hunter who remembers the emotions he felt at the sight of big game exposing itself as a target will understand what I was feeling, I who was still only a novice in the hunting profession. I had shot water birds for a few months in Sebastopol on the Cosumnes, partridges and rabbits at Anaheim, badgers near Orange, coyotes and sea birds at Anaheim Landing, but this was the first time I had leveled my sights on such a big speciman, twice as big as our deer in Poland. And in the meantime, gravel and stones kept falling, falling, with strange monotony; the animal was halting at every step. He sniffed the air, listened and gazed. Half an hour might have elapsed and still he had not covered half the distance. Suddenly he turned around and jumped back, as though unexpectedly frightened.

I managed to hold out. The squatter had not warned me in vain that deer use this strategy to entice from ambush rapacious animals who may be lurking by the water. Then, after a while, the animal started climbing down again, and again I heard falling gravel and stones; but none of this was happening any faster than before. It had been a long time since my patience had been exposed to such a great test. My hand was becoming

numb from holding the rifle, my heart was beating . . . "Only
fifty yards! Now!" whispers impatience. Forty yards . . . thirty
. . . even the squatter must be wondering why I do not fire.
Twenty-five yards! . . . I cannot endure any longer: I pulled
the trigger!

The echo of the roar shook the cliffs like a cannon shot. The
animal, hit with the conical bullet, tumbled down like a stone
to the bottom of the stream.

"All right!" said the squatter.

Letter VII

MY MOUNTAIN IDYLL CONTINUED

THUS began in the mountain canyon my life as a forest dweller, seemingly monotonous, and yet not lacking in exciting experiences. I rose daily when the skies were still grey and walked down into the valley where I usually found the fire already kindled and the squatter preparing breakfast. At breakfast the happenings of the previous night furnished subjects for conversation. Sometimes we discussed the damage done to the beehives by racoons; sometimes we found tracks of larger animals close by, and then we laid plans for hunting and setting an ambush for them; at other times we talked about the approaching rainy season and the need to lay in those food supplies which could be obtained only in town. These had to be procured early because when the streams and the Santa Ana River reached flood stage, the roads between the town and the canyon became impassable.

After breakfast, always finished before sunrise, the squatter would reach for his ax and resume the building of his cabin. I, on the other hand, would throw my rifle over my shoulder and head toward the deer trails. There were days when I returned empty handed; this would happen whenever I did not maintain the necessary caution; more frequently, however, I would bring home either an antelope or a wild goat. We cut the meat of these animals into thin slices and smoked it, or we hung it on a string to dry in the sun. At ten o'clock we would both lie down near the stream on a bed of moss and have our siesta until noon. At this time of day it is so hot that even in the winter it is impossible either to work or to tramp in the mountains. In the afternoon when the cool air blew in from the

Pacific, I would again take my gun, this time an ordinary double-barreled shotgun instead of a rifle, and go out to shoot birds.

Cock pheasants perched on the cacti would flee at the approach of a hunter. These were my favorite game, as well as large mountain partridges, millions of which lived on the mountain slopes and along the streams. During these excursions I often encountered rattlesnakes. These reptiles liked to crawl on unshaded rocks where they warmed themselves in the sun. Usually they fled when they saw me at a distance; sometimes, however, I had to wage battle with them. One morning when I went out before dawn, I spied a snake on the open road. I thought that the reptile would get out of my way, as is generally the case. Instead, he straightened himself to half the length of his body and tilting his head to one side, he began to hiss. I could then examine him closely. The tip of his tail, raised upward, shook from left to right so rapidly that the individual tremblings of the rattles combined to make a single high-pitched sound. The snake must have been either irritated or so full of food that he did not wish to escape. When I approached him from the side, he straightened himself even more and turned his head with every movement I made. This mutual inspection went on for some time. I saw no danger to myself, for in the end I could easily run away. Finally, I cut a long laurel branch with my bowie knife and trimming off the leaves, I moved forward. Standing erect as a candle, the snake was about to lunge at me when a blow from my stick killed him on the spot.

I cut off his tail on which I counted seventeen bells. This meant that the reptile was seventeen years of age and, therefore, old and dangerous. Since then I have accumulated a very fine collection of tails. Not counting those acquired personally, I received more than twenty from the squatters and Indians. The largest of these has eleven rattles even though much older snakes are quite common. In Woodward's garden in San Francisco,[1] for example, I saw a snake with forty bells on its tail.

But to return to my afternoon bird hunts—usually my efforts were well rewarded. Shooting all day long from morning until evening and sometimes even after sunset, I was gaining more and more skill. The surprisingly rapid development of my sight and hearing was responsible for my progress in the art of hunting. My way of life contributed to this transformation. Whereas in Warsaw I used to write far into the night until three and four a.m., here I retired at sunset and rose at dawn. But the main factor in perfecting my senses was my wild, sylvan life. The need constantly to study the terrain with my eyes, to look intently into the thick forest underbrush, into the dim rock crevices, the intensified caution and accuracy with which this must be done—this was real physical exercise which in a few months made my vision grow keener and sharp as a razor. It was all a matter of practice.

The same can be said of hearing. While the nights in the wilderness are noisy, the days are as silent as the grave, especially at the height of the heat when even the birds are still. The ear, accustomed to this quietness which is disturbed neither by human speech nor by animal sounds, ultimately becomes as fine and sensitive as the hearing of a prisoner condemned for life to a silent cell. Solitude and the attentive listening required while hunting train the ear still further. Finally you are able to hear, as Mickiewicz expressed it,

> How the butterfly rocks on the grass
> How the snake with its slippery breast
> Rustles through the leaves.[2]

Frequently, while I sat and wrote in the unfinished cabin and Jack worked several hundred yards away in the canyon, I could hear him speak to his dog; I heard him with such accuracy that

[1] Woodward's Garden, once the private garden of R. B. Woodward, became one of San Francisco's first public parks. It no longer exists.

[2] These lines are taken from the sonnet entitled "Akerman Steppes." Adam Mickiewicz (1798–1855) is Poland's greatest poet.

I could repeat every word. I could even tell when he was returning home and when he was going deeper into the forest. The
acuteness of my hearing was no doubt helped by the natural
acoustics of the rocks. These cause a rifle shot, rebounding from
one cliff to another, to roar like thunder and to reverberate in
several echoes until, dashed against fallen rubble, it tears itself
from the ravine and escapes into the forest.

Thus, hunting consumed most of each day but writing also
was a part of my daily occupation. Some irresistible force constantly compelled me to share with my readers this mountain
idyll which was so unique that to me it seemed imaginary, a
kind of dream. People of my profession rarely experience this
type of existence. It was so wholesome that it served as a great
tranquilizer after my life in the city and as the beginning of a
second youth before the first had vanished.

The desire to write came easily, but it was difficult to fulfill.
Aside from the fact that my stiff, bruised fingers would not
hold a pen, there were other obstacles. I always haul my writing equipment with me and I had it in my packsaddle at that
time. Jack, however, had neither table, nor chair, nor any
similar objects which we regard as necessities and which squatters look upon as inessential luxuries devised for effeminate
living. Jack sat and ate upon a rock in the canyon, and at night
went to sleep on a bed of moss in his tent. It is very probable
that even if he had chairs, he would never use them. It is true
that he did say that once the cabin was completed he would
like to arrange things differently, but I cannot guarantee that
tables and stools formed any part of his scheme.

Therefore I had to give some thought to arranging a suitable
study, for unsatisfactory working conditions do not allow a
writer to collect his thoughts, to concentrate, and to devote
himself exclusively to writing. Using only an ax, I succeeded
in constructing a splendid table from an empty cupboard-like
beehive. The table even had a drawer for protecting paper
from the dampness of the night dew. As for the chairs, I

followed the example of the Mexicans. While still residing in Anaheim, I visited several so-called *estancia* or cattle ranches. They consist of a shanty constructed carelessly from boards, frequently lacking a roof, and an enormous enclosure or corral capable of holding several hundred head of cattle which graze on the prairie during the day. The Mexicans and métises who reside on the ranches lead a semibarbaric life. During the day they gallop about the plains in pursuit of the cattle. In the evening they sit in the shanty around a fire of corn stocks and play cards—at the same time quarreling, fighting, and drinking. Like the squatters, they possess neither tables nor stools; cattle skulls propped against the walls comprise the only furnishings in the shanty. At nightfall the *vaqueros* place them around the fire and sit between the horns. I did likewise. Finding several cattle skeletons in the ravine, I picked out the largest skull and carried it home. By tying a bundle of moss between the horns, I had a chair worthy of the name on which I could loll like Voltaire in his *fauteuil*.

From this time forward I wrote practically every day and before a certain incident, which I shall mention later, tore me from my work, I finished all of those items which I sent you.[3] Meanwhile, however, a new task fell upon me. Jack Harrison, my Robinson Crusoe, had for several months been building a cabin and it was most likely that before he finished the roof and hoisted it up on the walls, much time would elapse.

I should not have been concerned about this, except that the nights became cooler and cooler as autumn approached. Such a heavy dew fell just before dawn that the top thick blanket with which I covered myself became as soaked as though exposed to a violent downpour. My health began to be affected since I was unaccustomed to sleeping under the open heavens, and daytime temperatures of 100° Fahrenheit and higher aggravated my plight. Jack offered me his tent but I refused to

[3] By this time Sienkiewicz had written not only the preceding *Letters*, but also *Charcoal Sketches* and *Selim Mirza*.

accept it, for I did not wish to take his place. Furthermore, the tent consisted merely of a piece of tattered canvas hung over a few stakes, which offered practically no protection.

I decided, therefore, that it would be best to help Jack with the construction of the roof. From that time forward the echo of two axes resounded daily. The work began to make rapid progress. To be sure, I knew nothing about carpentry and to this day have little knowledge of it. But the assistance of two hands, even though unskilled and possessing only physical strength, is of inestimable value in this type of work. Previously, for example, Jack had to carry one thin beam at a time for several miles. Now we carried two at a time, even three, tied with rope. I hit upon the idea of hitching my mustang to the heavy beams, but this proved impracticable. The only road leading into the heart of the forest was the bed of the stream. It was so full of rocks in some spots and so deep in others that not only a horse but even a man was constantly in danger of falling.

I had purchased this horse from Neblung for eight dollars, which was a rather high price. From the Indians and from the métises I could have bought one for as little as five dollars, especially with the help of a glass of whiskey. Max had taken him into the mountains, not to sell him, but primarily for my convenience. Likewise, when returning from the mountains, he intended to use him to carry back to the Landing goods purchased in Anaheim. Meanwhile, when Max was about to leave, I insisted on purchasing this unbroken mustang. Although it was rather awkward for Max to part with the horse at this time, he figured that he could transport his goods by hiring another mustang either at Anaheim or at almost any farm, and the deal was closed.

It became apparent later, however, that I had acquired no great prize. The horse was a young three-year-old of dappled grey, rather tall and strong, but like most mustangs, he was wild and very ill-natured. The Mexican saddles used exclusively in California and apparently throughout the country are equipped with enormous wooden stirrups completely covered with leather to protect the legs of the rider from the horse's teeth. Nevertheless, as soon as the horseman forgets himself for a moment and loosens the reins, immediately the mustang will turn his head and try to snap at the rider. In addition to the above faults, my horse would not allow anyone to approach him. Whenever I came near him to attach the saddle, he would roll his bloodshot eyes, prick up his ears, and begin to bite and kick so violently that I had to tighten my lasso around his neck with all my might. Only when he was half strangled was I able to do with him what I pleased. However, only the first months of living with a horse are generally so difficult. Later an animal becomes accustomed to the particular individual who attends him, gives him food, cleans him, and watches over him. Gradually the relationship becomes friendly even though it remains strict.

During the first few weeks I tried in vain to tame my mount. In vain, I gave him his barley, corn, and clover regularly. He filled out and became handsome but did not cease to be nervous and fearful. At times I became completely discouraged, believing that we would never live with one another in any other state except that of war.

Meanwhile, Jack advised that I try to tame him by means of hunger. I followed his advice. Purposely I tied the lasso short to the tree in order that the horse could not feed upon the succulent grass usually growing under the oaks, and I went away. At noon I gave him water but gave him no food. In the evening I brought some corn on a pan, let out the lasso a little, and standing at a distance called out, "Come." The mustang, according to his usual habit, pricked up his ears, jerked several times at the rope, but did not think of approaching. I tightened the rope and departed. Next morning the scene was similar. He moved his ears, stared at the corn, distended his nostrils, but would not come toward me. Meanwhile, the grass which he was able to nibble in the small area was all but gone. Hunger began to torment him more and more. At noon he came to the pan and ate greedily. I grasped his sensitive ears where he was especially ticklish, and stroked his forehead. This time he did not withdraw. Henceforth whenever I brought his fodder, I loosened the lasso and stood further and further away. He always approached me and in the end he would run toward me the moment I appeared, coming as far as the rope allowed, neighing, rising on his haunches, and prancing about with joy like a dog on a chain. While he ate, I covered him with caresses which later he himself demanded.

Only then did I realize what effect careful and solicitous rearing can have upon a horse. Like all mustangs, mine, too, had long, shaggy hair, overgrown fetlocks, and a bristling mane. After a month's care during which I covered him for the night with a blanket, fed him well, and cleaned him daily, his neck bent into the shape of a beautiful bow, his eyes sparkled with intelligence and spirit, his mane became narrow and fine, and his coat shone. In short, he became practically a thoroughbred at which the Mexicans and Indians looked with unconcealed covetousness.

Like the Indians, the Mexicans give their horses almost no care. When a Mexican comes in off the road, he removes the saddle and drives his horse out onto the prairie, as do our Cossacks in the Ukraine, and doesn't want to hear any more about him. I never saw a Mexican clean his horse or feed him fodder. The horse lives on what he finds. To be sure, in the spring and winter pasture is everywhere plentiful; but during the summer, in July and August, when the sun burns the grass to dust and the prairie looks like a cracked, clay threshing floor, the horses either die of starvation or survive only by eating the leaves of willows or other trees growing beside the dried-out stream beds. It is easy to understand why mustangs living under such conditions must be wild and vicious. As part of a herd throughout most of the year, they rarely see a human face. When occasionally a man or two does appear, it is only to whirl their long lassos over the frightened herd, to capture the horses, to strangle them, and then to mount them and to goad them with the kind of spurs formerly worn in Europe by medieval knights.

Were it not for their wild mode of life on the prairie, the mustangs could be transformed into beautiful thoroughbreds, especially suitable as saddle horses, for they possess within their veins the blood of ancient Spanish horses, descendants of those steeds which came to Spain from the East together with the Arabs in the year 711. As proof of this, those mustangs reared as race horses in certain parts of southern Texas are able to outrun the most famous full bloods of Canada and are worth fabulous sums of money. In general, however, the mustangs are not distinguished for handsomeness. They usually possess large heads, protruding foreheads, shaggy coats, and legs overgrown with hair. But they excel in endurance. Mexicans never ride in any other manner than at the gallop. The moment the horse feels the rider on his back, he lunges forward and starts to gallop. He does not change his pace, even though he must run twenty or thirty miles without a stop. The rider rocks in the saddle as in a hammock, twirls a *cigarittas* during the gallop sings O *dulce amiga!* [4] and only occasionally straightens out his huge sombrero when a gust of wind slides it too far off his brow.

When a horse leaves the herd and serves a single master constantly, he soon becomes clever and quick of comprehension. These qualities are especially apparent during the throwing of the lasso. When the rider casts the rope out in front of him, an experienced mustang reverses himself on the spot and begins to gallop at full speed in the opposite direction, thereby tightening the noose and strangling the captured victim. Some of the *vaqueros* have trained their animals so well that at the sound of a whistle their horses instantly come running to their masters at top speed. Such horses, however, are very scarce and highly valued.

[4] "Oh, sweet friend!"

Those mustangs sold in the cities become accustomed to the harness, but because they are usually harnessed while still too young, they look scraggly, rather like our peasant horses. They are best suited for packsaddles which are the common means of transporting small loads on the prairie.

My mustang gave excellent service as a packsaddle horse. The Mexican saddle, besides having a high pommel up front around which the lasso is wound, is equipped with six or even eight pair of straps made of exceptionally strong leather. On longer trips I would tie to these straps a bag of corn, another of flour, one small keg of whiskey, another of wine, plus a blanket and a rifle in the rear, a load totaling a hundred pounds or more not counting myself. With this cargo the horse would gallop several miles with little difficulty and I would dismount only in those places where I feared both the horse and I would break our necks. When Jack and I made some traces and tried to hitch him to a beam, however, he began to kick up his heels and to buck with such violence that I immediately unhitched him lest he be hurt. Henceforth, we carried the beams, rafters, and boards with our own hands.

The work of making boards occupied most of our time, for, lacking a large saw, we had to trim them with an ax. This not only took a long time but also meant that from an entire trunk we could make only a single board so heavy and unshapely that it resembled more a thin beam than a board. When the roof's skeleton of rafters was finally finished, we nailed on the boards crosswise with long nails. In two weeks we prepared ten wide laths and since Jack had already prepared twice this number, we completed the roof within another week and the cabin was ready.

We looked with pride and satisfaction at our creation, yet had we examined it with a less indulgent eye, we would have seen there was still much to be desired. The cabin consisted of a single room with space enough for two beds of moss, several cattle skulls, and my study. We built the door, quite according to the rules, of three short boards and nailed it to the hinges which Jack had purchased, together with other scrap iron, in Anaheim. But there were no window panes. Jack didn't even consider getting any, for the climate here makes them unnecessary. During the day the openings in the rear wall let in more than enough light. At night we covered these openings with shades made of thick canvas. The gently slanted roof, though somewhat unshapely, was sturdy and did protect us from the rains. Thus everything was in good order. Having finished the house, we surrounded it with a ditch which gave protection against the access of snakes. There was now nothing more to do except to plant fig, orange, peach, and almond trees.

But this was work for a later period, for above all we had to concern ourselves with gathering supplies for the rainy season. Unfortunately, at this time my health began to fail. The heavy and exhausting work in heat reaching more than 100° Fahrenheit caused me severe headaches, and then sitting by the fire during the cool nights, I caught a cold whose severity surpassed anything since the time of the Flood. Furthermore, when the dogs barked furiously in the night and when larger animals wailed close by, I had to get out of my warm moss bed, grab my gun, and make the rounds of the corral, the apiary, and sometimes shoot into the air, but above all catch cold unmercifully. One night my horse, apparently frightened by coyotes, jerked so strongly at the lasso in trying to break away, that he tangled it badly and I had to spend more than an hour untying the tightened knots. This was at four in the morning, and thus at the period of greatest chill. I froze like an anemone and had to spend the entire following day in bed.

If this had happened in another, less healthful climate, I should have become feverish or caught inflammation of the lungs [i.e., pneumonia]. But here no one has heard of fevers and my lungs do not inflame as readily as does my heart. Nevertheless, kindhearted Jack boiled Japan tea for me all day long and in the evening brought me a glass of some kind of herb decoction which was supposed to be very efficacious. The following day I was so much improved that I was able at dawn to go hunting.

The concern and friendship which Jack showed me won the affection of my heart. Jack was not a learned person, but like all Americans he had attended an elementary school and possessed many qualities rarely found even in the best educated people. He was, however, somewhat gloomy and reticent. In the evening beside the fire he did talk a good deal. But during the day while at work, we scarcely exchanged a word. Such reticence in a man of the world would indicate an irascible and unpleasant temperament, but with Harrison this was simply a habit resulting from his lonely life. I believe there are no people on the face of the earth who are as even-tempered as the squatters in general and Jack in particular. A changeable disposition usually occurs as a result of shattered nerves and unstable health, but squatters don't know what nerves are and they are as healthy as oak trees. In addition, the innate, masculine character common to the Americans and their complete lack of pettiness explain why these men of the frontier do not torture themselves with trifles or grow exasperated without just cause.

I have stated that lack of pettiness is a common attribute of Americans, and I repeat that there are no other people on earth who combine in themselves so well the various faults and virtues of true masculine character. The American does not possess the Frenchman's nimbleness of mind. He is not capable of the delicate feelings and discriminating sensitivity of the soul that mark the Frenchman or the Pole, for example. The Yankee considers the picture as a whole; he is oblivious of details, trifles, and minutiae. In everything he does he is a tough, resolute fellow. He knows how to love, but not how to whisper sentimentally. He knows how to hate, but not how to knife you behind your back. He despises gossip, the jabber of old women, and the embroidery of scandalous news at the expense of human dignity. When he hates, he destroys, but does not undermine. When he works, the chips fly. When he spends money, he scatters twenty-dollar bills like leaves. He does not understand what it is to pinch pennies. When he grows rich, he makes millions; when he goes bankrupt, he loses millions. He respects womankind as the highest gift of God. Frequently he allows a woman to lead him by the nose for the very reason that he doesn't do things by halves and so behaves like an enamoured lion. Finally, he loves his United States and is boastful and proud of them. When the republic is in danger, he doesn't stop to ponder or to look around, but instead takes down his Kentucky rifle, roars like a bull, and stands united as one man with his fellow Americans.

Whoever believes this characterization to be exaggerated or too generalized, to him I shall say that I did not search for it, nor did I find it in the large cities where all men fit a common pattern. The place where one should search for the real America, where her strength, wellbeing, and future lie, is in the small rural communities, on the farms as numerous as the sands of the sea, on the frontier, along the river banks, in the mountains, among the people of average means who are always active, industrious, and exuberant. Oh! It is very difficult for me to put into words how young, how eaglelike, and how full of ebullient, internal strength this people is! How happy I should be to send here for its health a certain nation known to me [5] where the public welfare counts for nothing, where everything has become trivial, where energy and work are mere words, where men are neurotic and anemic and for that reason wag their tongues and spin and carry to their womenfolk the latest filthy gossip.

As for the frontiersmen, they are clear-cut, excellent specimens who personify the qualities of the whole nation. Despite their rough appearances, the frontiersmen are for the most part

---

[5] There is little doubt that Sienkiewicz is referring to his native Poland when he speaks of "a certain nation known to me." As a columnist for the *Gazeta Polska*, he had been highly critical of many aspects of Polish society.

upright in character and mild in disposition. Leading a lonely
life, they do not experience the disillusionment and despair
that are so damaging to a man's nature. Jack possessed such a
mildness of disposition. His temperament was rather reserved
and his overflowing energy was absorbed by his work. Although
by nature he was little inclined toward meditation, yet his
Robinson Crusoe way of life tended to form within him that
habit so common to solitary individuals of constant introspec-
tion and self-analysis. In our confidential evening talks beside
the fire he told me that it sometimes seemed to him as though
there were two Jacks: one who was building a house, chopping
trees, cooking meals in the valley; and the other who was doing
nothing but simply gazing at the first. He told me this very
simply, interspersing his narrative with constant exclamations
of "By God! By God!" I even had to assist with the birth of
this idea, but the concept contained enough substance to
foster a certain philosophic mildness in his nature. If, for example, Jack the Extrovert became angry over some coyote or
racoon, and was tempted to explode, then Jack the Introvert
looked at him with a calm eye, laughed sympathetically, and
perhaps said, "Shame on you!" With these words any thought
of transgressing the usual bounds of good conduct vanished
like the light of a candle before a gust of wind.

It so happens that a person who lives alone thinks not only
for himself but also for the natural environment around him.
I tried to find out whether Jack asked himself if there was
a mind in these enormous rocks which cut the blue horizon,
in the streams scattered like a silver net over the mountainous expanse, in the trees, in the underbrush, in the animal
world, and in the sun and stars. I wanted to know if there
were in him a recognition of a spirit of nature or some kind
of vision of a unifying principle in nature. I had had occasion
to read about one such homespun philosopher. For example,
Giliat in Hugo's *Les travailleurs de la mer* peopled the air
with an imaginary world of unseen animals and became so

identified with nature that nature fell in love with him and revealed her secrets to him.

But I must confess with regret that I did not discover anything of the kind in Jack. Like every woodsman, he knew his environment. He knew when certain shrubs shake off their old leaves in order to dress themselves in new ones; he knew the medicinal properties of herbs and trees; he understood the speech of the mountains who announced rain for the next morning by hiding themselves in an evening blanket of cloud. In brief, he recognized the signs and read them like printed words in a book. But like Heine's fool,[6] no "why?" ever entered his head. When once I attempted to speak to him of these matters, he replied with the words of the Bible: that God created the world so that man might have a place in which to dwell and to gain a livelihood.

Jack was a religious person, as in fact were all the other squatters. This was the spiritual side of his character. In the evening as the fire was dying out in the valley, he always went a short distance uphill among the rocks and, baring his head, raised his eyes heavenward and began to say the Lord's Prayer. It was then that he seemed very poetic to me with that majestic strength which humbles itself before some still higher force. The silvery rays of the moon fell on his resolute, bearded face whose features seemed as though sculptured in stone. Sometimes I thought that I was living in the early Christian era and that I saw before me some kind of barbarian, a Cimbrian, placing his rough soul at the feet of God. The English words of the prayer which were strange to my ears intensified my illusion: "Our Father, Who art in Heaven, hallowed be Thy Name," Jack repeated as he gazed at the stars. Then he dropped his voice like a monk reading from the breviary, and later I again heard the isolated, solemn phrase: "Give us this day our daily bread." This prayer did not last long. If some ear in the depths

---

[6] The allusion is to the young man in Heine's poem, "Questions" (Second Cycle of "The North Sea").

of Heaven listens to the voices from the earth, surely it must have heard this voice from the wilderness.

After we had lived together for some time, Jack proposed that I should remain with him permanently.

"People in the cities have many more worries," he said to me, "and here it is peaceful. We shall raise bees, as many as we wish; we shall clear twice as much wilderness; we shall plant barley and corn; we shall plant tobacco and around the cabin we shall grow orange and fig trees and shrubs of white almond. The time will come when people will settle here, and the land will begin to have value; and then, when I shall be here no longer, you will become the owner of both your claim and mine, which together, by God! by God! will form such a farm as is not to be found anywhere between the ocean and Dry Lake.[7] In the forest one lives in peace. Do stay."

There was a brief moment when this temptation smiled at me and charmed me like a forest nymph. It was not the inheritance of Jack's land that tempted me. Jack really wasn't giving me anything. The countryside here is empty, the land belongs to no one, and I could, therefore, like every one else, take more of it than I could cultivate. But I did find a charm in this idyll, in this communion with nature, in this quiet port far from raging storms. After some lapse of time, however, the allurement paled. Unknown seas, lands, and peoples, the noble profession of a traveler, his life, his struggles, defeats, victories— ultimately would come the time of return when the traveler would shake the dust from his shoes at the threshold of his fatherland—all of this spoke with much greater force. I told Jack that having come into these mountains like a bird on the wing, I would, like a bird, fly from them.

What I am about to narrate occurred in the latter part of October. About noon such a quietness fell upon the region that

---

[7] As there are about twenty-five Dry Lakes in California alone, it is difficult to say which particular one is referred to here.

the mountains, cliffs, and wilderness seemed to be in the grip of an evil spell. Not a leaf stirred. While I wrote in the cabin, I could hear ripe acorns breaking loose from their pedicles and rustling through the leaves as they fell to the ground. The heat was unbearable and the air in the cabin became so stifling that after a while, being unable to write, I set down my pen. My heart and the pulse in my temples were beating with greater rapidity. I could not understand what was happening—whether I was ill or whether something unexpected was about to occur in nature. I wanted to ask Jack, but he had gone swimming in the stream an hour before and had not yet returned to the cabin. Therefore I lay down on the moss and began to wipe the perspiration which gathered abundantly on my brow.

Meanwhile, it became more and more stifling. I could no longer doubt that some kind of illness was coming over me when suddenly I heard Harrison's heavy footsteps from a distance. After a moment he entered the cabin. His cheeks were flushed, his eyes were dulled, and his brow was no less covered with perspiration than mine.

"What is happening to us, Jack?" I asked.

"The Santa Ana wind!" he replied.

I knew then what all of this meant. If the reader will look at a detailed map of California, he will easily recognize two practically parallel chains of mountains—Santa Ana and San Bernardino. The smaller and lower Santa Ana Range stretches nearer the ocean, whereas the more impressive San Bernardinos extend farther into the mainland, forming a kind of backbone of its southern portion.

Along the Gila River which empties into the Colorado, the wilderness becomes very barren. This portion of it is, in fact, called the Gila Desert. Its shifting sands are never covered with any greenness. There are no settlements either of whites or even of Indians. In the California section (between San Bernardino and Colorado) during springtime when the lakes are full of water and grass covers the depressions in the earth, silence gives way to the hum of life. Sometimes a herd of buffalo, which has wandered as far as the Arizona Mountains, parts the grass with their chests. In hot pursuit follow Indian riders crouched on their horses. Sometimes métises round up herds of mustangs. Sometimes cattle dealers pass on their way to ranches farther east. Sometimes a trapper from Prescott or Tucson loses his way. These are the things that happen in the desert beyond San Bernardino, but the Gila River remains always quiet, lifeless, and ominous.

But after the passage of spring the whole desert comes to resemble the Gila. It was for good reason that I called the Gila ominous, for everything that comes from there is like the breath of death. The locusts lay their eggs in the hot sand for the winter, and in the spring their progeny pass in the form of a cloud over the beautiful California valleys, leaving in their wake trees without leaves and a shameless, naked earth. Finally, it is from the Gila and the dry lakes that the Santa Ana wind blows through the Anaheim Valley.

It should really be called desert wind or Gila wind. It is a current of heated air from which the desert has sucked all freshness and dampness, and saturated it instead with static electricity. Sometimes this wind also blows up from the south from the direction of the Lower California peninsula, that is, from the Mexican side, which is likewise a desert. More frequently, however, it originates in the east from the Gila. For California it is the same as the sirocco for Sicily, the *solano* for Spain, and the simoom for Arabia. It is perhaps less dangerous than these others and less frequent, for it comes only in the fall and winter, irritating human nerves, drying up the muscles, wilting the leaves on trees, and seizing the animals with fear.

When Jack informed me of the wind's imminent arrival, I immediately went outside of the cabin. A certain restlessness could be sensed everywhere in nature despite the quietness, and the quietness itself seemed to me lifeless rather than restful. The air lost its transparency. The atmosphere seemed to be

filled with some kind of dust or smoke. The sun's light penetrating through this fog lost its splendid, brilliant gilt and its
light was sickly, sad, and rust-colored. The very orb of the sun,
devoid of its glittering rays and somewhat shaded and reddish,
permitted the eye to look with impunity upon it as though
through smoked glass. I thought that perhaps the air had become filled with smoke.

"Jack," I inquired, "could the Indians have set the forest on
fire somewhere?"

"No," replied Jack, "I think that it is dust from the desert."

But Jack must have been mistaken, for, after all, the dust
could not precede the wind. But in answer to my question
whether it always happened this way, he replied that it always
did. Meanwhile, the oaks suddenly trembled, rustled their
leaves, and showered the earth with acorns. Next Jack advised
me that I should loosen the noose of the lasso on which my
mustang was tied lest the animal might strangle himself by
jerking during the strong wind. When I approached him, I
noticed that his hair was ruffled, his head bowed, and his
nostrils near the ground. I loosened the noose, even too much.
Returning, I saw flocks of all kinds of birds hurrying to the
mountain slopes and from the valley toward the forest; thus
there were flocks of rose-colored turtledoves, ordinary partridges, mountain partridges with blue feathers, mockingbirds,
black woodpeckers with canary-yellow breasts and scarlet heads.
Grey cock pheasants tottered along on foot so close to our
cabin that I could have shot them from my window. Eagles
and crows hovered over the forest, but kept dropping into the
foliage. Finally everything grew silent; the haze became thicker,
the heat of the sun became even more intense, and then the
first blast of wind struck.

It seemed as though some kind of monstrous lung suddenly
blew hot air at me. Both Jack and I immediately sought shelter
in the cabin and, covering the windows with blankets, we lay

down on the moss. In the cabin the heat grew unbearable. I became slightly dizzy; the blood pounded in my veins like lead. I tried to read but could not. I could hardly breathe. The electricity which permeated the air acted upon my nerves in such a way that I wanted to quarrel with Jack. I tried to drink, but the water standing in the bucket in the corner of the cabin seemed distasteful to me. Finally, I wanted to smoke, but after the wind had blown for a quarter of an hour, my tobacco dried out so completely that it turned into powder in my fingers.

Being already accustomed to this wind, Jack withstood it much more easily than I did. I felt worse and worse. The individual blasts of air changed into a continuous hurricane. The forest bent down, the oaks fluttered their branches, and the air became so filled with leaves and sand that it was impossible to see. In the end the accursed wind transformed itself into intense heat filled with poisonous fumes which seemed to be shooting forth from an overheated stove. Jack brought me some water from the stream and I drank it greedily, but when meal time arrived I was unable to eat anything. We did not start a fire in the valley either at noon or in the evening, for the wind would have scattered the embers to the four corners of the earth, and what's worse, it might have carried sparks into the wilderness and caused a forest fire.

That night I could not close my eyes. The following day, instead of subsiding, the wind blew more violently. The trees crackled and broken branches fell in large numbers into the stream. Throughout this time there was not a single cloud in the heavens. I went outside only to feed my horse. I suffered unbearable pain. But on the third day at dawn or perhaps already in the night everything grew still.

Upon leaving the cabin, I took a deep breath. The air was cool and invigorating and the blue sky was clear. A gentle breeze was straying in from the ocean. In the east the rosy, pre-dawn light blushed like a girl. Everything was smiling. I looked about me—and swore like an ordinary sailor from Anaheim Landing.

My horse was gone!

My sad lasso hung near the tree. Apparently the horse had slipped his head through the noose, which was too loose, and escaped during the windstorm.

Harrison and I convoked a great council of war. Having slipped out of the noose, the horse could descend only down into the ravine, for there was no other exit. In the ravine he could either proceed eastward toward San Bernardino, or westward toward Anaheim. In the former instance, it would not be difficult to find him since the upper reaches of the stream cannot be forded. In the latter case, the search would be more difficult, for the stream widens as it descends and the canyon becomes more thickly forested. I thought also of scouring the wilderness surrounding our cabin; but Jack assured me that so large an animal as a horse could not penetrate the dense undergrowth with its tangled vines.

It was even doubtful whether it was worth searching for the horse. During the night he might have been devoured by such beasts of prey as a cougar or a lynx. Likewise, he might have been stolen by Mexicans. The search would entail many hardships, and in some ways might even be dangerous. But I had become very fond of my saddle horse and resolved to set out in search of him despite all difficulties. Furthermore, now that the cabin was finished, Jack and I had time to spare.

Immediately after breakfast, therefore, we began to make preparations for the expedition. Not knowing how long it would last, we each took a small supply of biscuits and dried meat. In addition, we each armed ourselves as if for war with a rifle, revolver, and bowie knife, as well as a lasso with which to lead back the horse.

Armed in this manner, we went first of all to the tree where he had been tied to look for tracks. There were a great many of them on the grass. They seemed to form a kind of trail, but this was only the path over which I led the horse to water. I could make nothing of it, but Jack lay on the grass and, after examining it closely, soon grunted in Indian fashion "Ugh!"

He had found, or at least insisted he had found, a fresh track although I could see no difference in it from the others. As far as we could determine, the horse had wandered down toward the stream. Succeeding tracks branching off from the path indicated this clearly. The horse could have gone upstream, or downstream toward Anaheim. Jack and I would have to separate.

I chose the direction toward Anaheim, for as I had traversed this route with Neblung in the night, I was somewhat familiar with it. I whistled for my dog, lighted my pipe, and started off.

The morning following the windstorm was enchanting. The breeze coming from the ocean was moist and cool. On both sides of the ravine birds sang as if paid to do so. In the open places where the stone corridor gave way to the valley the accessible banks of the stream teemed with animal life. Birds sipped water. Black squirrels squatted on their haunches, crunching laurel nuts and stroking their whiskers. My dog barked with joy, and the echo carried the bark into the distance, giving it a strange, powerful resonance. This was the morning's moment, the moment of that joy and awakening of nature when the trees and the flowers and the birds and all that is alive seem to call out "Evoe! [8] Let us be gay and love one another!" In such a moment the fire of life passes even through the chilled bones of an old man and in a youth the heart overflows with exuberance and the shoulders all but sprout wings.

This was the sort of mood I was in. New ravines, new stone formations, new trees constantly passed before my eyes. The entire route which I had previously traversed in the night appeared new and unfamiliar to me. Only one specific place remained in my memory. This valley, embracing about two square miles, was not so overgrown with dense and tangled

[8] The bacchanalian exclamation of joy.

vegetation as the others. It was, in fact, a Versailles garden in
the wilderness, embellished with marvelous bouquets of trees
and shrubs almost as though contrived by the hand of a
gardener-artist. Dark, splendid groves of oak and small, attractively placed clumps of maple covered most of the region.
Laurel bushes were set out in symmetrical beds. A row of trees
created a kind of avenue which stretched beyond my sight. It
was almost incredible that nature should have designed everything so artfully and harmoniously. A slight depression in the
center of the valley was covered with grass of a bright, fresh
greenness that betrayed the moistness of the soil. The tall
shrubs there were completely hidden under the tangle of
enormous wild grapevines. The illusion that these were simply
artificial arbors was so strong that it was dispelled only when on
closer approach I spied a grey-black, spotted wildcat spring out
from under the leaves.

There is nothing like it in any of the European mountains.
Nature overdid itself here in creating a magnificent park complete with a whole range of color and shadow, the artistic place-
ment of every detail, appropriate vistas, all reflecting discreet
good taste. So deceptive was this scene that involuntarily my
eyes searched the depths of this dark green forest for the sudden
gleam of a white marble palace, with windows glistening like
mirrors, with glamorous women thronging its balconies, and
with swans drifting on the blue waters of a nearby lake.[9]

But this region was uninhabited and silent, and only the
hum of large golden flies being pursued by birds broke the
quiet. Bewitched, I walked slowly and halted frequently. Meanwhile, the sun had risen high and it began to grow hot. Having
discovered a small hillock covered with moss, I lay down under

[9] Sienkiewicz's footnote: Later I learned that this charming spot, although
still uninhabited, already had a name, for it is known as "Picnic Place." The
residents of Anaheim, Orange, and Santa Ana, together with the surrounding farmers, gather here for a huge, annual celebration. "Picnic Place" no
longer belongs to the government but to one of the numerous California
land companies which own enormous tracts of virgin, uninhabited land.
Unoccupied government territories lie beyond "Picnic Place."

the shade of an oak, ate a piece of biscuit with dry meat, and, after telling the dog to be on guard, I fell asleep.

I slept so well that I did not awaken until about four o'clock. The sun had already traversed the greater part of its arc and was already bowing toward the west. I realized that before nightfall I should be unable to reach either the ranches at the foot of the mountains on the road to Anaheim or to return to Jack's cabin. I preferred, however, to spend the night closer to the settlements and therefore I continued forward.

The park soon ended and the amphitheater of red rock contracted again into a narrow, dark gorge. At its very entrance I met a horseman, a certain old Mexican with black hair like a horse's mane and a thievish face. In the manner of the Mexicans we began to converse with extravagant courtesy, using as frequently as possible the expressions *usted* and *caballero*. I made inquiries about my horse to which the *caballero*, leering like the worst pickpocket, replied that he had not seen my horse, but that he had seen the tracks of a grey bear, a remark which I did not believe for a moment. After this, with true Mexican politeness, excusing the boldness *de hacer cuestion*, he began to interrogate me: what was I doing in the mountains? did I have any friends here? where did I live? Perhaps he wanted to find out if he could with impunity throw his lasso around me the moment I turned my back and rob me of my weapons. But I was well acquainted with the Mexicans and despite all the *usteds*, I kept my finger on the trigger and was ready to shatter the skull of this rogue into bits as soon as I noticed that he was untying his rope. I was not at all afraid of him and conversed with him in a mocking tone which, in fact, disconcerted him. Nevertheless, I was determined not to be the first to set out on the road until my affable knight had removed himself by several lasso lengths. The moment I told him that I lived with Harrison, however, caution was no longer necessary. My *caballero* became enchanted: he told me that he knew Jack, that Jack was a distinguished (*considerable*), even a great (*grande*) person, and that Jack's friends must be the same. After these remarks he departed.

Apparently Jack had a reputation in the mountains which evoked respect. Although the Mexican *caballeros* generally have thievish inclinations, they are intensely fearful of the squatters because of the latter's solidarity. On behalf of one murdered squatter, the others immediately take up his cause even though they may live very far away, and they continue to beat up all the Indians and Mexicans they encounter until the latter themselves betray the guilty one.

I shall write later in greater detail about these people who are so unusual in many respects. At present, however, I should like to mention that here the culprit cannot easily escape being lynched. For while these scoundrels may kill and rob a person, they do not do so in order then to escape into the desert, but in order to drink and make merry in the nearest tavern. Here the frightful "Uncle Lynch" usually catches up with them. For this reason murders are not numerous, even though the squatters' dispersion seemingly assures impunity to the criminal.

But because caution is a traveler's best guide and guard, I did not set out on the road until my amiable *caballero* had removed himself out of gun-range. Soon there wafted toward me only his song and its accompaniment, the rhythmic clack of his knife handle against the pommel of the saddle.

I continued another four miles, until the sun began to set. Night was approaching rapidly, for in this climate the period of twilight is brief. The mournful harbingers of darkness, the coyotes, were already beginning to howl in the wooded valleys, the dog was becoming uneasy, and I had to think about a bed for the night. Taking advantage of the remaining light, I cut four armfuls of dry chaparral shrubs and gathered some fallen branches which were plentiful in the bed of the stream. Having chosen a suitable place among the stones, I kindled a fire.

I slept little during the night, for I had constantly to add branches to the fire in order to keep it going. All kinds of animal sounds, so common in the night, reached my ears, but I paid them little heed knowing that I had beside me a watchful dog and a trusty rifle. Furthermore, cougars and bears, the only dangerous animals, are not numerous here and never attack people unless first provoked, so there was nothing to fear. As for the dog, he ran from the fire every little while and disappeared in the darkness, barking loudly. With daybreak the wilderness grew silent. Only then did I fall asleep like a rock and not until nine o'clock did I start on my way.

Several score paces from where I had slept I came across a small rattlesnake crawling from stone to stone. Its tail bore five rattles. Walking along, I reached a place where on both sides of the stream stretched a narrow belt of fine sand mixed with golden mica. Once before along the Cosumnes River near Sacramento, I had been deceived by this same mica. Upon seeing huge quantities of it, I thought I had found such wealth that there would be nothing left for the Rothschilds to do but to become my bookkeepers. I gaped then, I remember, and could not believe my eyes. The entire bank of the river sparkled and changed colors; the rays of the sun were reflected from the larger pieces; everywhere there was gold, gold, gold. It could be hauled away by the wagon load. I pinched myself to make sure I was not asleep and, filling my pockets with my wealth, I hurried to Captain W.,[10] our compatriot, at whose home I was staying. Since he was an experienced miner, I wanted to share my news with him, to enter into a partnership, and to reap a few modest billions within a couple of months. I had no desire whatever for any more. You may easily imagine the expression on my face when the old miner burst into laughter and, shaking my treasure in the palm of his hand, uttered the one word, "Mica." Nevertheless, even the most ascetic traveler

[10] Captain Francis Wojciechowski, a refugee of the Polish Revolution of 1830. Sienkiewicz stayed for a while at his home in Sebastopol, California. The captain became the prototype of Podbipieta in Sienkiewicz's novel *With Fire and Sword.*

as he journeys through these mountains and deserts of California cannot repress the thought that almost any crevice or pile of stones may conceal wealth. Involuntarily your eyes roam from glistening streams to rocky fissures, expecting to be dazzled by a thick, antediluvian vein of golden ore. There is nothing fantastic in all this. If you ask where in California is gold found, the answer comes unhesitatingly—everywhere. To be sure, it is so scarce in some places that the cost of washing it two or three times would exceed the value of the metal. Yet if you take several loads of dirt and send them through the sluice, the quicksilver will invariably snatch a certain quantity of gold particles.

Not long ago I witnessed a curious example of that nightmare of gold which here torments everyone. A squatter and I, accompanied by a watchmaker compatriot of mine from Orange, were visiting a settlement located on the banks of a small stream. After a night spent in the wagon my countryman went to wash in the stream. He returned suddenly; his face was agitated and he had lost his hat.

"What has happened?" I inquired, thinking that he must have seen some dangerous animal.

"Hush!" he replied with a trembling voice, placing his finger to his lips.

"What is it then?"

"Gold!"

"Where?"

"Come and see."

I followed him, even though I did not believe for a moment that there was gold, for, had it been there, the residents of the settlement would have found it long ago. Having reached the bank, my friend showed me a small, round stone on whose surface glistened a golden, metallic scar. Then I, too, was convinced and we deliberated whether to reveal the secret to our companion. It seemed appropriate that we should, for he was a trustworthy and experienced person. He happened to approach just then and explained to us that the gold, metallic mark was simply the scratch left by brass-cleated shoes so commonly worn by farmers.

Such disenchantments, especially with mica, are daily occurrences since mica is so plentiful here. I saw huge quantities of it on the shores of the ocean at Anaheim Landing, Wilmington, and many other places. Mountain streams generally do not abound with it, but where the banks are sandy, some mica is usually found deposited in the depressions stamped by the feet of animals.

Among these tracks I searched for the hoof marks of my horse, but I found only the half-erased imprints of deer and the shallow but wide tracks of round paws, probably those of a lynx. I began to doubt that my horse had passed this way and for a moment the thought occured to me of turning back. But just to be sure, I wanted to inquire at the ranch lying at the foot of the mountains and therefore I continued forward. Meanwhile I was confronted with an unforseen development. The stream whose bank I had been following suddenly reached a perpendicular cliff and divided itself into two branches, creating with its main course a distinct letter Y. I did not know which branch would lead me to the foot of the mountain and to the road to Anaheim. The left branch seemed the more likely one and therefore I chose it. But after I had walked three miles, the left branch again divided itself in two. Apparently this was a whole network of waters which embraced a rather large area and as these streams emerged from the mountains, they flowed through the Anaheim Valley and the plain beyond toward the ocean. I realized that I had lost my way. The canyons were so primitive and silent that I speculated whether I might be the first human to have set foot in them.

Those banks of the stream not squeezed out by the cliffs were overgrown with a thick forest. Climbing vines hung all the way down to the water and, stretching from one bank to another, they hampered my passage to such a degree that I had to clear the way with my knife. Here nature remained in its pristine state. Even the birds seemed less fearful of a human being than in other canyons. A certain indescribable tranquillity prevailed that reflected the dignity and majesty of unconquered nature. Accordingly, all of the smaller canyons are uninhabited and many of them have never been visited by man.

Meanwhile I continued forward, unconcerned at having lost my way. I knew that every stream would lead me eventually to the foot of the mountains and to the valley where Anaheim, Santa Ana, and Orange are situated. Early in the afternoon I began to find my way out of the labyrinth of mountains. The cliffs on both sides of the stream were no longer so high; the stone corridor gave way to an extensive valley and an ever-broadening landscape. Finally I stopped to survey the view before me.

The mountains had ended. I stood on a kind of gigantic terrace some twenty feet high over whose edge the stream flowed at such a sharp angle as almost to create a waterfall. At the foot of the terrace a farmer's house could be seen, shining white amidst a mass of eucalyptus trees. Here began the Anaheim Valley, or rather that wide, airy, spacious plain extending to the very shores of the ocean. Leaning on my musket, I remained motionless for about a half hour and gazed at this enchanting valley. On the edge of the horizon stretched a grey-bluish mist or cloud illuminated by the purple of the sunset. This was the Pacific, Father of the Oceans, and lord of them all. In the hills protruding above the fog I recognized the island of Santa Catalina and Catalina Harbor which I had visited when I was still at Anaheim Landing. The sun was setting and above the ocean another ocean of purple and gold flooded the skies. I noticed first of all the wide sandy bed of the Santa Ana River flowing through this valley decked in royal colors. In the distance dark clusters of trees concealed Anaheim and Orange, while smaller clumps indicated farms scattered over the entire plain. This whole panorama lay at my feet. Like a bird aloft I surveyed villages and towns. The atmosphere was so transparent that every detail of this vast area was as distinct as if held in the palm of my hand. The stillness was complete. The beautiful clear sunset seemed to saturate everything with an incomparable charm and rosy peace. A pervasive feeling of bliss and serenity uplifted my heart and from my lips involuntarily escaped the words of that nostalgic ballad, "Oh my homeland, how I miss thee!" [11]

The sun had already set when I knocked on the door of the house at the foot of the terrace. It so happened that a certain Mitchell lived here, a cattle rancher and good friend of mine from Anaheim. Mitchell received me graciously and gave me an excellent bed which, after a night spent on the rocks in the mountains, seemed matchless.

The next day at dawn I set out on my way home into the mountains.

On hearing me approach, Jack came out happily to meet me. The horse had already been returned. Jack had found him about ten miles from our stream in a nearby canyon where Jack's fellow Louisianian, a squatter named Plesent, had his cabin. Jack began to tell me about Plesent, depicting him as a true king of the mountains who lorded it over all the Mexicans in the area. He had risen to such influence in part through his wealth in bees and livestock, but principally through his Mexican wife who was a woman of such wisdom that her words were accepted as oracles not only by her husband, but also by all her dark-haired cousins. Jack proposed that we visit them together. I readily agreed and, believing our conversation at an end, I was anxious to take a look at my horse. But Jack apparently had something further to tell me for, with a roguish twinkle in his eye, he held me back. His pipe was sending up a veritable cloud of smoke signals.

[11] The title and refrain of the ballad are "U nas inaczej." It was composed by Joseph Bohdan Zaleski (1802–1886) who is known as "the Ukrainian nightingale."

"Anything else new, Jack?" I inquired.

"Ahem, ahem," he mumbled.

"Is there something else on your mind?"

"Yes!" was the rejoinder. "Are you very tired?"

"A little. Why do you ask?"

"Well, if we are to go to Plesent's, we should get there by tonight."

"By God!"

"You see, sir, this is the way it is. At Plesent's there are gathered at the moment more than fifteen of his Mexican relatives, all with their lassos, horses, and guns. I must warn you that they are all hoodlums, although that's beside the point. But do you know why they have come? Well, Plesent discovered the tracks of a grey bear in the sand beside his stream. He has trailed him for two days and is convinced that 'Uncle Grizzly' has chosen a lair for himself less than two miles upstream."

"All right, Jack," I interrupted quickly.

"So Plesent sent old Ramon to the Mexicans, inviting them to join the hunt. They have brought wine which they are drinking unceasingly. At the same time they are playing cards and praising each other's courage, even though, by God, when a crisis does arise, they will invariably prove to be cowards. Old Ramon likewise came to me, but I was busy searching for your horse. In addition to us, Plesent is also expecting the two Shrewsbury brothers. Tomorrow at daybreak the hunt is to start. Will you go with me?"

Naturally I not only agreed, but almost embraced Jack with joy. We cleaned our guns, put things in order, and in two hours we were on our way.

Letter VIII

LIFE AMONG THE SQUATTERS

THE evening was already well advanced when my friend Jack and I arrived at the cabin of squatter Plesent. Plesent's abode was located in a spacious glen, heavily forested with ancient oaks. On one side the glen was enclosed by a huge, semicircular ridge and on the other by the steep banks of a stream. Beyond the stream was yet another, much deeper, valley surrounded by high mountains.

Plesent's homestead, which I saw for the first time by moonlight, had a certain romantic appearance, as did most of the squatter homesteads found in the canyons. The two valleys and the ridge resembled a gigantic Roman circus or a series of steps. At the foot of the steps a stream murmured along a stony corridor and pointed the way to Plesent's house. Moonlight drenched the entire amphitheater of hills and the valley-arena. Here everything was silent, as though asleep. It seemed as if the spectacle had just ended, the emperor had departed, and the mob had scattered into the streets of the city. But on the bloody sand of the arena there lay in eternal sleep the bodies of the gladiators. Seen from afar, the strangely symmetrical cliffs resembled in the moonlight the gloomy walls of a large city. Sometimes a splendid stage setting can create such an illusion and momentarily I had the impression that I was viewing the most magnificent setting of them all.

The barking of the dogs informed the inhabitants of the valley of our arrival. Through the branches of the oak trees I soon caught sight of the flaming fire and its red reflection on the white walls of the house. Human figures crossed back and forth before the fire while others squatted in front of it in Indian fashion. After climbing the steep banks of the stream, we finally reached the courtyard. Plesent, who came out to welcome us, greeted my companion with a casual "hello," and then introduced himself to me.

When we approached the fireplace, Plesent introduced me to his wife who, with typical Spanish politeness, immediately put aside her supper preparations and began to converse with me. Doña Refugio was a woman of about forty years of age and, though handsome of feature, her face seemed faded and spiritless. Never have I seen so mournful a countenance. When later I enquired about the cause for this melancholy, I learned that Doña Refugio's beloved younger sister, Monica, had died, poisoned by a rattlesnake. The childless Doña Refugio cherished her sister above all else and had not smiled since her death.

It was quite obvious that her husband as well as her guests respected Doña Refugio's grief. They treated her with special solicitude, attempting to fulfill her wishes even before she expressed them. Their concern for her puzzled me as I knew she was of Indian blood. This was easy to recognize by her very black, thick hair and dark complexion. But people of noble character, no matter what their racial origins may be, generally gain the esteem they deserve. Doña Refugio, as I later discovered, was well educated and unusually intelligent and thus had become a kind of oracle in this semiwilderness. People came to her for advice and assistance from the entire neighborhood—from Anaheim, Orange, and even from Los Nietos, her birthplace, where her parents still owned extensive lands. Being on her father's side of aristocratic lineage, she was highly respected by the Mexicans and, also through her father, related to them; on her mother's side, she had kinship with the métises. The comparative wealth of her family added luster and authority to her wisdom and virtues.

Like my friend Jack, Doña Refugio's husband hailed from Louisiana, but had moved to California after the Civil War. He was a husky fellow, several years younger than his wife, with honest, soft blue eyes set in a gentle but forceful face. In addition to Plesent, I met two more squatters from Madera Canyon, Samuel and Lucius Shrewsbury. Sam, the older of the two brothers, was a true American pioneer type. He was about six feet tall, with gigantic bony hands and legs, and a lean, well-developed physique that revealed great strength. His head resembled that of an old wolf; his eyes were friendly but shrewd. At times his appearance reminded me of Lincoln, who was also a splendid example of this type of Yankee. Whenever Sam talked, he would stretch out his big legs, thrust his head forward, and caressing his bristly chin, would begin with a drawling "w-e-ll." Also, Sam was a steady tobacco chewer and every so often would expectorate a loathsome stream of reddish juice. This practice was supposed to add a certain dignity to a man. Besides being a competent apiarist, Sam was also an incomparable hunter, builder, cabinetmaker, carpenter, smith, and painter. In other words, Sam could do everything.

Such jacks-of-all-trades are common amongst squatters. Living alone, and being always dependent exclusively on their own resources, they must of necessity learn various trades. These conditions of life result in certain attributes of character, such as self-confidence, a marked degree of independence, an attachment to republican ideas, plus boundless energy combined, strangely enough, with a certain deliberateness and placidness of temperament. It would be a mistake to assume the latter traits are symptoms of indolence and helplessness. Quite the contrary, they stem from the *sang-froid* inherent in the Anglo-Saxon race and from the habit of careful consideration of every contemplated action. The squatter thinks slowly, investigates, and deliberates, but once he decides upon a course of action, he is able to accomplish even the impossible.

To a high degree Sam personified the typical pioneer characteristics mentioned above, and for that reason I have described him at such length. Lucius, several years younger, had spent his entire life vagabonding in the forests. He, too, kept bees, but his older brother, who loved Lucius like a son, was the one who took care of them. The brothers lived together, since Lucius had little desire to build a house of his own. Sometimes he was not home for weeks or months on end. When at last he returned, however, he would be laden with a quantity of puma, bear, lynx, and deer skins. Lucius had a reputation for being an infallible marksman. In his expeditions he penetrated the desert on the other side of San Bernardino, often going as far as Arizona. All in all, he was a merry fellow in love with adventure. Trusting in his rifle and his powerful muscles, he had no care for the morrow.

These guests, together with almost a score of Mexicans, were sitting not in the house, since its only room was half-filled by a huge double bed, but around a fire at the side of the dwelling. Because of the warm climate, the prevailing custom among the mountain inhabitants is to sit, cook, and eat in the open air, and only to sleep under a roof. Mosquitoes, which are a real plague in warm countries and which sucked so much of my blood at Anaheim Landing, are not found here; thus there is nothing to serve as an obstacle to this life under the stars. The Plesents, like the other squatters, had built an open arbor not far from the house. It consisted of four thin maple poles which supported a roof interwoven with laurel branches and leaves. Under this primitive structure our hosts spent the greater part of their life. Under this shelter stood a table, or rather boards, on which Doña Refugio was preparing supper. The fire crackled loudly as the Mexicans kept adding dry laurel; its red flames danced even higher than the roof of the arbor, completely embracing the soot-blackened caldron in which the antelope meat and kidney beans were simmering. At one side in a frying pan pieces of salt pork, a favorite Mexican tidbit, were sputtering, hissing, and shriveling like condemned souls. Boiled Japan tea sweetened with honey was to conclude the supper.

The fire with the figures gathered around it presented a strange and original scene when, having momentarily withdrawn, I observed it from the darkness. Imagine, dear reader, bloody tongues of flame spitting thousands of sparks into a night drenched in moonlight. Imagine trees now blackened by the night, now silvered by the moon, or reddened by the splendor of the fire. Imagine the roar of numerous waterfalls as the stream rushed along its stony corridor. And imagine in the distance the dark majestic amphitheater of the mountains looming black against the silver background of the night. The figures sitting about the fire added romantic charm to the picture; one might have taken them for a band of brigands from Calabria or Pindus.[1] Far more ferocious in appearance than Sam, Lucius, or Plesent were the Mexicans squatting by the fire in customary Indian fashion. Their facial expressions, combining Indian dignity with Spanish haughtiness, contrasted strangely with the torn clothes that so inadequately covered their protruding knees and elbows. I was reminded of the gypsy camps seen in my childhood days. Here were the same faces with disheveled hair, the same beards black as a raven's feathers, the same tatters taking the place of clothes; only in their greater dignity, their unparalleled pride, and the consciousness of their own worth did they differ from the gypsies.

All of these *caballeros* were related to the mistress of the house and were closely akin to each other. When I was introduced to them, only their Christian names were given—Doroteo, Francisco, Antonio, Jesus, etc.; their surname, Salvadores y Guerra, was common to them all. As I was told later, they were the descendants of a once wealthy family that had possessed vast estates. During the settlement of the country by the Yankees, however, the family had lost everything and had taken up a roving life in the mountains.

This is the fate shared by the majority of the old landlords of Spanish descent. The more clever, ingenious, and industrious Americans replaced them, taking over in turn their lands,

---

[1] Calabria is the mountainous peninsula which forms the "toe" of Italy. Pindus is the mountain system in northern Greece.

wealth, and social position to such an extent that the proud *caballeros* were reduced to the local proletariat, either living in the uninhabited mountains, or tending sheep on the prairies, or working as day laborers in the neighboring settlements.

The decline in wealth and social position was followed by moral decline. As farm hands the Mexicans are excellent because they are strong and sturdy workers, but they outdrink even the Irish. Mexican stableboys and herdsmen give themselves over to gambling in their shanties and in the taverns whole days at a time. Mexican squatters are sluggards for the most part; how they manage to live, God only knows. Some of them keep horses, others trade in timber cut from barren canyons, contrary to Government order. But all of them are much given to fighting, robbing, and thieving. The Anglo-Saxon element displaced them from the farms, trade, and industry, not by any forcible measures nor by restrictive decrees of the Government, but simply by its greater energy, thriftiness, and superior gift for organization.

To be sure, there are still several Mexican families in California who have managed to maintain their wealth and social position, but these will eventually be merged with the new settlers or share the fate of their countrymen. Among these *morituri*,[2] extravagance and pride play a prominent role, just as they do in Poland. A Yankee, however rich he may be, works all the time and in all capacities. If he is a merchant, he takes care of his store. If he is a farmer, he himself sows, plows, and harrows; in short, he works side by side with his hired hands and eats at the same table with them. It seems almost incredible to the European visitor that such is the case, but I assure you it is true. Respect and unprecedented passion for work— this is the invincible power of the Yankees, this will assure them a brilliant future and world leadership. I repeat once again, Yankee is synonymous with worker; be he millionaire or pauper, he is always a worker. The Mexican represents the other extreme, for he is the antithesis of the Yankee.

[2] Those who are about to die.

A rich Mexican is a gentleman in the European sense of the word. In Los Angeles I have frequently seen these gentlemen of aristocratic bearing, fashionably dressed in black jackets and the finest linen, that contrasted strikingly against their dark complexions. Whether they were riding in carriages or on prancing steeds, they were usually accompanied by servants. Their distinguished outward appearance and the pride reflected in their demeanor attracted my attention. I noticed that whenever they desired to purchase something, they never entered a store but would halt on the street, and the merchant would hurry out to enquire what they desired. Upon asking who they were, I was informed with an ironic smile that they were the Señores Yorba, Mexican landowners to whom entire valleys in southern California had belonged not so very long ago. Some still possess large estates, comprising, however, less than one-tenth of their previous holdings. My storekeeper friend, Hobson, estimated the wealthiest of the Yorbas to be worth between forty and fifty thousand dollars, adding with evident satisfaction, "His wealth won't last very long."

"And afterwards?" I asked.

"Afterwards? They will tend our sheep. It's a very simple matter, it seems to me. Yorba has $40,000 and four sons; each of his sons will inherit $10,000; am I right?"

"Certainly! Of course, you are!"

"You can be sure, Sir," continued Hobson, "that the sons will follow their father's mode of living, even though each will have only one-fourth of the father's wealth. This will lead to inevitable ruin."

"How true, my friend!" I thought to myself, "How many Yorbas have I known across the sea! You are right! It is inevitable ruin. What is the cause? Could this be God's punishment? But enough! The Yorbas are no longer capable of understanding such simple logic." If Hobson had known Latin, he would certainly have described this family by the single word *morituri*.

Later I met the Yorbas personally. They are gentlemen in

the full sense of the word—hospitable, proud, polite, valiant —in short, chevaliers, possessing even the typical aristocratic virtue of not paying their creditors. Upon becoming better acquainted with them, I was convinced that they were truly well bred, unenlightened. They are the kind of people whose external refinement conceals internal obscurantism, numerous prejudices, and a lack of elementary knowledge. Any American storekeeper or worker who chews tobacco, never wears a tie, props his feet up, in short, any American whom Europeans would deem a boor knows more mathematics, history, geography, social and natural sciences than the elegant Señor Yorba. On the other hand, Señor Yorba frequently knows French. Señor Yorba lives in the United States where there are two political parties, Republican and Democratic. Imagine, dear reader, that you have just arrived from Poland and having no clear understanding of the parties, you ask Señor Yorba about them. Do you know what you will discover? That Señor Yorba understands these matters even less than you. And if you press him, he will tell you finally, "Vous savez . . . it's only the rabble quarreling about something, but we stay clear of it."

Of course, there are many exceptions to this general rule. There are among the Mexicans many wealthy merchant families who have achieved a reputation as "reliable houses." Some Mexicans hold important offices in the state of California. But in general, these people are being superseded under the pressure of brother Jonathan.[3] The best example is one I cited earlier—the displacement from their estates of the great landowners of Spanish descent. In the vicinity of Sacramento and San Francisco the huge territories formerly belonging to distinguished families are now dotted with the small farms of American settlers. Merely examine the place names in California. Starting from San Francisco or Sacramento and proceeding southwards, one encounters exclusively Spanish names like Merced, San Luis Obispo, Santa Barbara, Santa Monica,

---

[3] "Brother Jonathan" is a generic name formerly used for Americans.

Los Angeles, San Diego. I have enumerated only the names of more important communities, but the names of villages, rivers, mountains, and even the large ranches are also Spanish. This evidence proves that this region was formerly inhabited by a predominantly Mexican population. We know, of course, that California was seized from Mexico not so long ago. Today, however, Americans inhabit these Spanish towns, villages, farms, and mountains. The Spanish element has practically disappeared from northern California, while in the south it comprises only the lowest laboring stratum of society.

Never does it even enter the heads of the Americans or their Government to attempt to Americanize anybody or anything. In California not a single Spanish name has been Anglicized. If Germans establish a settlement, they call it Berlin, the French call theirs Paris, the Poles—Warsaw, the Russians— St. Petersburg, and it is perfectly "all right." A town could even be named Shanghai and to an American it would not matter. Moreover, there is not a single sizable town in the whole United States where various national groups do not have their own organizations for the express purpose of preserving their national traditions, language, and patriotism. The Government not only does not interfere in their activities, but it guarantees them the same legal rights and privileges to which all organizations are entitled.

Incidentally, I must admit that I have nowhere seen such rapid assimilation of minorities as takes place here. Children of recent German, French, Polish, or Russian immigrants, though they still know the language of their parents, prefer to speak English among themselves. The sole exception are the Chinese, of whom there are a great number in California and to whom I shall eventually devote a separate letter.[4]

To return to the Mexicans, no one ever tried to denationalize them, to drive them out, or to oppress them. On the contrary, those who still remember the old days frankly admit that

[4] See Letter XII.

the government of the United States is better than the former
Mexican regime, and they show no desire to be reunited with
their mother country. The Mexicans were guaranteed the same
equality and protection enjoyed by all other national groups,
and yet they have lost the ground from under their feet.

I found among the Mexicans still another trait which is
unique with them, namely, arrogant pride in their descent,
combined with a contempt for all other national groups, especially the Anglo-Saxons. Would you believe that every Mexican *caballero* whose bare knees peek from his trousers and
whose entire wealth consists of one blanket, one shirt, the one
pair of badly torn trousers already mentioned, a horse as lean
and bony as Don Quixote's Rosinante, a lasso, and a pack of
cigarittos—would you believe that such a *caballero*, simply because in his veins flows Spanish blood, is convinced deep down
in his soul that he is superior to those Yankees for whom he
must work? The well known simile, "proud as a Spanish beg-
gar," is perhaps nowhere so aptly applied as to this people.
Their pride may often be artificial, disguising under a ragged
coat a low deceitful character greedy for gain or gifts. In general, the moral standards of the Mexican lower classes are on
a level with their education. As I have already remarked, only
the energy of the Anglo-Saxon elements restrains the Mexican
populace from the plunder, robbery, and continuous turmoil
of which Mexico affords a permanent exhibition.

But from that pride, that sense of their own dignity, whether
genuine or feigned, has arisen another distinctive characteristic that sets this proletariat apart from all others; it is their
extraordinary politeness which they carry to a ridiculous extreme. In casual conversation one Mexican will never address
another except as *caballero*. If he disagrees with another, he
does so with the utmost tact, acknowledging his opponent's
profound wisdom and the validity of his point of view. Any
pair of ragged fellows about to enter a tavern will engage at
the threshold in all kinds of ceremonies and protestations as

to who should be the first to enter. In short, if a traveler accustomed to European politeness is offended by the lack of urbanity among the Americans, he will find it even to excess among the Mexicans.

As Plesent was introducing me to the Salvadores, the *caballeros* rose in turn and removed their hats, some of which were as riddled with holes as the roof of a Jewish tavern. After bowing ceremoniously, each extended his hand with an air of distinction, graciousness, and dignity that would have done credit to a Galician count. I also noticed that although all the Salvadores were related to each other—in some cases they were even brothers—they never failed to address each other with the polite form *usted* or *caballero*. Believing that I did not understand Spanish, they had no reason to represent themselves as being more polite than they actually were; therefore there was nothing artificial about their conversation. They stuck together, keeping a certain aloofness from the Shrewsburys, Jack, and even Plesent, although maintaining their customary politeness. This situation was, in fact, somewhat amusing, for the crude Americans were obviously incapable of appreciating this social behavior and politeness; on their part, being the wealthier ones, the Americans regarded themselves as superior and treated the dark-haired *caballeros* in a rather patronizing manner. Nevertheless, the best possible harmony existed between both sides, especially since none of the Mexicans, with the exception of Doña Refugio, knew any English and the squatters knew very little Spanish.

Finally supper was ready. We sat down to eat in the arbor, not on chairs but on discarded beehives shaped like boxes. Encouraged by me, Lucius began to tell about his hunting experiences.

"By God!" he said, "a year ago a bear almost finished me, and if it hadn't been for Sam, I swear by my right hand I would not be sitting here at this moment."

"Well," said Sam phlegmatically, as he rubbed his double

chin, "why don't you tell this gentleman about your expeditions to Arizona?"

Thus we turned to the subject of Arizona. Lucius claimed to be familiar with every corner of that country, having frequently visited it with an old adventurer named Rub. I questioned him concerning the Indians of Arizona, the Apaches and Comanches, about whose savageness and bravery I had heard so much. Lucius did not share this view; he stated that the Apaches are by no means as savage as people think they are. Although they often come into such towns as Prescott and Tucson to exchange pelts for various goods, they seem to be fearful of white men. Years ago it was a different story, he continued: raids, pillage, and murder occurred every day. Even larger settlements were in peril. Lucius well remembered those days. For example, he told me that on one occassion he and Rub went out to visit two French miners and found them both murdered and scalped. Lucius himself had many times participated in skirmishes with the redskins and spoke of their bravery with scorn and disdain. He asserted that in open battle they could not hold their own against the whites and that all their raids came without warning under cover of darkness. But the present generation of Indians living in the vicinity of settlements has been compelled by bloody experience to become peaceable. A few years ago rich veins of silver were discovered in the mountains which traverse this region in every direction. As a consequence of this discovery, there was an immediate influx of miners from California and as the population increased, the Indian menace diminished. Only the tribes living in the plains and mountains of the south and east have remained wild and predatory. The Mohave tribe living on the border of Sonora is especially noted for its savageness.

I questioned him closely about these details for it was my intention to join the first caravan of miners or settlers headed for Arizona in search of land. Such a plan can easily be fulfilled, for today throughout southern California there is a vigorous movement of emigrants in that direction. Despite this movement, however, the growth of population in Arizona cannot be rapid, for California itself is only sparsely populated. In an area of more than 150,000 square miles California still has less than one million inhabitants and its central and eastern parts remain practically unsettled. Today the enormous Territory of Arizona can still be described as largely uninhabited. Its major towns like Prescott and Tucson are communities numbering scarcely several hundred residents. Scattered among the mountains are small mining settlements; in the valleys where trees and water are abundant, an occasional farm or shepherd's *estancia* can be found; along the banks of the Gila and Colorado Rivers miners and shepherds camp in tents. Most of the settlers continue to lead a typical frontier life, that is, with a finger on the trigger of their rifles. But an endless expanse of mountains and plains still remains dreary, silent, and lacking all signs of human life.

This region does not yet produce enough to feed itself. Provisions must be brought either by the incredibly difficult route across the plains, or by sea around Lower California by way of the Gulf of California and finally through Colorado. This distance, coupled with the large supply of silver, has made all goods phenomenally expensive. A pound of flour costs a dollar, a pound of potatoes "four bits" or more than five Polish *zloty*. Similar conditions formerly existed in California. Possessing little legal tender but plenty of raw silver and gold dust, the miners of Arizona generally use these precious metals for commercial exchange. For this reason the merchants profit enormously by their transactions with the miners. In view of all these circumstances, Lucius advised me against going to Arizona.

"You simply can't imagine," he said, "what a gloomy, dreadful country it is. I have seen all kinds of deserts. Lower California is a desert, but at least it contains cacti and palms. In our own California a vast arid plain stretches from Los Angeles to San Francisco, yet it too is covered with palms. But Arizona has none of this."

"What is there, then, in Arizona?" I enquired.

"What is there?" he repeated. "I can tell you in a few words: mountains, cliffs, heaps of grey stones, and the desert—no water, no grass, no trees, nothing whatsoever, only piles of grey stones and bare mountains. True, there is silver everywhere, but let my tongue be damned if it is worth going there to get it."

Later I enquired further about the Gila and Colorado Rivers. Lucius admitted that the banks of these rivers are indeed fertile and rich in vegetation, but right behind the green belt begins the arid desert where the stifling Santa Ana winds originate. Finally I questioned Lucius about the canyons in the Arizona mountains.

"I know many of them," he replied, "but they have no such forests as the California canyons; their creeks are smaller and practically inaccessible. If you chance upon a forest, there you will find wigwams of the Apaches and it would be dangerous for a person alone or in a small group to wander there. Arizona be damned!" concluded Lucius. "I'll bet that people will never settle there."

I had no reason to doubt Lucius' account for I had myself seen areas which could match his description of Arizona. It would be futile to attempt to depict for the reader what a dreadful, oppressive effect Wyoming, Utah, and Nevada had upon me as I traveled through them on the transcontinental railroad. There the eye has nothing to rest upon other than endless desert, jagged Dantesque rocks, or precipices whose satanical names make one shudder. An occasional salt lake reflects a leaden, sullen sky. In areas as extensive as some European states I did not see even a single tree. From time to time small herds of antelope or deer flitted between the rocks, but what these animals eat and drink still remains a mystery to me. Even California, so esteemed by man and nature with its beautiful climate and fertile soil, has enormous stretches almost entirely without water, desertlike, and barren. Not so long ago I visited the huge desert in central California and I shall say only that I had the impression of being in the country of Dante, the land of death.

Having concluded his tale about Arizona, Lucius resumed the narration of his hunting adventures. Soon the conversation turned to the bear with which we were to deal the next day. Ramon, an old Indian living with the Plesents, took the floor and announced that the animal was *muy grande*—very big. At the same time I learned that the actual hunting team would be composed only of the two Shrewsburys, Jack, Plesent, and myself, for the Mexicans in our party possessed lassos and knives as their sole weapons. The Mexicans were to guard both exits from the valley and in the event that the animal should try to escape, they were to throw their ropes upon him and stop him on the spot. The old-timers of California frequently hunt bears with nothing but a lasso, but this incomparable weapon can be used effectively only from a horse; therefore, it is of no value among the cliffs and in the underbrush.

Meanwhile supper came to an end and we resumed our places around the fire. Old Ramon put to his lips an instrument known as a *chiote* and, fixing his eyes upon the heavens and assuming the pose of a concert artist, he began to play. In the distant darkness could be heard the snorting of the Mexican mustangs tied with lassos to the trees and the bells of the angora goats shut up in the corral on the hillside. These bells are tied to horses and goats in order to frighten wild animals away. Their ringing continued throughout the night; but it was a muted sound, like a distant echo, saddening, yet soothing, and inducing one to dream.

We all sat for some time in silence, a silence broken only by the crackle of burning wood and the quiet tones of the *chiote*. Soon, however, the stillness was interrupted by one of those events which occurs nightly in these mountains. A dog began to bark near the corral; almost immediately the other dogs joined in, and soon the whole valley resounded with their angry refrain. Lighting a long pine torch and shouldering his shotgun, Plesent went to investigate the cause of this commotion. Old Ramon and I followed after him. At the corral we found the white kids bleating in fright, while the dogs, gathered under a large tree, were baying furiously. Picking up several stones, Ramon threw them into the tree and at the same time uttered a piercing whistle. At first nothing happened, then suddenly a dark animal the size of an average dog jumped from one tree to another so swiftly that Plesent had no time to shoot.

"What was it?" I asked.

"A lynx! Damn his hide!" answered Plesent. "Every night I tie a good watchdog in the corral and still it doesn't help. Last year a mountain lion destroyed twelve kids and my old buck for which I paid seventy-five dollars in hard cash in Los Angeles."

We began to retrace our steps in silence. Soon I left the others, selecting what I thought would be a shorter route back. Suddenly Plesent shouted to me:

"Not that way! Not that way! Be careful! I have traps set there."

Indeed, I almost stepped into one of them. The two adjoining corrals, one with goats and the other with kids, were built like small fortresses difficult for the enemy to penetrate; but nothing so enticed all varieties of rapacious animals as the tasty booty inside. Plesent's life was a continuous struggle with these plunderers. One of the earliest squatters in the Santa Ana Mountains, Plesent had introduced the raising of angora goats in this region and had found it very profitable, for angora wool commands a much higher price then sheep's wool. Hundreds of thousands, perhaps even millions of sheep are raised in California, but this industry still has to overcome an almost insuperable handicap. All of the hills and mountains of California are covered with a certain variety of thistle whose small, practically microscopic burrs become entangled in the wool, thus making the spinning of the wool extremely difficult. Despite numerous efforts no remedy has yet been discovered, with the result that sheep wool does not bring the price it should. Angora goats are less troubled by the thistles, for their long straight hair does not catch so many burrs and can be more easily cleaned of them. I believe, therefore, that although the breeding of angora goats is possible only in the mountains, it will expand greatly in the future and provide a new, important source of national income.

From what I have observed, the raising of angora goats is not especially difficult. At daybreak the corral's gate is opened and the goats go into the mountains; they wander where they please, eat whatever they want, and return to the corral at night. During the day they are in no danger of attack from wild animals. Their unpleasant odor did not prevent me from watching them for hours at a time. Their large, gentle eyes and their silver or light-golden silken hair lend a certain charm to their appearance. The male goats in particular have such long hair that only their shins are visible. The most attractive, however, are the little kids with their short, fluffy hair and gazelle-like movements. All the goats climb over the rocks, cliffs, and precipices with unparalleled nimbleness.

The bearded buck, with the countenance of an old libertine, is the leader and despotic ruler of the herd. He is the first to leave the corral in the morning; nodding his head with dignity and jingling the bell at his neck, he leads the herd's procession. He is the one who selects the place of pasturage. He does not allow his consorts to scatter too far afield; he rewards the obedient with caresses and rebukes the disobedient with a mild butting from his horns. In general, he seems dissolute but at the same time dignified, sedate, and self-confident. His huge head, long horns, and abundant hair give him the appearance of a large animal, but in reality he is rather small and when he has been sheared, he looks like any hobbledehoy. Dogs do not frighten him. When he sees one, he goes straight at it, staring foolishly, tossing his head, and spitting loudly as if in loathing. If the dog does not give way but, as usually happens, stands his ground, sniffing and examining this extraordinary monster, then the buck advances a little, stops, sneezes even more threateningly, and finally, lowering his horns, lunges like lightning upon his enemy.

My dog was a constant object of such attacks. The belligerent buck will, upon occasion, even attack his master when the latter is opening the corral. In such a case the master seizes him around the neck and by the tail, and without further ceremony tosses the buck over the fence, a distance of ten feet. Insulted by such treatment, the buck-sultan expresses his indignation with loud spitting and retreats in a hurry.

These goats were the special care of the old Indian Ramon and he loved them like his own children. Returning from the corral on the night of the lynx episode, I became better acquainted with this *caballero*. He was a white-haired old man of seventy, but still hale and hearty. His face was the color of bronze. It was said that he was not a pure-blooded Indian, but if there was any white blood in him, the amount must have been very slight. A couple of swallows of brandy, which I offered him from my canteen, opened his heart. Later we sat next to each other by the fire and began to talk. When I asked him where he lived, he answered: "In the mountains!"

"But where is *la casa de usted?*

He replied: "Oh! *pobre* Ramon! he doesn't have a house. Sometimes he lives with the Plesents, sometimes with the Shrewsburys, sometimes in the Salvadores' tents, but most of the time with the Plesents because they are very, very kind people. In the past, a very long time ago, Ramon had his own wife, children, cabin, and his own herds. But later . . . that ill-fated firewater . . . Well, why talk about it? Now Ramon is *solo, solito,*" and he repeated the word mournfully, "*solito!*" Then he took up his *chiote* and began to strum with his eyes fixed upon the starry sky.

I observed this instrument with curiosity. Surely no more simple instrument was ever devised. It is a sort of harp with only one string, but the method of playing upon it is unique. Old Ramon put the narrow end to his lips, and by pressing the string in various places with the fingers of one hand, and by plucking the string with the other, he was able to produce different notes. In spite of the very limited range of sound Ramon was able to play a variety of Mexican melodies on this instrument. Most of these were melancholy, sentimental songs. From time to time one of the Salvadores accompanied Ramon with a deep, resonant baritone that many an opera star would have envied. Many of these songs were of a romantic nature.

> In the shade of the magnolia I dreamt of you.
> When I awoke and found you gone,
> I cried myself to sleep again.

When Francisco Salvadore finished singing this short verse, he paused a moment, and in that interval could be heard the tinkling goat bells and the tones of the *chiote*. Then with a voice of deepest yearning, the singer took up the refrain, "O Julia! O Julia!"

Even more moving was the song expressing the sorrow of the lover who lost his betrothed.

> The rain refreshed the air for you
> The breezes cooled you
> Mosquitoes did not trouble you
> The fig tree lowered its fruitful branches to you
> Flowers bloomed where'er you stepped
> I loved you, oh, how I loved you
> And yet you have forsaken me

There was a long spell of silence after the song ended. Memories of her deceased sister Monica came back to Doña Refugio and her eyes filled with tears; to conceal her emotions Doña Refugio rose and departed for the kitchen.

Meanwhile the evening passed quickly with these conversations, songs, and meditations. It was midnight when the elder Shrewsbury stretched out his legs, rubbed his chin and, turning to his host, said, "Well, tomorrow we have to get up at daybreak!"

We settled ourselves for the night. The Mexicans retired to the shed where there could be found some barley straw—and also an old buck segregated from the herd who poisoned the air around him. The two Shrewsburys, Jack, and I lay down beside the fire. In spite of my extreme fatigue, or perhaps because of it, I could not fall asleep. Thoughts of Lucius, Monica, old Ramon, and tomorrow's bear hunt whirled confusedly in my head. About 2 a.m. when only a few glowing embers of the fire remained, sleep closed my eyes.

Letter IX

BEAR HUNT

THE rattle of a rifle's steel bolt awakened me. In the dusky light I saw the huge figure of Lucius bent over the long barrel of his gun. Sam, too, was awake, the Mexicans were stirring near the shed, and in the small window of the Plesents' dwelling a light flickered. This moment of the day when Ormazd emerges victorious from his struggle with Ahriman,[1] the prince of darkness, always had an incomprehensible charm for me. It seemed to cast a mysterious spell over my bewildered soul, wandering in these endless forests under the hot California sky and yearning for its native land. In the meantime the night was fading away and in the distance the groves of trees were becoming more and more visible. An early woodpecker began rapping at a tree as though saying, "Knock, knock! Get up! The day is breaking in the hills and in the valleys!" In the gap between two hilltops appeared the first signs of daylight. Beautiful, blushing, "rosy-fingered dawn," as Homer has put it, flooded mountain and valley, changing dew drops suspended from oak leaves into glittering diamonds. There was an aura of joyfulness in this virgin, young world coming eagerly and confidently to life. Birds began to sing, goats to bleat, dogs to jump and run about. From the hillsides echoed the familiar "o ho! ho!" of the male partridge calling his mate. We all were in wonderful humor. Even serious Sam was singing a well-known American song whose refrain goes "Hi ho, Mississippi, Mississippi River!" Finally, after checking our weapons, we set out on the hunt.

Having reached the stony corridor, we proceeded upstream.

[1] Ormazd and Ahriman are the gods of Zorastrianism; the former represents light or the forces of good; the latter, darkness or evil.

Plesent and old Ramon, who knew the local terrain, took the lead; Lucius and I followed, while Sam and Jack brought up the rear. The Mexicans had departed much earlier, some of them going downstream, the others in the opposite direction. The latter could follow the river only a part of the way and then they branched off into the mountains. Their object was to penetrate deep into the mountains so that if the animal should try to flee, they could cut off his escape. The campaign plan, as drafted by Ramon and Lucius, called for our cavalry occupying the two exits from the valley to drive the animal into the arms of the infantry stationed in the center. The bear might, of course, try to escape up the sides of the valley, but since these were very steep and afforded no cover, we would surely spot him. Ramon, who was a skilled hunter, maintained that the bear would almost certainly be found on a particular hill which created a bend in the river and which jutted out sharply over the water.

About three miles from the Plesent homestead, Ramon began closely to observe the narrow path of sand mixed with mica. For a while this inspection was without result. Suddenly, however, the old Indian squatted down and from his throat came an inarticulate "ugh!" He showed us a deep track, made all the more evident by the glistening mica which had gathered in it. In all there were three imprints, only two of which were distinct; then the trail disappeared amid the rocks. Nevertheless, Ramon could follow it where others could see nothing. A strange sight was this old man with the bronzed face and white hair, tracking his game like a dog on the scent, stooping frequently and uttering his gutteral "ugh." Last night as he sat by the fire, resting his elbows on his knees and supporting his white-thatched head on his hand, he seemed almost decrepit. Today his nostrils were dilated and quivering as though gasping for air; his shiny eyes jumped from object to object with true Indian nimbleness, examining every piece of stone, every bush, the very ground under his feet.

Approaching the hill designated by Ramon as the bear's probable hideout, we proceeded slowly and so quietly that I could hear distinctly the murmur of the water over the rocks, the tapping of the woodpeckers, and the calls of the mountain partridges. It was a beautiful morning and already the sun was high in the sky. The air, permeated with the honeylike aroma of sage, would have been truly delightful, but here and there it was poisoned by the loathsome emanation of skunks, small black animals which are very numerous in these mountains. The dreadful smell which these creatures give off is nothing more than an excess of musk; but this substance so pleasing in small amounts is almost stifling in excess. A house under which a skunk takes shelter becomes absolutely uninhabitable. The odor saturates the lungs, causing choking and vomiting. Even dogs cannot endure it and chickens lapse into a faint. In the course of our trek we encountered this stench three or four times and only with the greatest effort did I keep from coughing.

Finally we reached the designated hill that protruded like a pyramid over the encircling stream. The hope of finding our quarry here became almost a certainty when old Ramon pointed out a large rock overgrown with a thin layer of slippery moss. The damp moss had been recently scuffed where the animal had climbed over it and in the furrows left by the enormous claws glittered the night dew. Showing us these tracks, Ramon whispered quietly: "Oso . . ." [2] and immediately we split up into two parties. Lucius, Sam, and Plesent circled the protruding promontory to climb the slope from the other side. The rest of us went directly up the hill. The underbrush here was so thick that we moved forward only very slowly. The three of us, Ramon, Jack, and I, likewise separated, each about forty steps apart.

And now the real hunt began. The whole hill was quiet as a grave. The sharpest eye could not have detected us as we

[2] *Oso* is the Spanish for bear.

crept forward in the underbrush, concealed even from each other. From time to time each would raise his head to determine the location of his companions by the trembling of the bushes. Once I caught a glimpse of Jack's blonde beard and another time Ramon's glowing eyes. Ten minutes passed, fifteen minutes passed, but we had advanced only a short distance up the hill. I encountered a place covered with gravel. The small stones began to roll down noisily, compelling me to drop to the ground and remain motionless. At last I moved forward again, but even more cautiously. A half hour must have gone by and I began to grow impatient. All was silent. Raising my head, I noticed on either side of me a slight trembling of the underbrush. My companions were moving forward. The thought struck me that if the animal was indeed close by, it would show up much sooner if we shouted and screamed. This was true, but on the other hand, should the bear be near the summit about six hundred yards away, it would disappear before we could cover half that distance.

But as it turned out, my patience was not to be put to the test much longer. A few more minutes passed when from the other side of the promontory resounded the explosion of a gun and immediately afterwards a frightful roar shook the air, then a loud shout, "Take care! Take care!" Then a second and a third shot. We jumped to our feet and began to run as fast as we could towards the commotion. Ramon who was nearest got there first. Immediately he raised his rifle and fired a shot. Two more shots followed, and again the roar of the bear, and then shouts, "Take care! Come here!"

At last Jack and I reached the curve and now I could see the whole scene of action. Above us side-by-side were the two Shrewsburys who were rapidly reloading their guns; a little further on stood Plesent who was calmly taking aim. At first I could not see the bear, but soon at the foot of the hill I spotted a huge grey bulk resembling a gigantic ball moving rapidly upwards. I could not understand what had happened.

I had expected to see the hunters below and the bear near the summit, but the situation was exactly reversed. There was no time for explanations for all of this was happening in a matter of seconds. Plesent fired, and the grey mass bellowed frantically again but continued its swift ascent. Then both Jack and I aimed. The bear stumbled in the underbrush but soon reappeared. Jack fired again. The bear reared up, fell backwards, and rolled all the way down to the stream. A tremendous "hurrah!" burst from our throats. I assumed it was all over, but the indomitable monster staggered up again, and clinging with his jaws and claws to the bushes, tried to reach the Shrewsburys. The brothers once more opened fire, while Jack and I with our fourteen-round Henry rifles sent one bullet after the other at the bear. At that moment the Mexican riders came galloping up on the other side of the stream, howling like wild beasts. Two of them, only the stream's-width away from the bear, whirled their dreadful lariats above their heads, but before the nooses could be thrown, a new salvo ended the drama. The animal once again rolled down towards the stream, but this time rose no more.

I started to run toward it when Jack halted me with a thunderous "stop!" Then we all began to descend slowly, each with his finger on the trigger. We stopped within ten steps of our quarry, ready to fire if necessary. The animal, still quivering, lay on its belly with its paws stretched out. A steady stream of blood gushed from the jaws and from time to time the death rattle could be heard. The sand and grass around him were torn up by the horrible claws. His bloody lips and snout were caked with sand from the furious gnashing of his fangs as he lay on the ground. Lucius placed the barrel of his Kentucky rifle against the animal's head and fired again. The rattling ceased; the miserable body of the bear strained once and became motionless.

"Enough!" said Sam in his phlegmatic manner.

Then we began to examine the carcass. It was as full of holes as a sieve. One bullet had hit him right under the ear, another below the eye, not taking into account the last one fired by Lucius and all the others over his entire body. This bear was not as huge as the one I had seen at the railroad station in Cheyenne, but it was still one of the largest of its kind. Even with both hands I could scarcely lift the enormous head from the ground. I also tried to spread apart his lips in order to take a look at his teeth. They were covered with drops of blood already coagulating. His front paws were armed with claws of such size that those of our Lithuanian white-necked bears seem tiny by comparison.

The American grey bear, known locally as the grizzly and in Latin as *ursus horribilis,* is the most dangerous member of the bear family. In strength, size, savageness, ferocity, and audacity it surpasses every variety of European bear. Never, at least very rarely, does the grizzly attack men first, but it is not afraid of them, and when hungry, it may force its way into the squatters' cabins or huts. Upon encountering a human being, it begins to snort with anger; its small eyes glare with fury; and if provoked, it will attack its victim with unparalleled ferocity. Because of its size and weight, it cannot, like the European bears, climb trees. Its physical endurance is so great that even when shot in the head it continues to struggle. Americans with their inclination to boastfulness take pride in the grizzly and tell fantastic tales of their bear-hunting experiences. They maintain dogmatically that neither African lions nor Indian tigers can compare with him. As for me, I am inclined to believe that the strength of the American grizzly surpasses that of the huge southern felines, but whether the latter are more dangerous to hunt, I have yet to discover.[3]

After a careful examination of the dead monster our group started homewards. Old Ramon and the Mexicans, however,

[3] Sienkiewicz actually made a hunting expedition to Africa in 1892 from where he wrote a series of *Letters from Africa.* Much later (1911), he wrote *In Desert and Jungle,* a tale set in the wilds of Africa, which became a children's classic in Poland.

remained behind to skin the animal and to cut off the delectable paws. I asked them to save the fangs and claws for me. At the cabin Doña Refugio was already waiting for us with breakfast. As we related our accounts of the hunt, I at last understood why the bear had been at the bottom of the hill and the hunters at the top, instead of the reverse. The circumstances were as follows: Lucius who was the first to spot the animal far up the hill shot and wounded him seriously. Immediately the bear rushed at Lucius like a whirlwind. It was then that we heard Sam's terrified shout, "Take care!" Somehow Lucius managed to leap to one side and the bear, unable to arrest his momentum, rolled to the very bottom of the slope. This often happens on hunting expeditions because a bear's hind legs are longer than the front ones, thus making it difficult for the animal to run downhill. In most instances, the bear loses balance and does not run but rolls down the slope. This was exactly what happened in our case.

An hour later Ramon and the Mexicans returned. Upon their arrival a veritable concert of barking and howling began, for the dogs, scenting the fresh skin, raised such a commotion that one would have thought that their own hides were in danger. That afternoon, in order to celebrate the successful outcome of our hunt, the Salvadores organized a sort of tournament or horse race. We all assembled on a wide plain that was almost treeless, except for a few oaks. All the Mexicans were on horseback, each holding in his hand a lasso or *reata*. When the race began, I did not know what to admire more—the nimbleness of the horses or that of their riders. One of the *caballeros* would pretend to be fleeing and would cling to his saddle so closely that head, hands, and feet became as one with the horse, leaving no protrusion on which a lasso could catch. Another, shouting and whirling his ominous rope above his head, would pursue his opponent in an attempt to capture him. At the appropriate moment the pursuer would throw his lasso and at the same instant his horse would wheel about at full speed and gallop in the opposite direction. If the lasso slipped off its fleeing target, then the roles were reversed and the pursuer became the pursued. Usually, however, the rope would fall over the head of the fugitive. The only way for the latter to avoid being choked and dragged from the saddle was to turn his mount quickly and gallop directly after his captor, overtake him, and engage in a hand-to-hand fight. This requires extraordinary skill and ability in horsemanship, for the rider who holds the rope purposely makes unexpected turns in order to pull his prisoner from the saddle.

The most dexterous and powerful of the Salvadores proved to be Jesus, a thirty-year-old, broad-shouldered Mexican with a black beard and eyes sharp as an eagle's. Jesus' *reata* never missed its mark. When captured, he always overtook his opponent and threw him from the horse. Jesus displayed his tremendous strength when, having been lassoed by his brother Doroteo, he caught up with him, and seizing his brother with one hand like a block of wood, he transferred him to his own mount, finally dropping his victim on the ground at our feet. This exhibition of strength aroused the envy of Lucius who, wishing to show off his own prowess before me, challenged Jesus to wrestle with him. At first the Mexican was reluctant but finally he agreed and the two men began to grapple. Within a few seconds the young Yankee lifted the Mexican athelete into the air and threw him to the ground, injuring Jesus' arm.

The horse racing had been preceded by a cock game. A hapless rooster borrowed from Doña Refugio was buried in the ground with its feet tied and with only its head and neck above the surface. Then from a distance of several score of paces each *caballero* in turn galloped past the bird at full speed and attempted to seize it by the head and pull it from the ground. After a few such attempts the cock was dead, and after several more the cock's head remained in the hand of one of the Salvadores. Later I learned that this cock game is a favorite among the Mexicans and that once a year similar contests take place with great ceremony near Los Angeles. The whole Mexican population, as well as many Yankees from the town and surrounding farms, assemble for these occasions.

That evening there came to Plesent's homestead three Indians from the still-wild Cachuilla tribe living on the other side of the Santa Ana Mountains. Their dark copper-colored faces were like those of gypsies. They wore neither braids nor feathers; instead their hair fell in thick tresses on both sides of their head. They were wearing moccasins of soft buckskin and a certain kind of shirt which did not cover their chest. In general, they looked more like beggars than warriors and in no way did they resemble the Sioux Indians I had encountered on my transcontinental journey. The pride, energy, and indifference so prominent in the Sioux were completely lacking in our visitors. Their bodies exuded a disagreeable odor that offended even the noses of our dogs. None of them possessed a rifle; bows, arrows, and tomahawks were their only weapons. Since they could speak neither English nor Spanish, I conversed with them with the assistance of old Ramon. The poor creatures told us that starvation reigned in their wigwams, and therefore they had come to beg the white man for food.

"Can't the red warriors kill deer and bighorns?" I asked them through Ramon.

U-wa-ka, who seemed to be the eldest, answered: "Ever since the rains fell in the mountains, the deer do not come down to drink at the springs, and the redskins cannot reach them on the mountain tops."

"Don't they have cows and sheep?"

"They did have, but many animals have died from lack of water and the redskins have eaten the rest."

"Did the whole tribe disperse?"

"No, the squaws, children, and old people remained, and the young men went out to find work among the whites."

I gave them some tobacco and whiskey. I also bought from them a bow and arrows, or rather, I received these in exchange for my knife. U-wa-ka showed me how to use the bow and then went with me among the oak trees where he shot a few woodpeckers and jays. I too tried my hand at it, but although I could draw the bow further than the famished Indian, my arrows failed to hit their mark by several yards, while U-wa-ka's rarely missed. Wishing to live for a while among the Indians, I enquired when the warriors would again return to these parts.

"Within a month," they replied.

"Will they accept me?"

"Of course! They will be happy to do so. The white brother will go hunting with the redskins in the canyons; he will come and go when he pleases; he will sit at the redskins' fireside and smoke a pipe with them; no one of the Cachuilla tribe will raise a hand against him."

Meanwhile Lucius, who had overheard our conversation, approached and asked: "What's this? Do you want to live in their reed tents?"

"Yes, I do."

"And you are not afraid?"

"Would they actually attack me?"

"No, but if one of those red devils dared to try it, dash his brains out in his own wigwam."

"That's exactly what I'll do."

"All right! But you will not be able to defend yourself from another danger, that is, the lice. By God! I know this from experience," Lucius continued. "If I had in my pocket today as many twenty-dollar gold pieces as each of those apes has lice in his head, I would found a bank in 'Frisco."

I must admit that Lucius' words somewhat dampened my enthusiasm to live among the redskins, and even, for the moment, diminished my sympathy for them. Nevertheless, these poor souls are deserving of pity. The tribes of the northern prairies and such southern tribes as the Apaches and the Comanches at least know how to defend themselves, and still possess some power of resistance. But the California Indians have given up the struggle. No one hears or knows anything about them. The best proof of this is that before I left for the mountains many Californians assured me that there were no longer any wild Indians to be found in their state. To be sure, there are nowadays only the remnants of them. Hidden in inaccessible canyons and deserted plains, these descendants of once-powerful tribes lead a roving life, keeping a few animals, hunting game, and living off wild fruits and vegetables. They are no longer persecuted since they disturb no one. The half-civilized among them hire themselves out in the fall to harvest the grapes and with the proceeds buy red cloth or dissipate their earnings on liquor. The uncivilized ones, however, frequently suffer hunger and God only knows how they manage to survive from day to day, especially since on this side of San Bernardino there are no buffalo, the main source of food for other tribes.

Doña Refugio provided these poor wretches with salt pork and beans. Since nightfall was approaching, the Indians found themselves a secluded spot among the nearby trees and went to sleep. Next morning they were gone.

We, too, tarried only one more day with the hospitable Plesents. Our host showed me his apiary which was bringing him a substantial income. In a clearing stood on wooden pedestals over two hundred white box-shaped hives. In every hive there were eleven frames which the bees fill with wax and honey. Once the wax is made, it is never destroyed; thus, by wasting no time in the production of new wax, the bees are able to make twice as much honey. The method by which the honey is extracted is an interesting one. This is done by a machine specially invented for this purpose. A frame with its wax and honey is placed in a cylinder that revolves at a high speed and the centrifugal force extracts the honey to the last drop. In this process not a single cell of the honeycomb is damaged. The frame with the wax is returned to the hive and the bees immediately begin to refill it. The output of honey here is truly remarkable and even in the poorest years it exceeds by five times the yield in Poland. There is an explanation for this: in the first place, the bees in a warm climate are more active; secondly, while the bees in Poland consume much of their honey during their long winter months of hibernation, the bees in California work practically the whole year round. Here the mountain slopes are covered with flowers both winter and summer. California honey also excels in taste, fragrance, and transparency even our best Lithuanian honey.

In general, beekeeping here is conducted, not in the old-fashioned manner in tree trunks as in Poland, but with all the innovations recently developed. Lack of adequate roads formerly hampered the growth of this industry. But from the moment when all the beekeepers organized themselves into the "Association of California Apiarists" and began to send their product directly to Liverpool, thereby eliminating the middleman, the price of honey began to rise. They now expect that apiculture will eventually become a most profitable branch of the economy.

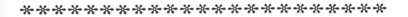

LIFE in the mountain canyons of California held an irresistible attraction for Sienkiewicz. "I am so happy here," he wrote, "that if I were blessed with eternal life, I should not wish to spend it anywhere else." Here he rid himself of "nerves, colds, and toothaches"; he slept "like a king." Above all, he loved the hunting. Even after the arrival of the Chlapowskis in Anaheim, Sienkiewicz did not join them immediately, for he could not tear himself away from the mountains at the height of the hunting season.

Only toward the end of the year (1876), looking sunburned, strong and healthy, did he join the colony in Anaheim. For several weeks he lived with his compatriots, but disillusionment had already begun to set in amongst the colonists. All grew nervous and morose, and a few, acutely homesick. Their initial enthusiasm evaporated as rapidly as did Count Chlapowski's capital, while "not a shadow of income" came in. "This latter crude reality gave the final blow to our cherished bubble," admitted Modjeska as she decided to recoup the family fortunes by returning to the stage. Early in 1877, she went to San Francisco to study English, preparatory to her American stage debut.

But proximity had served to transform Sienkiewicz's devoted friendship and admiration of Modjeska as an artist into sentiments of a more personal and ardent nature. Soon the young author followed his idol to San Francisco in order to be near her. Before long his attentions to her caused friction between

him and her husband Chlapowski, and under the circumstances
Sienkiewicz deemed it advisable to leave San Francisco at least
temporarily. By means of his correspondence with Julian
Horain, however, he kept himself informed of the actress and
her activities, and in every letter he would inquire about her
and ask to be remembered to her. He even sent letters to her
via Horain.

During his absence from San Francisco Sienkiewicz traveled
about the state. He journeyed by boat along the coast from
San Francisco to Los Angeles. He spent some time in the
Mohave Desert. He lived for a while with his elderly Polish
friend, Captain Francis Wojciechowski, at Sebastopol in Sacramento County. Later he moved to Haywards where he would
be but an hour's distance from San Francisco and Modjeska.

Sienkiewicz was visiting the forest of Mariposa at the time
the actress was about to give her first American theatrical performance. He hurried back to the city to be present at her opening on August 20, 1877, at the California Theater. For weeks
thereafter he could speak and write of nothing but "the celebrated Polish artist." He immediately dispatched a long, laudatory account of her debut to the *Gazeta Polska* so that her
friends and rivals back in Warsaw might know of her success.
She was still very much on his mind when on September 7,
1877, he wrote to a close but unnamed friend in Warsaw the
following letter describing her triumph and expressing his
thoughts on a variety of other subjects.

Letter X

THOUGHTS FROM SAN FRANCISCO

San Francisco
September 9, 1877

MY dear! [1]

I should have answered your last letter long ago. I was a little angry with you for printing my previous letter since neither in form nor style was it suitable for publication.[2] Furthermore, your editorial explanations in some places altered or generalized the meaning of my words. From the conclusion readers may get an impression that I have nothing but jeers for the Jews, whereas in reality I have a lot of respect for them.

It was only here that I became convinced what an energetic and enterprising people they are. It is less surprising in Poland that the Jews have gained control of commerce and, in part, of industry,[3] but here where the population is extremely industrious, where competition is especially keen and the struggle for survival is conducted ruthlessly, the real commercial abilities of the Jews become fully evident. In trade and commerce the Polish Jews hold their own against Yankee competition, and if need be, could do so against the devil himself. They come here in most instances without a cent, without a knowledge of the language or conditions, in other words, with only their two hands and a good head on their shoulders. The day after their arrival each one of them opens a business. If anyone tries to cheat them, he is himself cheated. In commercial transactions they are no less honest than other businessmen. I do not know

---

[1] This letter was addressed to a private, unknown party who had it printed in the Warsaw *Kurier Codzienny*.

[2] Since the "previous letter" referred to here contains nothing that is not found in Sienkiewicz's other letters, it is not reprinted in this volume.

[3] Occupational restrictions and restrictions on ownership of land compelled the Jews in Poland to enter commerce.

a single Jew who, after a year's residence, is still in poverty.
Each of them has money; each, as the Americans say, "is making a living"; and after a while each "is worth" such and such a
sum of money. Some of them manage to make millions. But
be that as it may. More important is the fact that the Jews
from the kingdom of Poland do not forget whence they have
come and where lie the bones of their forefathers, whereas
those from Austrian and Prussian Poland tend to identify themselves with the Germans. It cannot be denied that the Jews are
a hardy race. This element in our population should not be
discounted, for the Jews possess exactly those traits which we
Poles lack and which, added to our own, would make for a
strong nation.

Such is my frank opinion. Anyone who looks down upon the
Jews as being of inferior birth and ancestry is an imbecile. I
do not advocate that we court them with special favors. When
they do wrong, they should be punished like anybody else.
But under no circumstances can we exclude them from the
orbit of our lives. So much for the Jewish question.

You enquired about Madame Modrzejewska [4] and wrote
that only now everybody recognizes that she was "incomparable" and that no one can take her place. I am at last able to
inform you, not in confidence but openly, that she has already
appeared on the American stage. In a letter sent to the *Polish
Gazette* I described her opening performance here two weeks
ago.[5] She has played daily, appearing in three different roles, as
Adrienne, Ophelia, and Juliet. Even my best efforts would be
inadequate to describe the triumph of her appearances. The
cries of acclaim, the deluge of exotic flowers, the perspiring
crowds of spectators pushing and shoving, the clamor from the
upper balcony, the rhapsodies of the critics drawing compari-

---

[4] This is the Polish spelling of the name. The actress adopted the sim-
plified spelling "Modjeska" for stage use in this country.

[5] Madame Modjeska made her American debut on August 20, 1877, at
the California Theater. She played Adrienne in *Adrienne Lecouvreur* by
Eugene Scribe and Ernest Legouvé.

sons with Ristori and Rachel,[6] the ovations from the public and the press, the sonnets glorifying "the great daughter of Sarmatia"—all of these things only dimly reflect the luster of her success. Our countrymen who reside here permanently call her "our Madame M." So great is their pride and joy that they walk with their noses in the air and hardly speak to anyone. The newspapers, which previously were rather indifferent, now strive to outdo each other in compliments and expressions of enthusiasm. Since then various articles have appeared about the Slavs and the extraordinary talents of our race.

The Palace Hotel where Madame Modrzejewska stays is literally besieged by theatrical agents, critics, editors, and civic dignitaries. After her last performance representatives of the press handed her an address printed on a white satin scroll, together with a tricolor bouquet of flowers and a flag. The address was written in the form of a poem whose concluding lines read as follows:

> Keep Polish memories in your heart alone
> America now claims you for her own.

After these lines were affixed the signatures of the journalists. Even more beautiful was the sonnet written by Mr. Hinton, the editor of the *Evening Post,* and reprinted in other newspapers.

In short, we had in Warsaw perhaps the world's most famous actress and we lost her. Furthermore, how many times have various so-called critics written jeeringly of her in their papers so that later they could beat their chests and brag over their coffee cups: "I really gave Madame Modrzejewska a write-up." And so they continued to write until they wrote her out of Warsaw.

The theaters of New York, Boston, Washington, and Philadelphia have already sent her very attractive offers. This year she will very likely play in all of the important American cities. Then she intends to appear in London and later in Warsaw.

---

[6] Adelaide Ristori (1821–1906) and Elisa Rachel (1820–1858) were famous tragediennes, the one Italian and the other French.

The idea of appearing in Warsaw she will not give up for any price. After Warsaw she will return to England, America, and finally plans to visit Australia. Her debut on the American stage was very difficult. She did not even have the money to purchase her costumes. Her hopes for assistance from Warsaw were not realized. But she overcame all these difficulties. From the remnants of her Warsaw costumes she was able to design attractive new ones. After her first stage appearance her fortune was made. If I earned as much money in a year as she earns in a week, I would travel about the world in style and write my *feuilletons* gratis.

Well, there you have the news about Madame Modrzejewska. It all happened so suddenly and unexpectedly that it is hard to believe. I do not recall whether I mentioned that the lines of Ophelia were given in Polish and the effect was tremendous. *The Mail* wrote that it was the sweetest language ever heard by Americans. Because of the interest now kindled in all things Polish, the newspapers are clamoring for the artist to introduce Polish dramas. Madame Modrzejewska is considering the presentation of Slowacki, but I do not know whether this will be feasible.

Now a few words about myself. At the moment I am again in San Francisco, having come here from Mariposa especially to see Madame M. perform. Before going to Mariposa I had several exciting experiences. Here, as elsewhere in the United States, railroad workers were striking in protest against the cut in their daily wage rate. I witnessed exceedingly stormy meetings where the opposing forces resorted to paving bricks, fists, clubs, and revolvers. I was almost hit myself. Then before my very eyes the Guatemalan consul, Mr. Hangs, killed a certain Mr. Leslie.[7] I was among those who seized the murderer and took away his gun. Frankly, I regretted greatly that the authori-

---

[7] Sienkiewicz has the names somewhat confused. The murderer was a *former* Guatemalan consul by the name of Mr. Leslie C. Hanks. The murdered person was a San Francisco stockbroker named Mr. John E. Daily.

ties did not lock me up in the hoosegow too. Here it is customary to jail a witness in order to isolate him from the influence of the accused's family. Such a witness is paid five dollars a day, a sum of money that no writer could possibly earn for a day's work. Since I was not imprisoned, I set out for Mariposa.

Mariposa is one huge forest. A week after my arrival, I was crawling into a thicket in pursuit of a wounded vulture with my unloaded double-barreled shotgun, when whom should I meet nose to nose but *Madame La Cougouar*. Madame shrieked and snorted angrily at me. As for me, having had no formal introduction, I retreated with a haste that would have done credit to any well-mannered gentleman. I assure you, I almost collapsed from fright. Imagine, I did not even have a knife, and my unloaded shotgun was nothing but a worthless stick! Fortunately, *Madame La Cougouar* hid herself in an abandoned silver mine and I in the house. After regaining my composure, I took down my fourteen-shot Henry rifle and returned to the mine where I waited about thirty paces from the entrance throughout the night . . . without result. I vowed from that moment on never to be so foolish as to go into a thicket without my knife and loaded rifle.

What curious experiences are encountered in travel! Would it ever have occurred to me two years ago in Warsaw that I might be devoured? Once the danger is passed, such an experience has its comical side. Imagine for yourself a cougar and a Warsaw journalist, each born in a different hemisphere, but by some strange fate placed in each other's path so that one might eat the other. The only question is, who will eat whom? Will the cougar eat up the writer? If so, will this cursed beast have at least some conception of whom it is eating? Will it realize that in devouring me it is consuming at the same time about a thousand *feuilletons* in the *Polish Gazette*, about two hundred *Letters from my Travels*, my short stories "In Vain," "Humoresque," "Old Servant," "Hania," "Charcoal Sketches," and all those masterpieces which have yet to take flight from my imagination into the world like sparrows from a hayloft? Will this beast at least realize that it is a greater sin to eat an author than a calf or a sheep? Upon returning to her den, she is likely to say to her husband, "I feel nauseated. Today I ate something strangely unappetizing." What an ending!

Be that as it may, it is always better to travel than to sit like a stone in one place and allow one's talents to stagnate. Travel enables one to shake himself free of narrow partisanship, personal bias and antipathies, petty jealousies, mean pretensions, and preoccupation with trivialities. A traveler lives more fully, perhaps thinks more broadly and courageously, develops his own individuality, and does not become just another worn-out penny identical with every other; he is his own master and that counts more than anything else. But do not think I am trying to entice you to take up a life of vagabonding. Those whose duties and work keep them at home should remain there. But as for me, what did I do in Warsaw? I was writing. What will I be doing at the North or South Pole? I will be writing. In short, I shall always follow my own profession, and perhaps by traveling, I write about more interesting subjects.

Do you wish to know what are my plans for the immediate future? When some money I am awaiting as impatiently as a bridegroom his bride will have crossed the ocean and this continent and finally reached my hands, then posthaste I shall be on my way to Warsaw. There I plan to deliver a few lectures, to earn some funds for a new journey, and then to write more letters from my travels. So I shall continue until I undertake that least costly but longest voyage—to the other world. How soon I shall embark upon it I do not know, but if the proverb "a poor ax never sinks" is true, there is no danger of death by drowning for me.

I have tremendous admiration for many things in America, but not for the women. My observations are limited to those of California, however, for I am insufficiently acquainted with

the East. In general, the California women did not impress me
favorably. They dress as in Paris, indeed, even better. They
are so given to conspicuous extravagance that even in this California climate, be it summer or winter, they wear fur coats, fur
neckpieces, fur-trimmed jackets, and the like, for the sole purpose of showing off their expensive Alaskan sealskins. All day
long they sit in their rocking chairs exposing their legs, grinning, prattling, giggling, and coquetting in a naïve manner, but
doing no work at all. Each one of them strums on the piano,
but none of them plays well. They are not interested in the
study of languages, yet they assume airs and pretensions of
refinement that ill accord with republican equality and freedom. A complete lack of sentimentalism is characteristic of
them. They do not reveal the innermost affections of their
hearts in the moonlight, preferring to flirt gaily and boister-
ously. Frequently lacking in intelligence, concentration, reflection, and the qualities of mind and heart, they lead a life of
external superficiality like so many frolicsome kittens.

Again I remind you that I am speaking only of California,
being unfamiliar with the East. In California the people,
though simple and unrefined, are rich, and this wealth has
gone to the women's heads. Being *nouveaux riches,* they pose
as great ladies. This is not only comical but also undemocratic
and antirepublican.

My remarks apply, of course, only to the women of the
wealthier classes. The others, however, such as factory workers
and the wives of artisans and farmers, are decent, unpretentious
souls who diligently attend to their duties. They, too, are well
dressed, but only because their husbands wish them to be so.
American men care little about their own appearance and frequently go without tie or coat. But they cannot bear to see their
wives without silks, golden chains, long gloves reaching to the
elbows, and similar fineries.

In short, women here try in every respect to imitate their
European counterparts. This is not true of the men. You can-

not imagine what a difference there is in the customs of American and European men. The American is unceremonious and given to a simplicity of manner that verges on boorishness. When I first arrived here, they all seemed to me exceedingly impolite. Now that I have grown accustomed to it, I esteem this straightforwardness in the relations between men more highly than European gallantry.

Why, for heaven's sake, must one man strive to ingratiate himself with another? In Europe when two gentlemen are presented to each other, they spring at once from their seats, sweep off their hats and bow, flaunt the tails of their dress coats in great delight, shake hands, make sheep's eyes at each other, utter assurances of their immense pleasure at having the opportunity to meet, and then they toss at each other the most impudent compliments, such as, "For a long time I have been looking forward to making your acquaintance," or "I have heard so much about you," or "I feel fortunate to meet you." In other words, they prance about each other like two monkeys in ardent courtship. How ridiculous! You cannot imagine with what contempt Americans regard such behavior. It is for this reason they dislike Frenchmen.

Here when someone introduces two people he simply says: "Mister X, this is Mister Y." Mister X does not rise, does not remove his hat, does not even extend his hand, but simply nods his head and says "Hello." Mr. Y likewise nods and responds " 'Morning," and thereupon the two men are acquainted. At their next encounter they slap each other on the back with a "How do you do, old fellow?" It's as simple as all that.

At first, this informality shocked me very much. When, upon being introduced to someone, I would bow in the European manner and in return receive an indifferent nod of the head, I was many times tempted to box the fellow's ears. Now I have grown accustomed to American ways, and what's more, I have come to realize that although Americans may behave with too little ceremony, Europeans mince about with too much affectation. After all, what is the value of this bowing and grinning?

Would it not be much simpler for two people, upon meeting each other, to nod their heads and let it go at that? In a democratic republic this would be entirely natural. An acquaintance made in this fashion is as good as any other. If friendship follows, it is worth a hundred times more than any European friendship, for the American looks upon his friend as a brother and regards his friend's problems as his own. In Europe friends often promise more than they fulfill. Here relationships are more clearly defined: either it's every man for himself, or each man for his friend until death.

America with her institutions and customs has proved an immensely instructive country to me. Here has been resolved a perplexing social problem. Forty million people of all nationalities, many of them traditionally hostile to each other in Europe, live here as free, law-abiding citizens at peace with one another. But just as everything in this world has its good and bad side, it is quite possible that American freedom has its defects. Nevertheless, America provides living proof that its institutions, depite their deficiencies, can embrace the widest horizons, reconcile numerous nationalities, and encourage the development of a variety of interests.

Look at the countries of Europe, for example: France is a nation of Frenchmen; Prussia, a nation of Prussians. Although the United States is a political entity, it is not yet, strictly speaking, a nation. Here there are forty million people but not forty million Americans. Here is a state that is not national in character and yet does not hamper but protects and encourages the development of its different national groups. If the Germans wish to remain German, all right; likewise, the Irish, the Swedes, the English, all are free to retain their national identity. But all of them will be good American citizens.

✳ ✳

W HILE in California Sienkiewicz maintained close contact with his numerous Polish friends, but he did not restrict his social life to them. In San Francisco, for example, he often mingled in other circles and met some of the wealthy local residents. Among the latter was a certain Mr. Woothrup who was a member of the California Club, a society of sportsmen. Thanks to this connection, Sienkiewicz received an invitation from the club to join a buffalo hunting expedition into Wyoming that was to be headed by Woothrup. Naturally, he accepted the invitation with delight, for he never missed an opportunity to hunt.

During the expedition which lasted throughout October, 1877, the enthusiastic huntsman bagged his first buffalo and had other exciting adventures. But his pleasure in this trip was somewhat marred when, toward the end, he fell seriously ill. Woothrup and his companions took excellent care of him and by the time the group returned to San Francisco, he was much improved, though still very weak.

His illness and slow convalescence compelled Sienkiewicz to remain in San Francisco even though he was anxious now to begin his journey homeward. Helena Modjeska was no longer on the West Coast; she had departed for the East where she was to achieve new triumphs in New York and other large cities. Her departure saddened the entire Polish community in San Francisco, most of all Sienkiewicz. He was neither so sad nor so ill as to be unable to write, however, and in articles sent to the *Gazeta Polska* he described his recent hunting adventures in Wyoming. The articles made no mention of Virginia City which he had visited en route to Wyoming and which he made the subject of the following letter written to an unknown friend in Warsaw.

Letter XI

VIRGINIA CITY

San Francisco
December 18, 1877

CONTRARY to my expectations, I am still in San Francisco, being detained here by the illness which I contracted during my recent expedition to Wyoming. While en route to Wyoming we spent a day in Virginia City, Nevada. This city is only two hours' distance from the main line of the transcontinental railroad. Since the leader of our expedition, Woothrup, was a stockholder in the mines of that area and had some connection with their operation, and since I wanted to inspect the silver veins, we set out in that direction from the Reno station.

Before I describe my impressions of the mines, I shall tell you a few words about Nevada itself. This spacious state, contiguous with California, is separated from the latter by the peaks of the beautiful, lofty Sierra Nevadas. Their summits, disappearing among the clouds, are permanently covered with snow, but their slopes rustle with one great forest of American pines which in Latin are called *pinus ponderosa*. On the California slopes spring reigns eternally. Imagine swollen waters the year around, a multitude of rushing streams, a warm, moist breeze, trees turning green, grass glittering with dew, and this refreshing, young, springlike charm permeating the whole atmosphere, and you will have some conception of these mountainsides. From the coach windows can be seen many cabins of lumberjacks and squatters; further on appear sawmills, watermills, miners' settlements, piles of logs, and, finally, sluices conducting water to the gold mines. These sluices are a characteristic feature of this region. Sometimes they run close to the railroad tracks, descend into the valleys, leap from one mountain to another, pass over ravines, and sometimes stretch over a distance of several English miles. Built of boards, they resemble large troughs through which the water flows rapidly. They appear to be suspended in the air, although they are actually supported by tall poles crossed in the form of the letter X. These boards and poles would look ugly indeed were it not for the moss, ivy, bindweed, wild-peas, and other climbing plants which, clinging to the soil caught in the crevices between the boards, cover their nakedness with an impenetrable curtain of greenness. In the troughs every few yards are small riffles in which lies quicksilver.

The process of extracting the gold consists of the following: Into the running water of the sluices the miners continually pour gold-bearing mud, sand, and earth. Being heavier, the grains of gold sink to the bottom and near each riffle come in contact with the quicksilver which has the property of attracting and dissolving the gold. After a certain amount of earth has been washed in this manner, there remains only the task of removing the gold-saturated mercury, distilling it, and pocketing the pure gold.

Such is the appearance of the western slopes of the Sierra Nevadas. On the other hand, the eastern slopes are quite different, for here there is no spring, the vegetation is stunted, the landscape is monotonous. In general, Nevada has a rather gloomy appearance. Through the central portion of the state runs a vast tangle of large and small mountain ranges, extending to the middle of Utah. The railroad runs between the mountains in a valley that seems to open *ad infinitum* before the locomotive. As in Utah, the soil is in many places saturated with salt and appears white as though sprinkled with snow. Of course, nothing grows upon this salt except some small fat plants from which a sticky, salty substance oozes out when they are broken. The lack of any trees and shrubs gives the region a completely barren character. Nor is there a single sizable river in this area; there are only lakes here, some of them rather large, situated close to the California boundary and usually referred to as "mud lakes."

In the southern part of the state the mountains disappear entirely and the region becomes a prairie. Here the lakes have been replaced by large stretches of land covered with soda, the so-called Soda Lagoon, or by sandy hollows which fill with water during the rainy season, but otherwise remain dry throughout most of the year. The mountains, on the other hand, abound with great mineral wealth. Rich deposits of gold, silver, and copper are found here and therefore most of the local towns have grown out of miners' settlements.

One of these communities which has been transformed into a city of several tens of thousands is Virginia City. It is also known as Silver City, and rightly so, inasmuch as silver is found not only within the bowels of the earth but everywhere. Virginia City has an unusually attractive location on a mountain overlooking a large portion of the surrounding countryside. Because of the high altitude, the climate is cold, the wind blows continuously as in a smithy, and snow falls occasionally. Water is scarce and not very safe to drink; it is drunk, therefore, only when mixed with California wine.

Upon arriving in town, we made our way immediately to the mines. Amidst piles of earth and torn-up terrain there suddenly opened before us a black pit. Soon our guide crawled out from underground and Woothrup, much to my surprise, presented him to me in a very formal manner. Before we entered the pit, the guide led us to a hut where he suggested that we don suits of bladder—damp, dirty, loathsome garments. After putting these on, we returned to the pit, took seats in a kind of basket made of boards standing at the entrance to the pit, and all at once everything became pitch black.

We began to descend into the pit at breakneck speed. By the faltering glimmer of a lantern I caught sight of ropes, or perhaps chains, unwinding themselves with frightening rapidity. Down, down, down sped the basket. I thought that it would never stop. . . . But finally it did stop, or rather it came to such an abrupt halt that we nearly knocked our heads together.

I asked the guide, "Does such a mad ride ever result in an accident?"

"Occasionally," he replied. "If the chains break, those sitting in the basket are killed, of course."

"And does this really happen?"

Again a calm reply: "Sometimes."

"After all, there must be winches which can stop the elevator?" enquired Woothrup.

"Sometimes," answered the ragged fellow who was serving as our guide. "Once in ten times they stop it."

I take it, then, that accidents do not happen very often because, after all, if they did occur daily, they could hardly be called accidents. Such reassurance is enough for Americans. But as for me, while I was rushing downwards in the darkness, I almost regretted having come here.

Upon reaching the bottom, we found ourselves in a labyrinth of underground corridors, rooms, and chapels where lights twinkled. Our guide, as amiable as he was dirty and ragged, conducted us around, generously explaining everything. Occasionally wagons filled with silver-bearing ore went by us and were hoisted to the surface by means of chains. Scattered groups of laborers worked with determination, breaking up the quartz with pickaxes. Imagine for yourselves these silver veins, distinguishable on the walls by their lighter color, running in all directions, downwards, upwards, now vanishing, now reappearing. You can scarcely believe your eyes at the sight of these millions that you can touch with your hand here. These must surely be the richest mines in the world. In them work locomotives, wagons, men, and horses, as well as steam engines that tear out the ore from the rocks. We descended nearly nine hundred feet. The flickering light in these galleries created a bewitching spectacle. In places the galleries widened to resemble chapels and halls whose walls, arches, and floors were decorated in a natural mosaic by the silver veins. Believe me, when I realized that everything I was touching, gazing at, and standing upon was of silver, it seemed to me that I had been carried back to the era of King Midas, or that I was viewing a scene from *A Thousand and One Nights.*

Subterranean water seeped out of the ground where we walked, creating here and there a mud puddle or small pond. In some places water trickled from the rocks. The whistle, roar, and clanging of the steam engines, the clatter of wagons, and the shouts of human voices could be heard in some underground passages, while in others a dead silence reigned. Occasionally this silence was broken by a human voice which echoed eerily as a result of the strange underground acoustics.

For someone like myself who had rarely visited a mine, these were new experiences, unusual and intriguing. In all of this I saw new evidences of the power of man. This creature seemingly insignificant in relation to the whole world nevertheless crosses oceans, bores his way into the interior of the earth, commands iron monsters to bite rocks, reverses the course of rivers, drills tunnels into mountains or demolishes them if they are presumptuous enough to stand in his way. Here beneath the surface of the earth amidst the clangor of work, I sensed the enterprising nature of man—that constant drive "forward! forward!"; that certain stubbornness and perseverance in perfecting his living conditions, in acquiring wealth, in improving his status, as though life were eternal. But, of course, life is eternal, for while individuals may die, the human race remains. To be sure, the vast amount of silver disgorged year in and year out by mines like this will change hands, but once extracted it will continue to provide a forward impetus by lubricating the wheel of progress so that it turns at an ever faster pace.

We did not descend beyond nine hundred feet since my friend was eager to return to town to look after various business affairs. Besides, it was too wet, smoky, and hot. Only now did I understand the need for the protective garb that we had donned at the entrance. We hurried back to the elevator, a loud "all right!" resounded and we were snatched upwards.

Upon emerging into the daylight, I drew a deep breath. We began to thank our guide. As I have already mentioned, he was a rather ragged and dirty individual dressed in a flannel shirt, a battered hat, and torn rubber boots. His face, although begrimed with soot, nevertheless bore a certain air of distinction, and his light blue eyes revealed intelligence. Since he had been very polite, I wondered upon leaving, "Should I or should I not give him a dollar? If he is a European, he'll take it; if he's an American, perhaps he'll be offended . . . I, for one, don't know. He certainly does look very shabby . . ." Finally, I decided to behave as my companion did, who, as an American, ought to know what to do.

I must confess that I was somewhat surprised that Woothrup not only gave him nothing, but said goodbye to him as to a friend and stated that he would visit him that same evening. The tattered workman nodded his head and invited me, too, for the evening. I nodded in response and we departed.

Once we were seated in the buggy, I said to Woothrup, "Perhaps we should have given something to the guide?"

Woothrup looked at me with surprise. "How long have you been in America?"

"About two years."

"Oh, you foreigners! It certainly takes you a long time before you even begin to understand our society."

"What's this all about?"

"Never mind. You'll see this evening."

"Aren't we supposed to be at that workman's house this evening?"

"Yes, but before that we have to be in many places."

Accordingly, upon reaching town, we made our rounds, and about eight o'clock in the evening we stood before a beautiful

marble mansion separated from the street by a railing and a
splendid lawn graced by a fountain.

"Is the master at home?" Woothrup asked the person who
opened the door.

"Yes, Sir! Please come into the parlor."

We entered the parlor, a room furnished in true oriental
luxury, full of bronze statues, paintings, mirrors, velvets, and
the like. In a few moments the host entered and . . . please
imagine my surprise when I recognized Mr. James Little, our
guide of that morning. I confess I was embarrassed. Mr. Little,
now dressed not ostentatiously but in good taste, with an im-
maculate white shirt, his face washed and his hair combed,
had the appearance if not of a prince (since there are none in
the United States) at least of a banker. Then his beautiful,
blonde wife entered, dressed in a silken gown and wearing a
golden necklace. She was followed by the even more striking
Miss Ellinor, the sister of Mrs. Little.

When these ladies learned that I was a Pole, we had a
ready subject for conversation since a few weeks previously
Madame Modrzejewska had performed in a play in Virginia
City just before her departure for New York. When I told
them that I was not only a compatriot of the great actress, but
that I had the honor of knowing her personally, my standing in
the esteem of Mrs. Little and Miss Ellinor literally increased
twofold. Both ladies could not find words enough to praise
"the greatest artist in the world," as Miss Ellinor put it. Both
were quick to boast of the fact that they had been introduced
to her. Mrs. Little showed me all the reviews which she had
kept from the local newspapers. These not only praised our
actress to the skies, but even reported her every private remark.

"Since our town lies practically on the direct route between
San Francisco and New York and since its per capita wealth is
perhaps the greatest in America," stated Mrs. Little, "all of the
most famous artists stop here even though our population
numbers only a few thousand. We have seen Janauschek, Clara

Morris, Mrs. Bowers, and Miss Eytinge, but we have never seen, nor do we expect to see, an actress comparable to Modjeska. What talent! What sweetness! What ladylike bearing! These were qualities unknown on our stage until now."

"Yes, indeed," added Mr. Little, suddenly interrupting the conversation on business matters that he had been conducting with Woothrup in the corner. "I had the pleasure of showing Lady Modjeska through our mines."

"And didn't you receive a couple of dollars for your services?" enquired Woothrup.[1]

Reddening up to my ears, I threw him a murderous look, but Woothrup, pretending not to notice it, continued unperturbed: "And I know a certain Polish gentleman who this morning wanted to offer you a dollar. Do you hear that, James?"

Everyone laughed heartily. Mr. Little then commented, "This happens rather frequently with the foreigners who visit our mines. Not long ago an Englishman offered me five dollars, and when I refused, he insisted, 'Take them, take them, my friend. Five dollars have their value, and it seems to me you need them.'

" 'I don't deny,' I answered, 'that five dollars have their value, but I cannot say I need them as I have half a million of them in the bank, not counting the ones I hold in shares.'

"The Englishman gaped at me and after a minute muttered, 'You would then have half a million and five,'—upon which we parted friends."

Surely I need not explain that Mr. Little is not a laborer, but the chief engineer and one of the major shareholders of the mine. His dirty clothing and face could, indeed, easily lead someone to make an error. On the other hand, it is impossible to use any other type of apparel in the mine. Therefore, visitors don special outfits since below ground all clothes are torn by jagged rocks, spotted by dampness, and blackened by smoke and soot. Of course, an engineer who spends the greater

[1] Madame Modjeska herself speaks of this incident in her memoirs.

part of his day in the mine must soon acquire the appearance of a ragamuffin. Besides, as I have mentioned in a previous letter, American men bedeck their wives with finery but pay little attention to their own dress.

But to get back to Virginia City, it is a town of fabulous riches. Millionaire mine owners reside here. Because of the abundance of wealth everything is extremely expensive. For instance, a night in a hotel, including supper and breakfast, costs five dollars. The engineers, the office workers, and the miners, all earn scores of dollars daily. I give you my word that the most prolific writer in Poland does not earn as much as any Irishman here who carries out rubbish. But should you see these people on the street with their flannel shirts, tattered hats, and dirty faces, you would not consider them worth two cents. It is true, however, that you would not see women dressed in anything but silks. As you look at the town, at the little palaces three times more beautiful than the villas along Belvedere Avenue in Warsaw, at the gardens coaxed forth by artificial and expensive means from the barren earth, you will surmise that there is no lack of money here and that the town deserves the nickname "Silver City" given to it by its inhabitants.

In this region new mines are constantly being discovered and towns arise beside them in a twinkling of an eye. Miners build rows of houses; merchants arrive with wares to be sold to the miners at tremendous profits; stores are opened; hordes of businessmen flock here, so hotels are constructed; since money is plentiful, banks are founded. Thus, where yesterday the wolf howled and the Indian scalped his fellow Indian, today stands a town. To this vast mineral wealth can be attributed the rise of San Francisco, Sacramento, Virginia City, and many others. Darwin, California, is even now being established before my own eyes. It is also true that when a mine gives out, the town vanishes as quickly as it appeared. This happened, for example, to Sebastopol, a small town built in Sacramento

County during the Crimean War. Houses and stores lined its streets, mail coaches stopped there, its inhabitants numbered several thousands—and now its population consists of the aged Captain Wojciechowski and his French servant. Where once were streets, the earth is plowed and barely sown, and "nec locus ubi Troia fuit." [2]

Were it not for the mines, Nevada would surely have remained empty to this day, for neither its climate nor the fertility of its soil attracts anyone. Who would be so stupid as to sit among the rocks under cloudy skies on salt or soda deposits when next door lies a beautiful, warm, and productive country! But when one sits on silver or gold, then the sitting pays. Perhaps in time when land becomes scarce, people will come even to Nevada, and perhaps they will make a garden of Nevada just as the Mormons have done with the much worse state of Utah. But that time lies in the distant future since at present only one-fourth of the states are populated. Apart from California, the remainder of the immeasurable expanse stretching practically from the Mississippi to the Pacific Ocean is still nearly empty.

Speaking of Mormons, would you believe that among the Latter-day Saints there is a certain Polish worthy from Lithuania? I do not know his name as he had changed it for an English one. Nor do I have any idea how many wives he has, but I do know that he wrote Horain (from whom I have these details) addressing him as "My dear brother" and urging him to become a Mormon. Horain also told me that in New York he once saw through his window a Negro selling cucumbers, and like a true Lithuanian he wanted to eat a couple of them with honey. He therefore sent some children to catch up with the Negro and to buy some cucumbers. The children bought the cucumbers and began to make various observations to each other concerning the Negro. Whereupon the latter enquired in purest Polish: "You speak Polish, do you?"

[2] Not even the spot where Troy existed.

The surprise of the children is easily understandable. They brought the Negro home where the family began to question him on how he happened to learn Polish. It developed that he was the ex-slave of a certain Pole living in the vicinity of New York under the adopted name of Major. The Negro had been purchased in the South; however, when his master moved to the North where slavery was nonexistent, he had to be freed. But as he and his master had grown fond of one another, they had not parted.

"And does your master always talk to you in Polish?" asked Horain.

"At present he always does," the Negro replied, "but when he first bought me, he spoke Polish only when he was angry."

"And what did he say then?"

The Negro began to utter in true Mazovian spirit: [3] "S—— — ——— . . ." and a host of other profanities.

This country, where no one is surprised at anything, lends itself to the development of originality. That is why there is no lack of "characters" among our compatriots here, especially the older ones. Not long ago there died here an old man by the name of Sielawa. He was a very unfortunate person. It would be difficult to enumerate regions where he had not roamed, or hardships which he had not suffered. He wandered among the Indians and knocked about the four corners of the world; here he earned a dollar, there he lost it; in short, he was a leaf tossed about in a storm.

But he did find two years of happiness in his life. He became a lighthouse-keeper at Aspinwall, New Granada, not far from the equator. Sitting on the solitary rock, seeing no human being for months at a time, the strange old man felt happy. He imagined that this was the end of his wanderings and that quietly he would await the twilight of life and the moment when he would embark upon his final, eternal journey. Every

[3] Mazovia was the old name of central Poland whose inhabitants, the Mazurians, were considered rude and unrestrained people.

two weeks supplies were brought for him and stacked on the shore. The lighthouse-keeper would gather up the cases, leaving empty ones in their place, and return to his tower. At six in the evening he lighted the lantern; at six in the morning he extinguished it. In addition to this, he fished. At times he watched the sails that appeared on the blue horizon and gazed into the distance, lost in his own visions and dreams.

Suddenly his happiness came to an end—and do you know who was responsible? It was Zygmunt Kaczkowski.[4] On one occasion the old man found among his supplies a package of Polish books. At the sight of them he fell upon his knees and wept. Who had sent them to him, or how that person had learned his address, he could not guess. He carried off the books to his tower, opened the first one at hand, and began to read. The volume was Kaczkowski's *Murdelio*. The old man read and read, not merely with his eyes but with his whole heart and soul. It grew dark. He lighted a lamp and continued to read. . . . The following day he was removed from his post and turned over to the court. He had forgotten to light the beacon, and as a result a ship had run upon the rocks.

Later Sielawa came to New York where he poisoned himself, apparently because of poverty. Beside him lay a copy of *Murdelio*.[5]

Here in California the memory is still fresh of a similar character by the name of Kowalewski. He lived in Sebastopol with Wojciechowski, but often they did not see each other for years at a time. One morning Kowalewski tied his clothes in a bundle and prepared to set out on the road.

"Where are you going, Kowalewski?" his companion enquired.

"Oh, I'm bored with sitting around."

[4] Zygmunt Kaczkowski (1826–1896) was a Polish historical novelist. *Murdelio* is one of his longer and more interesting novels in the cycle entitled *Tales of the Last of the Nieczujas*.

[5] The episode which Sienkiewicz relates here was the basis for one of his best-known short stories, *The Lighthouse-keeper of Aspinwall*.

"But, man, you don't even have any firearms; you may meet up with a bear or some other misfortune, and that will be the end of you."

"And what would this be for?" retorted Kowalewski, brandishing with ease a terrifying iron pike that any other man could barely lift off the ground.

And so he would go out "for a walk" and sometimes would not return for several years. This happened during the days when the country was still wild and empty, and danger lurked everywhere. But this did not bother Kowalewski. Upon his return he would greet his companion as if he had been gone only an hour. If he returned at dinner time, he would sit down quietly at the table; or if it was time to work, he would quietly get busy. What he had done and where he had traveled during his absences, no one ever knew. One day he returned weak, wasted away, and lacking his pike.

"I could not carry it any longer," he said. "Soon I shall die."

And indeed, he did die shortly afterwards.

Primitive nature and solitude develop in man a certain inner mysticism that frequently expresses itself as eccentricity. Among the squatters of the Santa Ana Mountains I saw several Europeans who once belonged to the intelligentsia. Each of them possessed some peculiarity. Only simple individuals or Americans who accept things as they are can endure without damage to their character the mysterious influences of nature and solitude.

I have made this letter longer than I intended, yet I ought still to answer the questions you raised in your last letter. You asked what is happening to our actress. She has gone to New York where she is to appear at the Fifth Avenue Theater, the most fashionable playhouse in New York. Her performances will begin on December 22. News about her generally reaches us here through the newspapers which from time to time tell about the receptions given for her on the East Coast and which occasionally quote what "the great artist" said on this or that occasion, what is her opinion of San Francisco, etc. You wrote me that some people in Warsaw are trying to minimize the importance of her triumphs in San Francisco, claiming that the stage here is provincial and that her triumphs here are no guarantee of success in New York. Just let them wait for New York. As for San Francisco, ask them if they have ever been here. Do they know that the city's population, together with Oakland, reaches 400,000? Do they know that there are seven permanent theaters here? The number alone indicates the development and importance of artistic life. And finally, do they know that Ristori, Janauschek, Bowers, Morris, and other notables have played here? Let her detractors make fools of themselves. Each man does that for which he is best suited. I find this situation easy to comprehend. When the news reached Warsaw of the great actress' pending appearances in America, inevitably there were many who on one alleged basis or another stated dogmatically and foresaw in advance that she would not succeed. But now how can these prophets admit that their foreseeing, critical brains were as improperly placed as the eyes of a lobster?

Take care of yourself. As soon as my health improves, I shall board ship and "anchors aweigh"—and after a month or two, if the ship does not sink, I shall have the pleasure of shaking hands with you.

S IENKIEWICZ was sometimes immobilized, but he was never idle. During his last months in San Francisco while still recuperating from his illness, he freelanced with articles on the Chinese and Poles in this country. It is easy to understand why he wrote on these subjects. Minority groups, whether Indians, Chinese, Poles, or others, were of great interest to him. Agitation over the Chinese was at that time reaching its height in California and he had ample opportunities, therefore, to observe the controversy at close range. Further, he was able to secure additional authoritative information on this subject from Captain Piotrowski, the former California Commissioner of Immigration, with whom he lived briefly.

As for the Polish settlements in the United States, Sienkiewicz was prompted to write about them because he knew that such a report would be of absorbing interest to his fellow countrymen. Polish immigration to America had only begun; the flood gates were to open in the next decade. Sienkiewicz's report must have answered many questions for prospective immigrants, but it would be impossible to know whether any of his compatriots were actually encouraged to emigrate by what he wrote. Unlike the glowing descriptions of "the promised land" distributed widely by railroad and steamship companies, his account presented a harsh but realistic picture of what Polish immigrants might expect in the New World.

By January, 1878, Sienkiewicz recovered from his illness and left San Francisco for the East in order to be once more at the side of Helena Modjeska. He followed the track of her theatrical circuit, visiting her in Boston, Pittsburgh, and New York.

Toward the end of March, exactly two years after his arrival in this country, Sienkiewicz sailed from New York for Europe. He settled in France for a year and awaited the clarification of the political situation in the Near East resulting from the Russo-Turkish War of 1877–78. Possible renewal of the war threatened him with the draft into the Russian army. Not until November, 1879, after a visit to Austrian Poland and Italy, did Sienkiewicz finally return to Warsaw. Refreshed and stimulated by his travels, he now embarked upon his great literary creations.

Letter XII

THE CHINESE IN CALIFORNIA

THE north side of the city of San Francisco, beginning with Clay Street, is occupied by the Chinese district. Were it not for the brick buildings built in the European style, it might appear to a visitor in this part of the town that he had, by some miracle, been transported to Canton or Shanghai. A strange impression is made by these noisy, nimble people, dressed in uniform costumes, with their yellow complexions, slanted eyes, and long pigtails braided of hair and black silk reaching almost to the ground.

During the afternoon market hours the district presents a very animated picture. The sidewalks literally teem with buyers and sellers. Authentic Chinese stores, bearing Chinese inscriptions and filled with the products of Chinese industry, stand with their doors wide open and attract many customers. At every step you encounter something new and different. Here is the shop of a Chinese goldsmith; a bronze dragon displayed in the window reveals his trade. And here is an apothecary's shop. The old Chinaman, who is not only an apothecary but also a doctor, is preparing some kind of drug, examining it closely through his gold-rimmed spectacles. The adjoining shop contains porcelain ware and palm fans. Further on is a restaurant. Through its window you can see the cooks dressed in white with their pigtails tied about their heads. Like marionettes they skip around the table, cutting the dough which they are about to boil. In a nearby barbership five or six Chinese are kneeling in front of the barbers with their heads resting in the barbers' laps. The barber raises the pigtail of his patient with one hand, while with the other he guides a razor carefully over the curve of the skull. In the smoking houses old and young

Chinese smoke tobacco (or perhaps even the forbidden opium) in small metal pipes.

On the streets the hubbub grows constantly greater. Hard-working coolies pass carrying long bamboo poles at either end of which are tied baskets filled with vegetables, bundles of sugar cane, bananas, or strangely shaped ocean fish. In front of the houses stand Chinese women dressed in trousers, with their hair combed in butterfly style and ornamented with bronze pins. Cries and supplications can sometimes be distinguished in the strange Chinese speech whose monosyllabic sounds often give the effect of sighs or clapping. Few white people can be seen in this district. Only on the street corners stand serious-looking policemen dressed in grey overcoats with silver stars on their chests. Perhaps the only other evidence of American civilization are the omnibuses which are drawn over the hills that cover the district neither by horses nor steam but by hidden chains. American stores are few here. Most stores bear Chinese inscriptions whose queer letters written in vertical columns are reflected from a red, varnished paper.

But we have not yet entered the most interesting places which are designated by multicolored paper lanterns. These are the Buddhist temples. In front of each of them hang five or six such lanterns in order that the faithful may at a single glance distinguish the temples from other ordinary buildings. Let us go inside; everyone is allowed to enter here. Now we are really in China. A large room transformed into a temple is illuminated by colored lamps and multicolored window panes. In the corners stand silk umbrellas set on long handles, flags with suns, moons, and dragons, or long poles at the top of which are bronze emblems of indefinable forms, similar sometimes to fantastic flowers or animals, or representing a bewildering mixture of both. The variegated light from the window panes and the lamps throws a certain mysterious luster over the entire nave. In the center is erected the first altar in the form of a low, wide table on which stands a pair of silver dragons two feet high. In the middle of the table rises a bronze pyramid covered with carvings in the shape of animals or humans. This pyramid also serves as a *sanctuarium* in which are preserved the holy books of Buddha.

The main altar stands in the innermost part of the temple. There in the mysterious twilight, illuminated only by the glittering light of two lamps suspended by chains and surrounded by dragons, tigers, and bronze lotus flowers, looms from behind the silk curtains the statue of a great Buddha. Buddha is portrayed in a sitting position, with his hand and forefinger pointed upward as though he were teaching. The hairs of his beard are entwined between the fingers of his upraised hand; the expression on his golden-bronze colored face is a mixture of boredom and stupidity.

In traveling from India to China he apparently lost his Indian physiognomy, for his eyes are slanted, his cheek bones protruding, his nose flat, his face in general representing a stout Chinese type. Likewise, he is dressed in the robe of a Chinese mandarin, consisting of a richly embroidered coat rather like the apparel of Moscow coachmen, of trousers tied at the ankles, and of slippers with thick, white soles whose tips turn upward. In front of his statue on that part of the altar which in a Catholic church is called the *mensa* lie small sticks made of black wood and shaped somewhat like a weaver's shuttle. Every Chinaman who enters takes these sticks and taps one against the other for several minutes in greater praise of Buddha and, considering his prayer completed, he returns as quickly as possible to his business.

I have not observed any other kind of prayers in these temples, though I visited them quite frequently. I noticed also that on the faces of those who prayed by tapping there could be detected no concentration of thought, nor any uplifting of a spirit either towards Buddah or towards meditation over the great truths preached by him. In the first place, the entire activity lasts but a short time, and secondly, it appears to be performed in a purely mechanical manner. It reminded me of those prayers of the bonzes recited with the help of a spinning wheel on whose spokes prayers are inscribed. According to the belief of the bonzes, as the wheel is turned, the prayers are repeated a thousand times and sent to heaven.

San Francisco has about a score of these temples for its entire Chinese population professes the principles of Buddhism. Among the coolies who come from Mongolia and Manchuria are supposed to be a certain number of Shamanists. These, however, do not have separate places of worship. Neither are there any Mohammedans nor followers of Confucius.

Mohammedanism, although it had at one time been strongly propagandized in the western parts of the Celestial Empire, especially in Bukhara, never found many followers among the real Chinese. It captivated the imaginations of the Eastern peoples and spread even to the Indies during the reign of the Moguls. But with its fantastic content, full of passion and emotion, Mohammedanism had no appeal for the cold Chinese reason which appears to be the embodiment of practical positivism.

As for the teachings of Confucius, they are professed only by the Emperor, the Court, the upper classes, and perhaps by the more enlightened inhabitants of the capital. It is an official religion, if these tenets may be called a religion, for Confucianism is more an exposition in morality. As far as I remember the titles of the five books which Confucius has left, they indicate that in all of his teachings there is no reference to theology. There are books dealing with the state, parental respect, ceremonial hymns, duties, etc., but not one of the books concerns the Supreme Being.

The masses of the Chinese people, on the other hand, profess almost without exception the religion, or more accurately, the philosophy of Buddha. All of the oppressed, all of the poor, the lower castes of India and the coolies of China —these will continue to find comfort in Buddhism for a long time to come. Buddha, as is known, does not recognize caste, and thus makes people equal not only in spiritual affairs and in heaven, but also on earth. Furthermore, he regards life in the same manner as does a poor, overworked man, namely, as a penance or as a period of misfortune. Buddhism is a kind of philosophy of pessimism which anticipated Schopenhauer and Hartmann by a thousand years. This life is regarded as transitory and unstable, as a misfortune, and in its place Buddhism holds out the promise of Nirvana.

There can be no question that Buddhism in India differs from that in China. It is a difference that has been created by the national character of the two peoples. In India Buddhism has transformed itself into a very strong asceticism; in China, into one more support for utilitarianism. While the pious Indian "yogi" sits motionless on the ground for several or even a score of years with his eyes focused on the tip of his nose in order better to forget about the affairs of the world, the sober Chinaman reasons that although life is a misfortune and penance, this penance will be easier to bear if he has something to eat and to drink and if he has the means to buy himself a small piece of land for his old age. Thus, the Chinaman toils and toils unceasingly; he hoards every penny and cultivates every inch of soil. And when employment and land is unavailable in his native country, he packs his dragons and his Buddha into a small box and sails across the sea to find work in Australia or in California.

In a sense, he takes all of China with him, for he does not abandon his religion, his customs, or even his dress. All proselyting efforts among the Chinese have come to naught. Christian propaganda succeeds among young, primitive nations, full of feeling and poetry. In the Chinaman it finds none of these qualities. A Chinaman is incapable of exaltation or of sacrifice. He is an old, wise man who, even if he wished, could not understand that it is a virtue and not a folly to die for one's principles, to sacrifice oneself for another, or to give to one's neighbor what one has earned. As far as I know, the California missions have failed to convert a single Chinese. Every one of them prefers to visit the temple of his Buddha, to tap the pieces of wood, and then to consider himself relieved of any further obligation either toward God or his fellow man.

But I return to the picture of Chinese life in California which I had begun to describe. From the temple I lead my readers to the theater. This structure, like all structures inhabited by the Chinese, has no characteristic external features. It is an old, long, one-storey brick building, converted into a theater. The inside is also arranged in an ordinary manner with benches and standing places, and in front of these the stage. The play begins after eight in the evening and continues far into the night. The spectators assemble as early as possible. It is dangerous for a person to come here alone, for he may easily lose his watch, money, or at least his pocket handkerchief. This can easily happen since in addition to the Chinese, so-called "hoodlums" congregate here, that is, scamps of the worst type from the entire city. The theater is packed and the stuffiness and heat here are unbearable. Quarrels and fights frequently occur between the Chinese and the "hoodlums," sometimes ending with the thrust of a knife. In the midst of the noise, laughter, and shouting you hear "ho Ah Ming! Ah-wong! Tsen-Fu!" and the like; also you hear the cracking of beechnuts which the audience is breaking open and eating not only before but throughout the performance.

Finally the curtain rises. On the stage illuminated by paper lamps greased with tallow are seen paper trees, small houses with curved roofs, and the inevitable dragons. First one actor enters, then another, and the play begins. I have in my time written dramatic criticism, but I have never found myself in similar difficulties—how to give a concise and accurate review of a play? If it only were one of those plays in which a dragon emerges from the right of the stage, the sun from the left, the dragon tries to swallow the sun, and the sun resists—following which the curtain falls amidst the general rapture of the audience! Not at all! The play which I witnessed was of the type that Americans describe by the word "emotional." I believe the play concerned a writer who was in love with a girl much wealthier than himself. *Tout comme chez nous!* The girl, however, did not appear on the stage, for women do not take part in plays. I do not know what followed, what had taken place before, or how the play ended. I can only speculate with regard to what happened. Since in China events occur which according to our conceptions are exceedingly improbable, the wealthy girl undoubtedly gave her hand to the impoverished writer.

The vagueness of my review is explained very simply. First, I did not understand a word of what was said; secondly, the play did not end that evening. The actors walked back and forth, conversed with one another, and some even jumped up and down. But in the end there was neither a marriage nor a funeral. To the sober Chinese mind it is inconceivable that a play often dealing with several years of the hero's life could be completed in one evening. This would be incompatible with reality and altogether incongruous. A play ought to last as many years as it represents—if three, then three; if more, then more. There is in all of this a certain Chinese logic. If a drama is to be a reality, let it be the reality that it claims. Thanks to this principle, a play here is presented in the same way that we in Poland publish a novel in serial form. Every evening the play closes with the words "to be continued," and whoever wishes to see it, let him come again. Even as I pen these lines, the enamoured writer has not yet succeeded in winning the hand of the comely "Flower of tea"; but it may be that he has already won over several influential relatives with whose help it will be easier for him to reach his desired goal.

Accompanied by a policeman, you may visit all kinds of Chinese establishments, entrance to which is forbidden to private persons. These include brothels, houses where people play cards secretly or smoke opium, dark dens which serve as shelters to conceal Chinese misery or as havens for recently arrived coolies who have not yet been able to find jobs. In one such house of refuge I saw more than a score of people crowded into a small room. Some of the newcomers lay asleep on the straw, while others were drinking tea or eating rice from large, tin utensils with the help of two wooden sticks which take the place of our tableware. The dexterity with which the Chinese use their chopsticks is truly astonishing. While even the larger lumps of rice eluded me, the Chinamen grasped with their chopsticks the smallest, individual grains, picking them out as accurately as a bird with his beak. The general appearance of such a house of temporary refuge makes a very unpleasant impression. Everything here is dirty, shabby, suffocating; the women are mixed with the men, the ill with the well. The entire Chinese population leads a precarious existence, slovenly and unhealthy. Chinese dwellings, always overcrowded, are contagious holes in which syphilis and smallpox rage. They have no conception of scientific hygiene. Anything and everything is eaten not only by those who have just arrived and are without jobs but also by the wealthy, for Chinese niggardliness surpasses all imagination.

In general, the Chinese are a peaceful and timid people, but amongst themselves they quarrel quite frequently and with equal frequency the quarrels end with a stabbing. They are also much given to stealing; for that reason in no other district do the police have as much work as they do in the Chinese quarter. And yet there is nothing more difficult than to maintain a close check on these people whose names are not established, are difficult to remember and to spell, and are almost all alike. Ah-Wongs, Ah-Mings, Jeh-Hangs are here numbered by the thousands, and each one taken separately resembles another as two drops of water. Each one has the same slanted eyes, the same long pigtail, flattened nose, and uniform dress —in a word, everything. Therefore, the apprehension of a

Chinese criminal is fraught with innumerable difficulties, especially since they all stand by one another and since the police here are not permitted to use violent methods on any individual, whether he be white, yellow, or black.

The morals of the California Chinese stand at a very low level. Among them every type of gambling flourishes, and especially prevalent is prostitution which is caused by the lack of women, for nine out of every ten inhabitants here are men.[1] Very few bring wives with them, and for that reason it so happens that when among ten Chinese occupying a dwelling there is but one woman, they all live together with her. I encountered such examples of polyandry quite frequently, particularly in the country. In the cities brothels tend to restrain it, but only to a certain degree, for the state government tolerates neither public houses nor the importation of prostitutes. These evidences of licentiousness make an unfavorable impression upon the white population of San Francisco, furnishing the anti-Chinese party here with still another argument against Chinese importation.

This slant-eyed population is brought to California by Chinese companies of which there are six in San Francisco closely connected with one another. I shall not cite their names as they would have no significance for my readers. These companies lease ships principally from the Pacific Steamship Company and load their decks with coolies from Canton, Shanghai, and other port cities. Indeed, the companies pay the coolies' passage and support them until they find work in San Francisco. This is one of the most abominable monopolies in the world, comparable in essence to slavery itself. Upon assuming the financial obligations for his passage, for the first necessities of life, for clothing, for agricultural or mining tools, and at the same time paying a commission for the job found for him, the impoverished coolie, even with such great frugality as only

[1] According to the U.S. Census of 1880 there were in California 71,244 Chinese men and 3,888 Chinese women.

a Chinaman is capable of, practically never succeeds in paying off his indebtedness to the company. Thus, the Chinese are simply slaves and all of their earnings are profit for the company. If we add that the company governs and judges them, that it requires them to make all of their purchases in company stores where credit is extended to them, we shall easily understand how the Chinese, especially the laborers, are rarely able to free themselves from the company's stranglehold.

Having set foot upon American soil, every coolie is theoretically free. He may at once sever all ties with the company and transform his relationship with the company to that of a debtor to a creditor. He could even refuse to pay his contracted debts or pay them in installments at his own discretion. Having found a job, he could refuse to buy in the Chinese company stores. In short, he could start life on his own. But this rarely happens. First of all, arriving in a strange country without funds, without a knowledge of the language, among a foreign and unsympathetic people, the Chinaman sees in the company his sole guardian and protector, in short, his Chinese camp. Further, accustomed in his homeland to the despotism of the mandarins, to the bamboo rod, shackles, and other similar tortures, he does not feel the full weight of the company's oppression. Finally, he does not realize that local laws more powerful than the company will in most instances take his side with little concern for the company.

Later, upon coming in contact with white people and becoming acquainted with the language, the laws, and with freedom, he becomes conscious of his position. But even then fear retains him in the company's hands. Local laws can, in fact, shield him from open violence, but they do not protect him from the stab of a knife by an unseen hand—a danger to which every coolie is subjected who would like to cut all ties which bind him to the company.

The American spirit of freedom would long ago have undermined and destroyed this disgraceful monopoly were it not for the fact that there are no legal grounds upon which to attack the companies. The law permits the existence of all kinds of associations and allows the extension of credit to the worker. The Chinese are not slaves—the relationship is one of debtor to creditor. The monopoly exists privately, not officially. In short, from a legal standpoint, the companies are all in order. But public opinion is so hostile to all of this and anti-Chinese agitation has assumed such proportions that it can definitely be said that the days of the companies' existence and of the importation of Chinese are already numbered.

Let us now look at the kind of work the Chinese perform in California. A single word describes it accurately—everything. A significant proportion of them has turned to agriculture. The whole of San Francisco is situated on arid dunes and sandy hills, and yet whoever goes to the outskirts of the city will perceive at the ends of unfinished streets, on the hills, valleys, and slopes, on the roadsides, in fact, everywhere, small vegetable gardens encircling the city with one belt of greenness. The antlike labor of the Chinese has transformed the sterile sand into the most fertile black earth. How and when this was accomplished they alone can tell, but suffice it to say that all the fruits and vegetables, raspberries and strawberries, under the care of Chinese gardeners grow to a fabulous size. I have seen strawberries as large as small pears, heads of cabbage four times the size of European ones, and pumpkins the size of our washtubs.

The Chinese hut stands in the center of the garden. At every hour of the day you will observe the long-pigtailed, yellow gardeners now digging, now spreading manure upon the soil, now watering the vegetables. In the interests of one's own appetite it is sometimes better not to see the latter, for I have myself had the experience of observing Chinamen pouring a liquid created from human excrement diluted with water between the leaves of heads of cabbage still unfolded. Yet the whole of San Francisco lives on the fruits and vegetables bought from the Chinese. Every morning you see their loaded wagons headed toward the markets in the center of town or stopping in front of private homes. It may even be said that in all of California this branch of industry has passed exclusively into the hands of the Chinese. Rarely, however, do they work on their own lands, but rather on leased lands. They do not purchase land as no Chinaman comes to California to settle here permanently, but to earn several hundred dollars and to return to spend his last years in his native land. In addition to attachment to his homeland and religious motives, the great disparity in the value of money in California and in China influences him to go back. In the Celestial Empire where money goes a long way, a few hundred dollars constitute a fortune that permits the owner to retire. "Here I am a nobody," said a Chinaman to me, "but in China, with three hundred dollars I am a big, very big gentleman."

A large number of Chinese likewise work for white farmers, especially in the orchards. In California, beginning with San Francisco and all the way down to San Diego in the south, the cultivation of grain plays a minor role, for with the exception of barley, the climate is too hot for rye, wheat, and others of our grains. Thus, the growing of grapes and oranges constitutes the principal branch of agriculture in the south, whereas fruit trees and hops predominate in the north. In the vicinity of San Francisco, and in Alameda County along the railroad, are whole orchards of apple trees, pear trees, peach trees, and almond trees; here and there fields comprising scores of acres are covered with red currant bushes; near Sacramento are extensive hop gardens. The work on these fields and in these orchards is done almost exclusively by hired Chinese. What is more, the farmers assert that such work as picking currants or hops, which requires minute care, cannot be done as well by whites. In addition, since white labor costs twice as much as that of the Chinese, it would not be at all profitable.

Because of the intense and widespread anti-Chinese agitation, an attempt has been made to replace the Chinese with children. Not to mention the fact that the children became ill with diarrhea from eating too much fruit while picking it, their labor proved so careless and so much fruit remained on the bushes that the owners suffered losses instead of making profits.

In the cultivation of grain in northern California the Chinese cannot compete with the whites. For plowing, harrowing, and harvesting, the white worker, being twice as strong, is much more in demand, for he works faster and with greater energy. Where there are no whites, however, Chinese are used even for these jobs.

In southern California where vineyards abound, there, too, very few Chinese are employed. In this area Mexican and Indian laborers who are as strong as the Yankees and who work as cheaply as the Chinese are easily obtainable. At Anaheim and in the vicinity of Los Angeles, Mexicans are engaged in cultivating the vineyards, while the picking and pressing of the grapes is done almost exclusively by the half-civilized Indians. The Indians provide additional profit to their employers by usually drinking up at the employers' all of their earnings. But the cultivation of vegetable gardens remains here, as everywhere else, in the hands of the Chinese. This is also true of all the household duties which in Europe are performed by women.

Among the squatters settled on government lands in the Coast Ranges, Santa Ana, San Bernardino, and Santa Lucia, I rarely encountered any Chinese. Life on the prairie and in the forests requires powerful, physical work of which the Chinaman is not capable. There is no law which would prevent them from staking out agricultural claims, settling on them, and after a certain lapse of time becoming proprietors; but this is never done by the Chinese. Life on the prairie may assure one a quiet life until death, but it does not provide cash income which is the main concern of the Chinese who are anxious to return to the Celestial Empire when they retire.

Another occupation of the rural population is the panning of gold. However, a much smaller number of Chinese is engaged in this occupation than in agriculture. Those engaged in it lead a life of hardship and very few of them acquire riches. The most famous gold mines have long since become the property of various wealthy companies, and it is, therefore, more difficult now than formerly to stake out a mining claim.

Formerly, when gold was discovered in a certain area, everyone coming into the area in search of gold staked out a claim on which he alone had the right to dig for gold. There was no written law barring Chinese from staking out mining claims, but such was, in fact, the unwritten law. The simple truth is that white prospectors could not endure the Chinese as neighbors and when the latter took up claims first, they were driven out with the aid of revolvers.[2] Now that all has passed into the hands of companies, now that the mines are simply large business enterprises, and now that new beds are rarely discovered on unoccupied government land; even the whites cannot locate claims, let alone the Chinese. Thus, the Chinese take over lands which have long since been abandoned either by individual miners or by companies. To be sure, their earnings must be very small, especially since the equipment they use for panning the gold is very primitive, not at all comparable to the equipment used by the rich and powerful companies.

I visited such Chinese mining settlements in the vicinity of Sebastopol. On the hillsides made ragged by previous miners and left torn, eroded, and pulverized, stand the miserable Chinese shacks in a deserted area. Their inhabitants depart for work at the break of day, take some meager supply of food with them and return only in the evening. A whole day's work

[2] Anti-Chinese agitation in California began in the mining camps. In 1850 the state legislature passed a law imposing a tax on foreign miners which was aimed at the Chinese and which was applied primarily against them.

brings them no more than 25 cents. This amount is so small that, if some company were to pan these hills, it would have to contribute from its own pocket at least two dollars daily to each of its workers. But a Chinaman eats most anything, drinks plain water, a handful of rice and a cup of tea is all he needs for the entire day. He therefore puts aside one cent at a time until he saves several hundred dollars or dies of exhaustion, as frequently happens.

I now turn to the urban population. The lot of the Chinese working in the cities is incomparably better than that of the miners. There is not a single type of work in which Chinese are not engaged. They are engaged in business; in the factories they serve as laborers; they are hired by the owners of handicraft shops; in the hotels they perform all the more menial tasks; in private homes they are responsible for orderliness and cleanliness; in restaurants and on the railroads they serve as cooks and waiters. Practically all of the laundries in town are in their hands and it must be admitted that they do the laundry neatly, quickly, and cheaply. They serve as nurses for children. In a private home the Chinaman fulfills all of the duties of a maid; he puts things away, sweeps the floors, makes the beds, cooks the meals, washes the dishes, and does the shopping in town; he is a quiet, sober, industrious, gentle, and obedient servant, and he costs much less than a white servant. Ever since the Chinese have become numerous in California, all prices have declined considerably. Everything from the cigars wrapped by Chinese hands to items of food—everything now costs less because the cost of labor is less. The salary of a Chinese servant will seem to Polish readers incredibly high, but I assure them that for California it is extremely low. It is only half the salary that is paid to white men, or even to white women. It is equivalent to fifteen or twenty dollars (thirty to forty rubles) per month. In the country a servant who does not live in can be employed for even less. A hired white man doing heavy work here generally receives two dollars daily.

A Chinaman, it is true, works more slowly and somewhat longer, but he is satisfied with a dollar per day. Thus, the Chinese have reduced the cost of labor and this has been followed by the reduction in price of all products and all the necessities of life.[3]

Taking these things into consideration, one might deem the Chinese a blessing to California were it not for the keen competition they create for the white working class, in some places even depriving the latter of the means of subsistence. A white man cannot work as cheaply as a Chinaman, for he requires more food and better living quarters instead of suffocating with a score of others in one hole. Finally, a white worker usually has a family, wife and children, whereas the Chinaman is alone. We shall get a clear picture of the position of the white working class in California when we consider the fact that 100,000 Chinese workers in California have deprived 100,000 white men of their jobs.[4] In the factories, in the workshops, on the railroads—everywhere the yellow men have forced out the white. The result is that if the Chinese are a blessing at all it is only for the wealthy classes who need servants and workers. In the conflict between capital and labor the Chinese have tipped the scales decisively in favor of capital. Even though white workers should offer their services more cheaply, some employers would prefer Chinese as workers who stand beyond the social pale, as workers who are not fellow citizens but half-slaves, quiet, obedient, and docile. In short, the Chinese are a threat to the working class, and as they become more numerous, they begin to create dangerous competition for small business, small farmers, and small industries.

A powerful anti-Chinese movement, involving thousands of

[3] A more serious cause of price reductions was the Panic of 1873, the effects of which reached California in 1876. Crop failures due to drought and a sharp decline in gold output also contributed to the economic difficulties in California.

[4] The figure 100,000 more accurately represents the number of Chinese in the country as a whole; about three-fourths of these resided in California.

people, has consequently grown up in San Francisco and all of California. Its object is to prevent the further importation of coolies into California and to drive out by whatever means possible those who are already here. To this movement belong people of all classes, but mainly workers who are often inclined to resort to violent measures. The menacing social disturbances which have occurred in the Eastern states have also been repeated here, but here they have had an anti-Chinese character.[5]

I was in San Francisco the night a massacre of the Chinese was expected. By the light streaming from burning buildings along the coast marched huge, menacing crowds of workers, carrying banners bearing such inscriptions as the following: "Self-preservation is the first law of nature." The stores were closed. The Chinese, fortified on their hills and armed with hand grenades, awaited the attack at any moment. Somehow the mob sensed that these people, though generally peaceful and timid, would defend themselves to the bitter end. From the other direction there appeared the local militia and citizens armed with heavy clubs and revolvers. Occasional shots echoed in the streets. Shooting occurred near the burning houses for the crowds would not permit the fires to be extinguished. The mass meeting of the workers was a stormy one, but there was no spilling of blood. It was decided to send a deputation to Congress and to boycott all Chinese products. The crowds then dispersed, but the fires lasted for several days. Order was at last restored, but only after the railroads, which had provoked the disturbances by reducing the wages of white men, agreed not to reduce wages and to dismiss their Chinese employees.

Besides this particular, threatening demonstration, I witnessed numerous meetings which were peaceful in character, but perhaps for that very reason more significant in the anti-Chinese movement. At present not only do the workers belong

[5] The continuing effects of the Panic of 1873 resulted in numerous strikes and riots in the Eastern states. In Califonia the anti-Chinese agitation was led in 1877 by Denis Kearney and the "Sand-Lotters."

to the movement, but also the majority of the journalists, ordinary citizens, merchants, craftsmen—in a word, the majority of the inhabitants of California. In joining the anti-Chinese movement, thoughtful citizens are motivated not only by personal reasons but also by their patriotism. Analyzing the problem objectively, one must admit that California perhaps loses more than it gains from the Chinese. They leave their jobs behind them—that is true—but they take their earnings with them out of the country. The Chinaman does not enrich local commerce and industry, for he buys exclusively in the Chinese stores. The Chinaman does not purchase land and does not settle on it, as does a farmer who then hands it down to his sons and grandsons. The Chinaman rarely accepts American citizenship even though the Burlingame Treaty concluded in 1868 gives the yellow races equal rights with others.[6] Finally, after the Chinaman has accumulated a certain amount of money, he leaves the country never to return to it again.

Furthermore, the Chinese have not only deprived the white working class of its means of livelihood, but they are also the cause of far greater injury to the country: they hinder the flow of white emigration from the Eastern states and from Europe, that emigration which would take up permanent residence, accept citizenship, and produce a population which would settle the country instead of exploiting it and then departing from it.[7]

One final point: by not accepting citizenship and by working as hired men, the Chinese are introducing a certain element of

---

[6] Although a few Chinese were naturalized both before and after the ratification of the Burlingame Treaty, the courts generally regarded them as ineligible for citizenship under the terms of the naturalization law of 1790 which reserved this privilege for "free white" persons. The Chinese Exclusion Act of 1882 specifically barred Chinese from acquiring citizenship.

[7] By their labor, especially on the railroads, the Chinese contributed greatly to the growth of the national economy. But anti-Chinese agitators commonly accused them of "exploiting" the country and of taking money out of it.

servitude into this society, perhaps the only one in the world in which equality is not a meaningless word. Whether a farmer, a craftsman, or someone else employing Chinese and becoming accustomed to the relationship of master to slave, he will find it difficult to forget this role in his relations with other white men. This is perhaps the most important aspect of the problem, for such a relationship is a sin against democratic morality on which all institutions and the very existence of this society has till now been based.

These are the reasons why most of the more intelligent people of California, as well as the workers, belong to the anti-Chinese party. If the state had the legal authority to deport the Chinese, this would have been done long ago. They are protected, however, by the Constitution of the United States. The state government has done all within its power. It has established the position of Commissioner of Immigration whose duties consist of watching over the Chinese companies, searching the ships importing coolies, barring diseased persons and prostitutes, and, frankly, restricting and making more difficult the importation of Chinese. Until recently the Commissioner of Immigration was our compatriot, Rudolf Korwin Piotrowski, to whom I am grateful for much of my information about the Chinese.[8] In addition, the municipal authorities have taken certain measures, the most important of which was the ban on the deportation of the corpses of deceased Chinese to the Celestial Empire. The Chinese are known to pay particular honor to their dead. According to their conceptions formulated on the basis of religion and age-long custom, a deceased person should be buried within the limits of the

[8] Rudolf Korwin Piotrowski (1814–1883) came to the United States in 1848 and for thirty years worked in gold and silver mines. He used his first earnings to purchase a large tract of land not far from San Francisco. Here he founded the colony of Sebastopol, so named for the defeat suffered by Russia in the Crimean War. For his services to the Union cause during the Civil War, he was rewarded by the governor of California with the position of Commissioner of Immigration. Piotrowski became the prototype for Zagloba in Sienkiewicz's *With Fire and Sword*.

Celestial Empire to pass to Nirvana and to rest in peace. Thus, year after year the same ships that imported the living, exported the dead. Now the deportation of the dead has been forbidden once and for all. This regulation has the effect of restraining the Chinese in China from departing for the country of the "barbarians" and inducing the California Chinese to return to their native land as soon as possible.

Such is the status of the Chinese question in California. It has already reached the Congress in Washington where it will no doubt cause much trouble for it will involve certain changes, or at least interpretations, of the Constitution. The Constitution clearly allows all foreigners to enter the United States, to become naturalized or not, to engage in business, or to become laborers—in short, to do whatever they please. From a legal point of view, the Chinese have the Constitution on their side. On the other hand, the dangers to which the states lying on the Pacific Ocean may in time be exposed as a result of Chinese immigration—dangers which are already very evident in California and imminent in the Washington Territory, Oregon, Arizona, and Nevada—will no doubt weigh heavily on the minds of those who have the power to alter the Constitution.

There is no doubt that the Chinese question could in time cause such discord as to threaten the unity between the East and the West as was recently caused between the North and the South over the question of slavery. Such is not yet the case. Today it is scarcely a small dark cloud on the fair horizon of the Union. However, precaution calls for early insurance against storm and lightning. Apparently, the opponents of the Chinese in California have succeeded in bringing the question to the attention of President Hayes. How Congress will deal with it we shall know in the near future.[9]

[9] The response of Congress was to pass a series of Chinese Exclusion Laws, beginning with the act of May 6, 1882.

Letter XIII

POLISH COMMUNITIES IN AMERICA

MY task is to give the readers a report on my visit to America, but the diverse manifestations of human life in this land make this no easy assignment. Indeed, should I be asked what kind of nation inhabits this country whose northern frontiers slumber under eternal snows and whose southern regions rustle with palm forests, my answer would be: there you will find not one nation but many nations—in fact, all the races of mankind. The Aryan, the Semite, the prognathic Negro, the son of the Celestial Empire with his slant eyes and long pigtail, and finally the original owner of these lands, the proud, redskinned warrior—all of them live in the same climate, under the same skies, frequently side by side. There the Caucasian race has sent representatives of all of its branches and nationalities, beginning with the Greeks and ending with the Scots and the Irish.

To answer the question of how these national groups live together and what institutions were responsible for uniting them into a single political entity, I should have to follow in the footsteps of Alexis de Tocqueville and write an exhaustive treatise on American social institutions. For this I lack both talent and time. Therefore, I shall reply only with this generalization: in the United States there has been no attempt to assimilate or to force allegiance upon anyone, and therein lies the secret of the harmony in which the various elements live. This enigma can be explained by the single word "freedom" —a word which in Europe represents only an idea and a claim, but in the United States a practical reality.

It is the social, political, and religious freedom, the complete decentralization that stems from it, the loose political ties and unlimited respect for the individual which create the above-mentioned diversities and prevent the formation of a uniform national character. The relationship of the state to its citizens, the federal Constitution, the laws of the individual states, counties, and cities, the variety of social organizations, and a host of other matters—all of these are subjects too rich and too abundant for superficial treatment. Since it is impossible to follow several roads simultaneously without getting lost, I have selected the one that seemed to me the most interesting: the Poles and the Polish settlements in the United States.

On the ships sailing between Hamburg and New York there is a place even for the poorest passengers known as the steerage. On the English and French ships these accommodations are passable, but on the German vessels they are much inferior. Usually the steerage consists of a large dark room where the light of day enters not through windows opening along the deck, but through ordinary portholes in the ship's side. There are no cabins; the beds are attached directly to the wall; only a corner is assigned to the women and set off by a railing. When the sea is rough, the waves strike noisily against the portholes and fill the room with an ominous green light. Here the odors of the kitchen and the exhalations of human beings are mingled with the strong smell of ocean spray, tar, and wet rope. The air is heavy and damp and the room is dark. In the evenings lamps cast a dim light; glasses and tin utensils upon the tables tinkle from the rocking of the boat; the beams squeak; and from above are heard the angry shouting of the sailors and the shrill sounds of the petty officers' whistles. In such rooms as this the emigrants travel.

On small ships where the fares are lowest of all, one can obtain accommodations of this sort for some twenty dollars from Hamburg to New York, Boston, Baltimore, or other American ports. But this is a miserable and exhausting mode of travel. To every Pole journeying comfortably in first class I should recommend that out of curiosity he visit the steerage, especially during a stormy night when gigantic masses of water are pouring over the decks, when wind is tossing the ship, and when air, water, and darkness seem blended in a single chaos. On how many ships will the traveler, before his eyes become accustomed to the gloom, hear words whispered by frightened voices and by shapes crouched in corners—words in our native tongue: "We seek refuge in Your protection, O Holy Mother of God!"

When asked "Are you from Poland?" these dark figures spring forward as if propelled by some mysterious force. They surround the traveler on all sides and their voices, agitated and trembling with tears, bombard him with questions.

"Sir! Most illustrious sir! We come from Poland. And you, too, sir?"

When asked from what part of Poland, there is a chorus of replies: "From under the yoke of the Prussian, of the Austrian, of the Muscovite." [1]

These are men of our own blood, bone of our bones— these are our Mazurians, Poznanians, and Silesians. They are on their way . . . on their way to what destination?

"To Hamerika!" replies a Mazurian.

"To the Freeland," explains a Silesian.

"And for what purpose?"

"In search of bread and freedom which we did not have back home."

Soon, however, they begin to complain, for they are lonely for the thatched cottages in which they were born. They were persuaded to undertake the journey by some passenger agent or other who receives a fixed commission per head. But they did not know that it would be like this, that such oceans and

---

[1] The word *Moskale*, translated here as "Muscovites," is an old Polish and Ukrainian term for the inhabitants of the Grand Duchy of Muscovy. Still used today with reference to the Russians, it carries the connotation that Russians are hated eastern barbarians.

stormy seas had to be crossed, that they would be so herded into the steerage. Nor did they realize that there would be no one with whom they could speak in the "Catholic" language.[2] What will now become of them they did not know. They are at God's mercy like the sea gulls floating in the air in the wake of the ship. Everything here is strange to them—the mountainous waves, the ship itself, even its crew. The roar of the propeller and the nocturnal flapping of the sails whipped by the wind fill them with a superstitious fear. Most of all, however, they are frightened by the endlessness of the ocean. They do not know what to make of all that surrounds them. They are oppressed by the unknown. Yet they endure all these strange elements, the weariness, tediousness, scornful abuse, discomforts, unfamiliar impressions, and fears by their inexhaustible, stolid, humble, peasant patience. They are sustained by their faith in St. Mary of Czestochowa with her somber face and radiant crown who is their guiding star in the midst of these stormy nights and boundless waters.[3]

Meanwhile, the days and nights pass. The ship with its prow pointed westward laboriously climbs wave after wave. It moves forward until at last, after a score of days or more, the land for which they had been heading begins to appear on the horizon as though emerging from the sea. The shores can now be seen ever more clearly. The quarantine house on Sandy Hook looms above the waves; further on, the enormous estuary of the East River can be perceived; still further, forests of masts, and beyond them a conglomeration of roofs, factory chimneys, and steeples. Over all of this rise columns of smoke unraveling in downy wisps at their summits. This is New York and its environs.

Our voyagers throng on deck, excited and happy. Whoever has crossed the ocean will easily comprehend their joy at the

---

[2] In many parts of Poland, religion was the criterion for determining nationality. If a person was Catholic in religion, he was regarded as a Pole.

[3] Poles make annual pilgrimages to the famous shrine of St. Mary at Czestochowa.

sight of land. Thus it seems to them that God has taken mercy
upon them as upon some caravan lost in the desert, and having
led them safely across the ocean, has shown them the promised
land. Having grown accustomed to the silence and monotonous
emptiness of the sea, they are now surrounded by the hum
and noise of seething life. The small boat of the pilot rushes
over the waves towards the ship with the swiftness of a swallow
and it is followed by another from the quarantine office. The
propeller begins to churn the water, pushing the ship first
backward, then forward. You can hear the clanging of the unwinding winches, the shouting, calling, and cursing of the
sailors. Another hour goes by. The ship eases its way into the
narrow dock and disgorges its passengers. They have arrived!
Through the large customs house located on the wharves they
walk out into the street. And now what?

Matthew looks at Bartholomew, Bartholomew at Francis.
What to do next? To whom should they turn? Where should
they go? The ship had literally thrown them out on the street
and that was the end. The agent in Hamburg had, of course,
promised them that when they arrived there would be someone waiting for them, but that "someone" existed only in the
words of the agent. The agent and the shipping company have
fulfilled their obligations and owe the immigrants nothing more.
The former had packed them into the steerage and the latter
had transported them across the ocean. They may now do
whatever they please. They have arrived in a metropolis. An
unfamiliar life teems about them, elevated trains whistle above
their heads, buses and carriages crisscross one another, crowds
of white and colored persons hurry about with feverish speed
in all directions, hucksters of every variety bellow as though
possessed by the devil. And they—those peasants of ours—
in the midst of this hubbub, splendor, and magnificence, feel
even more lonely and forsaken than on the ocean wastes.
Again they are at God's mercy. They have no conception of
how much more they must endure before they encounter some

Polish priest who will tell them which way to turn, where to secure employment, where to find a crust of bread. Even before this, greedy proprietors of boarding houses located close to the port will have squeezed the last penny out of them. They will have suffered cold in the filthy basements of various lodgings. Many a drunken Irishman, surprised at the size and strength of the Mazurian fist and anxious to test its power, will have blackened the eyes of these poor souls who dare not even defend themselves for fear of striking a "gentleman."

Their lot is a severe and terrifying one and whoever would depict it accurately would create an epic of human misery.[4] To write or to hear of the days without a morsel of bread when hunger tears one's insides with an iron hand, of the nights spent on the docks under the open heavens, and of the dreams interrupted by the humming of mosquitoes in summer or the howling of the wind in winter, is easier than to feel or to experience these things yourself. Is there anyone whose hand is not against them? Their early history is a tale of misery, loneliness, painful despair, and humiliation. Do not think, however, that I am narrating the history of some particular group of Polish immigrants. Not at all! Almost a hundred thousand peasants sent by our land across the ocean have gone through such a Dantean inferno—in search of a better life. The Polish immigrants in America have nothing in common with those living in France or in Switzerland. The latter are political exiles, expelled by revolutionary storms. In America there are practically no Polish political *émigrés*. They are primarily peasants and workers who have come in quest of bread. Thus you will easily understand that in a country inhabited by a people who are not at all sentimental, but rather energetic, industrious, and whose competition it is difficult to survive, the fate of these newcomers, poorly educated, unfamiliar with

[4] Sienkiewicz was so attracted by this theme that he himself attempted to depict the plight of peasant immigrants in his intensely moving short story, "In Search of Bread."

American conditions, ignorant of the language, uncertain how to proceed, must truly be lamentable.

America or, strictly speaking, the United States, is not a land lacking in hospitality. These coarse Yankee democrats, eternally occupied with business, are at heart more generous than is superficially apparent. This is a country of simple people with simple feelings. A healthy young man will almost invariably hear one piece of advice: "Help yourself!" And if he does not know how to follow this advice, he may even die of starvation. On the other hand, a man who is old and infirm, a woman, or a child, receive more assistance in the United States than anywhere else. This, however, is private assistance which would be wholly inadequate in the case of immigrants. Yet if the government is to provide assistance, it must be in the interest of the government to do so. Thus, for example, while the influx of Chinese is dangerous to the young republic, that of white immigrants is beneficial. The latter become citizens, they settle on the land and transform the prairie into arable fields, they found towns, establish new trade relations, and contribute to economic expansion. It is, therefore, in the interest of the Union to encourage European immigration.

That is the purpose of the immigrant homes in New York where the new arrivals can find shelter, food, and instruction in the English language and in some handicraft. The work done by the immigrants in these houses covers the cost of their maintenance. After a certain period when the immigrant is prepared for the struggle with life, he leaves the establishment and begins to work on his own.

But such institutions, giving creditable evidence of the wisdom and generosity of the Americans, are entirely inadequate. To begin with, these institutions cannot accommodate even half the immigrants who need shelter. Secondly, only trades are taught in them while many immigrants, especially the Poles, yearn for the soil. Furthermore, these establishments are a form of guardianship, in fact, regular workhouses. Men, women, and children work there separately, according to the nature of their skills; thus, families cannot remain together. For these reasons and because of the aversion of our peasants to all similar institutions such as hospitals, workhouses, and the like, very few of them take advantage of the immigrant houses.

But the main reason is that our peasants know nothing of the existence of these institutions. I happened to meet some Poles who had already been living in the United States for several years and who learned of the existence of immigrant workhouses only when, in conversation, the expression fell from my lips. Then, too, the immigrant houses do not have their own agents, as do the hotels, to hunt out the new arrivals in the port.

And yet, is there nothing that our peasants bring to the New World that might guarantee them a peaceful life and a secure livelihood? Of course there is! They bring with them the habit of being content with little, true peasant endurance, patience, and an iron constitution. A German or French immigrant overcomes only with difficulty those hardships and inconveniences to which our peasant adjusts himself with ease, accustomed as he is to walking barefoot, eating whatever is at hand, and sleeping under any kind of roof. He does not even comprehend the need for various comforts that the German and French immigrant regard as necessities of life. Sun does not burn him; rain does not harm him; snow and wind do not chill him. In cold Wisconsin and Minnesota he is not perturbed by the snow drifts; in semitropical Texas, once he throws off the fever, he works in the scorching heat like a Negro. Perhaps he may be less skillful than others, but he has greater endurance and is a humble and quiet worker.

In a country where areas as vast as the German Empire and France combined still stand vacant, where limitless mineral and agricultural resources merely await exploitation by human hands, where labor is as costly as it is hard to find, our settlers

should be assured of success. Unfortunately, they often find
the road to success as agonizing as the road to the Cross.
Whereas the Atlantic states are practically overpopulated, the
Western states, i.e., those on the other side of the Mississippi,
are still uninhabited. Here there would be room for the population of the whole of central Europe and from the agricultural
and mineral wealth another such civilization could be created.
The land here belongs to no one. Gradually an agricultural
population is beginning to flow into the area just west of
Chicago, but tremendous empty regions still stretch out in
front of those settling on the frontiers. On these frontiers
everyone may become a landowner. But our peasant undergoes
much suffering before he understands the advice tossed at him
so casually in the East: "Go to the Far West and there you
will find land and work."

Aside from the fact that one must know of the existence
of the Far West in order to go there—and our newly arrived
immigrant has no such knowledge—getting there is not easy.
The railroad fare alone from New York to Chicago, even by
immigrant coach, costs more than the passage from Hamburg
to New York. Once having reached the unoccupied land, the
peasant needs a plow, ax, scythe, wagon, horse, mule, gun to
protect him from wild animals, seed for sowing—in short, a
complete supply of settler's effects. But our peasant, whose last
penny was squeezed from him in New York, either cannot
get to the Far West, or if he gets there, finds himself solitary
and defenseless in the midst of a wilderness. The story of leaves
buffeted by a storm begins to assume a tragic aspect. And yet
under threat of death by starvation most of the immigrants
must leave the overpopulated Atlantic seaboard and move into
the interior of the country. There, not only is land more
easily secured, but more hands are needed and jobs are readily
available. This journey is a difficult one, however.

Nowadays the newcomer is better off than formerly. Polish
newspapers are now published in the United States that can

give publicity to adversity. Organizations exist which have relief funds at their disposal for unexpected disasters. But even today success comes slowly. Before the immigrant is able to earn a decent livelihood, he frequently experiences pain and bitter tears. Many leaves will be lost in the storm before the remainder come to rest around some Polish church on the remote prairies of Wisconsin, Illinois, Texas, or Nebraska.

As I have indicated, nearly everyone undergoes a similar series of experiences. There is a saying in the United States that he who comes here is critical during the first year, begins to understand the country in the second year, and falls in love with it during the third year. I have myself experienced the truth of this saying. As for the Poles who have long resided in the United States, I have only this comment: to an immigrant living in France or in Switzerland you may say what you please about these countries, but it would be dangerous to speak disparagingly of the United States to any Pole residing here. He does not cease to love his former fatherland, but after Poland he loves most the United States.

There is nothing strange about this. A Pole in France remains always an immigrant, while this vast land recognizes him immediately as her own. The new arrival appears before a federal judge and declares that he wishes to become a citizen of the Union. The reply is short and always the same: "All right!" The judge reads a declaration on the strength of which the newcomer renounces his former allegiance and any noble privileges he may have possessed—and the whole affair is finished. From this moment forward he is under the protection of the Star-Spangled Banner; he is now at home; he is no longer in a foreign country, but in his own. After five years he has the right to vote, to become a congressman, a senator, a cabinet minister; in short, he possesses the same rights and privileges as all other American citizens. To be sure, whoever is not born on American soil cannot become the President of the Union. I can assure you, however, that our ordinary Matthew or

Bartholomew has few ambitions in this direction. Otherwise, he enjoys full rights.

Other lands grant only asylum; this land recognizes the immigrant as a son and grants him rights. This is the other side of the coin on which I had first depicted the misery of the immigrants. Whoever has once overcome this misery and has by superhuman effort succeeded in getting out of the overcrowded port cities and settled on a farm or in a town of the Far West will find his lot much easier. Many of the newcomers, especially those of the working class, settle in growing communities where increasing human needs and the resulting industry require many hands.

Since the cities along the shores of the Great Lakes were undergoing industrial expansion and needed workers, it was principally here that Polish laborers settled. Buffalo, Detroit, Chicago, and Milwaukee are full of them. The chief Polish center is Chicago, situated in the state of Illinois on enormous Lake Michigan. In this city of almost a half-million inhabitants there are said to be about 20,000 of our compatriots. The small area occupied by them in the city—a sector sneeringly referred to by the Germans as *Polakei* [5]—leads me to think that this figure is somewhat exaggerated. Most Poles reside along Milwaukee Avenue where they have purchased homes. When I arrived in Chicago at daybreak and visited this part of the city, it seemed at times as though I were in Poland. The morning sun rising from the waters of Lake Michigan illuminated Polish inscriptions and names on the buildings. Only the innumerable telegraph wires and posts—a sight unfamiliar in Europe—and the limitless lake spoiled the illusion. Meanwhile the sun climbed steadily higher. Doors and windows began to open and the illusion was restored for the first words I heard were uttered in Polish. A few minutes later I caught sight of the church of St. Stanislaw Kostka at the corner of Noble and Bradley Streets. About eight o'clock in the morning

[5] *Polackei* is a derogatory German term for Poland.

flocks of children began to swarm here on the way to the school maintained by the priests and situated beside the church. Their childish chirping made a strange impression upon me for despite the fact that these children were studying in a Polish school an English influence was clearly perceptible in their speech.

After the children disappeared behind the school doors, I strolled along further to see the other church between Milwaukee Avenue and Division Street. It was, in a sense, only a branch of the first church, which had proved inadequate for the constantly increasing number of Poles. Unfortunately the new structure was soon seized for nonpayment of its debts.

The Poles of Chicago are united through Polish societies whose aims are to assist new arrivals, to protect their members from foreign influences, and to preserve their national spirit. There are nine such societies, but seven of these are purely religious in character. The two secular organizations are known as the "Polish Village" and the "Kosciuszko Society." Unfortunately, all of these groups do not always work together, following, in this respect, the example of their newspapers, the *Polish Catholic Gazette* and the *Chicago Polish Gazette*. At election time this disunity is harmful to Polish candidates and diminishes the influence that the Poles in Illinois might have in view of their numbers.

Another center where numerous Poles have congregated is Milwaukee, Wisconsin, on the shores of Lake Michigan. The number of Poles residing here is supposed to equal that of Chicago. Being an older settlement, the Poles of Milwaukee are better off than those living in other towns. They have both an elementary and secondary school. All of their organizations are associated with the Church.

Likewise in Wisconsin is situated the town of Northeim, a Polish colony in the midst of immense forests which have scarcely been cleared. The land occupied by this colony was acquired very cheaply or without charge. Later, when commerce, industry, and agriculture began to prosper in the region, the price of land rose rapidly, with the result that the settlers found themselves in possession of very valuable properties. The peasant population here remains under the control of the Church which also conducts the school attended by ninety students. Northeim, together with the neighboring settlement at Manitowoc, constitute a single parish. At Manitowoc there is a Polish academy supported by the state.

In New York City there are about eight thousand Poles. They used to have their own newspaper, the New York *Courier*, which recently ceased publication. In addition, Poles in varying numbers reside in all of the larger cities. If they belong primarily to the intelligentsia, they combine in secular societies; if they are peasants and laborers, they unite in church-parish organizations.

Exclusively Polish settlements are to be found at Radom, Illinois; Krakow, Missouri; Polonia, Wisconsin; and Panna Maria, Texas.[6] These are small agricultural towns of several hundred families, possessing their own schools, churches, and local government in the American pattern. Their character is so typically Polish that they scarcely differ from similar towns in Poland itself. Even Jews are to be found in these communities, but not in the same numbers as in Poland, for here they are attracted to the large commercial centers.

The Polish Jews whom I met in America were rather numerous in the large towns and were generally quite wealthy. Americans call all newcomers "greenhorns" and exploit them at every opportunity. But our Polish Jew, thanks to his innate talent for business and to his enterprise, will arrive in New York on Sunday, let us say, open a small business on Monday, and already by Tuesday he will lead into the field the most cunning American who tries to cheat him. Here the scythe strikes a stone, and for this reason the designation "Polish Jew" arouses justifiable wariness among American profiteers.

[6] Panna Maria, Texas, is the oldest Polish settlement in the United States.

Because of their acuteness, knowledge of the German language, and business initiative, our Polish Jews fare rather well in the United States and do not suffer the hardships of our peasants. At the recently discovered gold mines where adventurers quickly congregate, where the knife, the revolver, and the terrifying lynch law still prevail, where an American merchant hesitates to open shop out of fear both for his merchandise and his life, the first stores are generally established by our Jews. By their courtesy, kind words, and, above all, extension of credit, they win the favor of the most dangerous adventurers and regulators. And once having the revolvers of these desperadoes on their side, the storekeepers conduct their affairs with complete safety. Profits are enormous in such localities because the miners pay for their goods with unweighed gold dust instead of with money. I saw our Jews operating stores under the conditions I have just described at Deadwood, Dakota; Darwin, California; and Virginia City, Nevada. Perhaps within a few years their proprietors will become millionaires.

When I consider the status of the Jewish population in the United States, I come to the conclusion that while peasant emigration is perilous both to the mother country and the peasant himself, the emigration of the Jews is beneficial to them. In Polish villages there are hundreds of Jewish families who do not possess the means of livelihood and are engaged only in the harmful, unproductive tasks of middlemen. In the United States where willing hands and an enterprising head can make one wealthy, where many branches of commerce have not yet been developed, wide possibilities for prosperity and profits would open to them.

I cannot devote any more time to this subject and I return to the Polish settlements. Such Polish colonies as Radom and Panna Maria are not purely commercial towns. Their inhabitants occupy themselves chiefly with cattle raising and agriculture. In Illinois, Wisconsin, and Indiana they plant potatoes and sow wheat as in Poland; in hot Texas, they grow corn and even cotton. Although their condition is far from opulent, in fact, rather modest, they are able to satisfy their needs and their earnings are sufficient to build churches, establish schools, and defray municipal expenditures. The older settlers, if they are thrifty, are comparatively well off. A certain degree of prosperity is achieved most easily by those who are married, especially those having many children, for in the United States where labor is costly, children are a real blessing for the settler.

In the cities a considerable portion of the Polish population are workers who live on daily wages earned in the factories. They are much poorer than the American, German, English, or Scottish workers. When there is prosperity in the United States, however, they earn a better livelihood than they knew in Poland, and the more thrifty among them even achieve some measure of security. In many Polish workers' homes I saw floors completely covered with carpeting as is the American fashion. In the so-called "parlor" or drawing room, there was no shortage of rocking chairs; at dinner beefsteak or meat pudding and beer were served.

I must always warn, however, that I am writing only of those who had the necessary health and strength of character to overcome the hardships of the first days. On the other hand, even the more fortunate lose their jobs and find themselves in desperate circumstances during periods of economic depression. This frequently results in new migrations into regions where business is better, or the movement of city dwellers to rural settlements. During my sojourn in the States two new Polish settlements arose in this manner: New Posen in Nebraska and Warren Hoino in Arkansas. Established under unfavorable circumstances, the latter is not expected to survive for long.

From what I have said thus far, we see that Poles are scattered throughout the whole United States from the Atlantic Ocean to the Pacific and from the Gulf of Mexico to the St.

Lawrence River—in other words, over a territory as vast as the whole of Europe. They are linked together through their societies, their newspapers, and the publications of the Polish bookstores in Chicago, Milwaukee, and Detroit.

The main force, however, which maintains some degree of moral unity among the Poles is the Church and the Polish priests. The Church gathers around itself the leading workers or peasants and is constantly creating new parishes. The priest marries, baptizes, and buries, but above all, teaches. Not only do these functions provide a source of income for the priest, but they also enable him to wield political influence for he controls the votes of his flock. That such a state of affairs may be displeasing to some does not prevent its existence. It is even possible that this preponderance of purely clerical influence engenders a certain exclusiveness and diminishes the size of the Polish-American community by excluding, for example, the Protestants of whom there are many among the Prussian Silesians and Mazurians. On the other hand, one must admit that the Church brings together the Polish masses, creates from them a social entity, does not allow them to become scattered and to disappear unnoticed among foreign elements; and, finally, the Church provides the only refuge for those new arrivals whose fate I described at the beginning of this sketch.

In the founding of new settlements the clergy play a very important role. It frequently happens, especially in the larger American cities, that the workers suddenly display a desire to exchange their life in the factories for the plow and the pioneer's ax. The reason for this is economic depression with its accompanying unemployment. Although difficult at first, the settler's life is more secure than that of a laborer. He can stake out a land claim with payment over a period of ten years at $1.50 per acre,[7] or acquire it likewise on installment

[7] See Letter IV, footnote 4.

payments from the railroad. After surviving the initial hardships, the settler eventually comes to possess his own property and to earn a decent livelihood.

But, of course, a solitary individual cannot settle on the prairie far from other people. Cooperative action is necessary here. A sizable group of people must be ready to set out together and to work as a unit. To provide unity of action, leadership is necessary. Families that intend to establish a settlement usually select one or more representatives who go out in advance to view the land. These men negotiate contracts with the railroad companies, endeavor to secure the best possible terms, and, finally, subdivide the acquired territories. In settling on government lands such intermediaries are not so necessary, for government land actually belongs to no one and legally may be settled upon without previous agreements with anyone. Once the $1.50 per acre is paid in the nearest land office, or even after the first installment is paid, the land is regarded as private property. Thus, when occupying land, it is necessary simply to make sure that someone else does not already have a claim to it—otherwise no difficulties exist. But settlers usually prefer lands belonging to railroad companies since locations along railroad lines have greater prospects of development in the future. In such instances, the role of the emissaries is exceptionally important, for everything depends on the kind of terms that are included in the contract with the railroad management. For example, the management may promise a new station to the growing colony, it may sell the land at a higher or lower price, it may spread out the payments over a very long period—all of this depends on the skill of the emissaries as negotiators.

Almost without exception priests serve as such envoys for our colonists, and were it not for them, settlements like Radom, Czestochowa, and others would never have arisen, for peasants would not know how to handle these matters. The clerical plenipotentiary has this further advantage over the secular that the latter might be bribed into accepting the worst possible land and the least desirable terms for the settlers and thereupon wash his hands of the whole affair and depart; conversely, the priest usually remains with the settlement, becomes its father-confessor, and is thus directly affected by the fate of the colony. This is entirely natural and I had an opportunity to be convinced of this superiority of the clerical leaders over the secular during my sojourn in the United States.

Two new Polish settlements were being founded at that time. A secular leader bought land in Arkansas, named the prospective colony Warren Hoino, and by protraying it in truly golden colors, succeeded in assembling over a hundred families. The whole enterprise was strongly supported by Dyniewicz's *Chicago Polish Gazette*, a bitter rival of the *Polish Catholic Gazette*, edited by the clergy. The latter, or rather its partisans, decided to oppose the venture, fearing that the *Chicago Polish Gazette* might gain in popular favor by backing so important an undertaking. On their initiative the proposal was made to establish simultaneously another Polish colony in Nebraska to be called New Posen. Since interested participants were not lacking, lands were soon bought and New Posen passed from the realm of fancy to that of reality.

Each newspaper now began to praise its own colony and could not find enough derogatory terms to describe the settlement of its rival. New Posen was accused of being situated in a treeless region which lacked materials for building homes and which was devasted from time to time by locusts. There was some truth in this accusation. Nebraska is one gigantic prairie where even to this day the Pawnee Indians roam and where trees are found only along the Platte River and its tributaries. The locust does, indeed, frequently lay waste to this remarkable prairie. On the other hand, the fertility of the virgin soil rewards the settlers for all their misfortunes. In refuting the accusations the *Catholic Gazette* stated that the lands in

Arkansas were covered with oaks whose clearance might take so long that the settlers would first die of starvation. It was further alleged that the terms of the contract were unfavorable, that the purchased territories had only a thin layer of black earth, and, finally, that the Arkansas River annually flooded the whole region, causing deadly fevers and other diseases which decimated the population. Both sides sent out commissions to determine the true state of affairs, but being highly partisan, these commissions declared pro and con according to the views of each group.

In the end, the situation in Warren Hoino took a turn for the worse. Arkansas is, indeed, famed for the fertility of its soil, and the abundance of its forests is an added attraction for any colony. Nor is its climate as unhealthy, for example, as that of Texas. Yet I came to the conclusion that, despite these favorable attributes, the colony founded there had no real future. Apparently the land was purchased rashly, without foresight, and subdivided so as to please various private interests; and even the administration of the funds was not above reproach. Most of the settlers who had already gone to Warren Hoino returned posthaste, raising a cry that they had been duped. Others, having spent all of their money for the journey and not wishing to remain in the colony, found themselves in truly desperate straits. The expedition to Warren Hoino was termed an expedition to Siberia. In short, it appears that much blame may be attached to the secular promoters of the new colony. Meanwhile New Posen, which at first glance did not appear to have as many possibilities for successful development, was established from the very beginning on a firm foundation and as far as I know, its prospects for the future are improving daily.[8]

I have devoted a few lines to the history of these two colonies

---

[8] Both communities still exist and have retained some of their Polish character. Their names, however, have been changed: Warren Hoino is today called Marche and New Posen is known as Farwell.

in order to give my readers an example of the manner in which new colonies are founded and, at the same time, to show the importance of the role and activity of the Polish priests in the United States. The care and conscientiousness with which the New Posen affair was conducted may undoubtedly be attributed to the intention of the clerical negotiators to settle in the colony and create a parish. Thus, whatever would concern New Posen would concern them, and their own future success would depend upon that of the colony. I do not mean to imply that personal interests alone gave assurance of the honesty of their actions; but it is an axiom that the general interest is always and everywhere the more vigorously defended the more closely and directly it is tied to the personal interests of those at the helm.

From what I have said thus far it is clear that the clergy are largely responsible for such organization as exists among the Poles residing in America. To be sure, the existing organization is insufficient. Colonies are scattered throughout the breadth of the United States and know very little about each other. The newspapers published in Chicago lack news reports from the multitude of Polish colonies, making it difficult to compile any accurate statistical data. Truthfully speaking, no one knows exactly how many Poles there are in the United States. The figures cited in the Polish press are not based on any accurate calculation; they are always exaggerated, for the editors wish to give the impression that their newspapers are widely read and are the organs of large political parties. On the one hand, this brings them paid commercial advertisements, the main source of their income; on the other, it gives them a certain political importance during elections.

Actually, in a city like Chicago, Milwaukee, or Detroit, where the Polish population is densely settled, it is no small matter for a candidate to have the votes of this group behind him. Their votes alone cannot place a candidate in office; but if it is a question of deciding between a Republican and a Democrat, they may tip the scales in favor of one or the other. Of course, a candidate wishing to obtain the votes of a particular national group does not appeal to its individual members, but to its newspaper, bestowing various favors or promising benefits commensurate with the number of votes. This is the reason why all newspapers exaggerate the number of their subscribers and of their compatriots. The figures which appear in the Polish-American press and which indicate the Polish population to be two hundred, three hundred, or even five hundred thousand have no relationship to truth.[9] Yet no one is concerned with verifying these statistics and no one has any conception, therefore, what influence the Poles in the United States might wield, providing they worked together.

The task of organizing the Poles as a group still leaves much to be desired. But to bring all the Poles together into a single territory or state and to create a strong social entity would be out of the question. Such *pia desideria*[10] have entered the heads of Poles—but not those living in the United States. The latter realize that these idealistic objectives would inevitably be shattered against practical considerations. Only a few new religious sects which inspire fanaticism can unite their coreligionists in the manner that Brigham Young united the Mormons. During my sojourn in the States the suggestion was made amongst the Poles of establishing a *sejm*[11] and a senate to provide unity in their public life—but after closer examination even this proposal proved impractical.

Above and beyond their religious and social functions, the clergy are principally concerned with preserving Polish national

[9] The difficulty of arriving at accurate figures stems from the fact that in the U.S. Census Poles were listed not as Poles but as subjects of Germany, Austria, or Russia, the three powers among whom the Polish state had been partitioned.
[10] Objects of one's fond affections.
[11] The lower house of the Polish parliament.

identity. This is likewise the objective of Polish newspapers, secular societies, and veterans' groups—in short, of all Polish institutions in America.[12]

Unfortunately, however, all their efforts are in vain. In my opinion, despite the most noble endeavors on the part of their leaders, American Poles will sooner or later become denationalized and be completely assimilated by the Americans. Stronger elements than the Polish have been unable to resist the influence of the Anglo-Saxon language and civilization. No one attempts to Americanize you or to force anything upon you. Each national group is free to set up newspapers, schools, and even an army. In the latter case the government intercedes only to the extent of furnishing the rifles.

And yet American influence is irresistible. Foreigners who come to America and who obtain citizenship live under American laws, take part in public life, and sooner or later transform themselves into Americans in spirit. After that, it is only a matter of time before the acceptance of the English language becomes an inexorable necessity. All of the national groups living side by side must, of course, use a common language; otherwise, a Pole in Haywood would never be able to understand his Portuguese neighbor. Then, too, English is the common social, commercial, and official language. In addition, Poles, Italians, Czechs, Spaniards, etc., who come to the United States do not have in their tongues the numerous expressions which serve to define purely local American concepts, relationships, and conditions. English expressions soon

[12] Although the Poles failed to preserve their state, they were determined to preserve the Polish nation. Intense nationalism prevailed not only among the intellectuals but among the common people as well, and the attempts at Prussianization and Russification merely had the effect of adding oil to the flame. As political exiles and emigrants they carried their nationalism with them. At heart, they remained Poles no matter how far removed they were from their native land. Sienkiewicz foresaw, however, that neither Polish nationalism nor the nationalism of other immigrant groups would thrive long on American soil; here it could not be transmitted from one generation to the next as was the case in Europe.

force their way into these linguistic gaps and fissures, and the decay of the native speech inevitably sets in. One might say that the English language is wafted in the wind and somehow is inhaled involuntarily by those who arrive from Europe. It is like a flood, gradual to be sure, but moving forward without interruption. In the purely German settlement of Anaheim in southern California, the parents spank their children because the latter insist on speaking English with one another. And yet this community, situated in the midst of a predominantly Mexican population, does not even have direct contact with the Anglo-Saxon element. I saw this same influence of English language and manners on the German youth of Cincinnati, the strongest German hearth in the whole United States. As for the Poles, even their clergy, even their newspaper editors and reporters, have been unable to resist the pervasive effects of English; and yet these are people who are well educated and who consciously defend themselves against this ascendancy. I would say that under the influence of the English language there is being created here a separate Polish-American dialect whose common words are Polish, while all aspects of American life differing from that of Poland, such as commerce, society, government, customs, and agricultural methods, are described by English terms and expressions.[13]

Newspapers, however, guard the purity of the Polish tongue. The bookstores of Dyniewicz, Piotrowski, and the Barzynskis sell Polish books, and Polish societies attempt to conduct their proceedings in correct language. In short, the American Poles are not lacking in good intentions and in patriotism, but their speech, torn from the maternal stem, inevitably deteriorates and decays, loses its original spirit, and undergoes a transformation like a plant transplanted to a strange soil.

[13] English words appropriated by the Poles were given a Polish spelling and even declined whenever necessary. The following are but a few of the examples cited by Sienkiewicz: rajlrod (railroad), tykiet (ticket), stymer (steamer), morgedz (mortgage), drajwer (driver), czyken-jard (chicken yard), salon (saloon), biznes (business), etc.

The bringing together of all the Poles in some one state, their union into a single entity, and the enactment of their own protective measures could delay the process of denationalization. But since nothing of the sort exists nor can exist because the Poles live scattered throughout the states, the denationalization of future generations is only a matter of time. Nor will a new wave of immigration stop the process, for emigration fever and the conditions causing this malady are transitory phenomena; once they reach their crisis, they become weaker. Neither in the kingdom of Poland, including Lithuania, nor in Galicia, nor in the Grand Duchy of Posen is our situation comparable to that of Germany or England which each year must expell their surplus population under threat of misery and starvation. Thus the enticements of the emigration agents will never in Poland be founded on a valid or objective basis. This is an exceptionally fortunate situation for us.

As the number of Polish immigrants in the United States declines, the denationalization of those who came earlier will gain momentum. Furthermore, all immigrant groups are composed primarily of men who, unable to find enough women of their own nationality, take wives from among the local inhabitants. Thus, I am unacquainted with a single Pole, married to an American woman, whose children know the Polish language. I do not exclude even the intelligentsia. This is inevitable. Such children are unable to read Polish books and newspapers. But even if they learn Polish, it will no longer be their mother tongue. Exclusively Polish settlements, such as Radom or Czestochowa, and especially those founded on the prairie far removed from large cities, as New Posen in Nebraska, will hold out longer, perhaps even very much longer, but with the passage of years even these will succumb to the common fate. It should be added that people who are poor invariably come under the influence of those who are rich and the native Americans are richer than the Poles. Thus everything conspires against the best intentions of the Poles. This small segment of the Polish nation will sooner or later by the irresistible force of circumstances become absorbed within the foreign element. A shoot grafted on another trunk is transformed into another kind of tree.

We must remember only the first generation lives here and it will hold out. Whether on the shores of the Great Lakes or the Pacific Ocean those who have been born in the fatherland will not forget it and will remain faithful to it. Settlers in Illinois and in Texas preserve lumps of Polish earth as if they were relics. These they place in the coffin under the head or over the heart of the deceased. The Polish peasant loves his homeland more than he realizes. Today on the prairies of Nebraska and Arkansas many a Polish peasant pauses to ponder and frequently to weep as he strikes his scythe against the whetstone, for the sound reminds him of his native village. Or somewhere under the hot skies of Texas when the church organ resounds and the people begin to sing "Holy Father," their eyes fill with tears and their peasant thoughts wing their way back across the ocean like sea gulls and return to the thatched huts in their native Poland.

But what of the second, third, and fourth generations? What of the children born of German, Irish, or American mothers? Sooner or later they will forget. They will change everything, even their names, which English teeth find too difficult to chew and which interfere with business. How long this will take is difficult to say. But just as Poland disappeared, so will this same, sad fate inevitably befall her children who, today, are scattered throughout the world.

INDEX